Cover Photograph:
Anne C. Maguire ashore at Portland Head, Maine.
Courtesy of ©Mystic Seaport Museum, Inc.

THE BELL TOLLS SERIES

SHIPWRECKS & LIGHTHOUSES
OF EASTERN LONG ISLAND

Henry Keatts
George Farr

ISBN 0-936849-05-03

Fathom Press
Post Office Box 191
Eastport, New York 11941

DEDICATION

To our readers
and all who are lured
to the sea around us.

The Bell Tolls

Henry Keatts

George Farr

ABOUT THE AUTHORS

Henry Keatts is Professor of Biology and Oceanography, Suffolk Community College, Long Island, NY. In addition to being widely published in his field, Keatts is the author of *New England's Legacy of Shipwrecks* and *Field Guide to Sunken U-boats,* both published by the American Merchant Marine Museum Press (United States Merchant Marine Academy), *Guide to Shipwreck Diving: New York and New Jersey* published by Pisces Books, and *Beachcomber's Guide: From Cape Cod to Cape Hatteras* published by Gulf Publishing Company. He is co-author of *Complete Wreck Diving: A Guide to Diving Wrecks* published by Aqua Quest Publications. He is a Fellow of the prestigious Explorers Club (Manhattan, NY), an associate member of the Boston Sea Rovers, and an honorary member of the Gillmen Club (Hartford, CT) and the Adirondack Underwater Explorers (Saratoga Springs, NY). He is president of the American Society of Oceanographers.

George Farr is a Research Diver who retired from IBM management in 1975 with a thirst for new fields of study and involvement. That interest brought him into contact with Professor Keatts, first as a student in Keatts' Oceanography course, then as a fellow scuba diver. In addition to free-lance writing he has co-authored with Keatts the *Dive into History* series (*Vol. 1: Warships, Vol. 2: U.S. Submarines,* and *Vol. 3: U-boats*) published by Pisces Books.

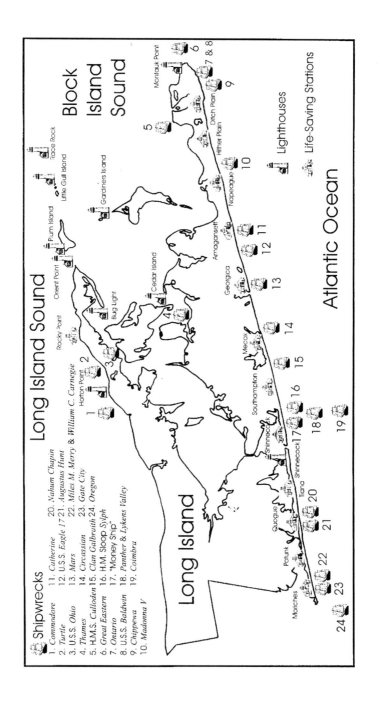

Shipwrecks

1. *Commodore*
2. *Turtle*
3. *U.S.S. Ohio*
4. *Thames*
5. *H.M.S. Culloden*
6. *Great Eastern*
7. *Ontario*
8. *U.S.S. Baldwin*
9. *Chippewa*
10. *Madonna V*
11. *Catherine*
12. *U.S.S. Eagle 17*
13. *Mars*
14. *Circassian*
15. *Clan Galbraith*
16. *H.M. Sloop Sylph*
17. *"Money Ship"*
18. *Panther & Lykens Valley*
19. *Coimbra*
20. *Nahum Chapin*
21. *Augustus Hunt*
22. *Miles M. Merry & William C. Carnegie*
23. *Gate City*
24. *Oregon*

Long Island Sound

Long Island

Block Island Sound

Atlantic Ocean

Race Rock
Little Gull Island
Plum Island
Orient Point
Gardiners Island
Montauk Point
Ditch Plain
Hither Plain
Napeague
Amagansett
Georgica
Cedar Island
Bug Light
Rocky Point
Horton Point
Mecox
Southampton
Shinnecock
Tiana
Quogue
Potunk
Moriches

Lighthouses

Life-Saving Stations

ACKNOWLEDGMENTS

The authors gratefully acknowledge the contributions and cooperation of the following individuals and organizations:

Aaron Hirsh

Clifford Benfield
Curator, Southold Historical Society Nautical Musuem

Antonia Booth
Southold Town Historian

Paul M. Bradley, Jr., Frank Braynard, James Christley, Vincent Quatroche, and the U.S. Lighthouse Society
for their superb illustrations

Mary A. Casey-Smith

Chris and Shawn Keatts

East Hampton Library

Suzan Smyth Habib
Curator of the Sag Harbor History Room, John Hermain Memorial Library (Sag Harbor)

National Archives

Naval Historical Center, Washington Navy Yard

Jacqueline Rea
Photo Collection Curator, Bridgehampton Historical Society and East Hampton Historical Society

Anne Realmuto
Director, Quogue Library

Riverhead Free Library

Pat Shuttleworth
Chairman, The Quogue Historical Society

Southold Historical Society

Southold Library

Steamship Historical Society of America

Submarine Force Library & Musuem, Groton, Connecticut

Suffolk County Historical Society

Tom Roach

Wayne Wheeler
President, U.S. Lighthouse Society

Special thanks to Trelleborg Viking, Inc. Diving Division for use of their excellent dry suits.

This book covers both shipwrecks and lighthouses because without shipwrecks there would be no lighthouses. The number of ships that failed to navigate dangerous waters determined the strategic location of lighthouses along rocky shores or shoals. Many ships were lost, even after a warning from a tower high above a tall cliff or one swept by waves, but without them the toll would have been much greater.

Just as there would be no lighthouses without shipwrecks, shipwrecks would never occur without ships, and no record of distaster at sea would be complete without lifesaving (hyphenated during the 19th century). The hyphen is retained for reference to the Life-Saving Service and for a specific Life-Saving Station (e.g., Quogue Life-Saving Station), as was the custom of the time. Elsewhere, we do not hyphenate lifesaving, hoping that the practice does not confuse our readers. Eastern Long Island offers far too many shipwrecks for all to be covered in this work. Selection for inclusion was based on historic significance, popularity, accessibility, and available information on the ship and circumstances of her sinking. This volume provides the background of each vessel and description of its present condition when appropriate.

The three topics, Shipwrecks, Lifesaving and Lighthouses are presented as general introduction in the first three chapters, grouped as Book I. We hope you will find them informative, and perhaps a useful reference while reading the chapters that follow in Book II.

Book II covers Eastern Long Island, with the introduction devoted to its history, people, and geography. The episodes that follow describe prominent shipwrecks, their sinking, salvage, and current condition, and the island's lighthouses.

We hope that you, the reader, will enjoy this volume as much as we have enjoyed writing it. One imperative that has dictated its preparation is historic accuracy. It has been pursued to the fullest extent possible. In some cases, dialog and description have been added for emotional influence, but always within the context of supporting records. If incorrect data, misinterpretation, or lack of information are noted, input would be most welcome. Additional information, photographs, or slides forwarded to Professor Henry Keatts, Suffolk Community College, Riverhead, NY 11901 will receive appreciative attention and confirming research for inclusion in further editions of this work. Also, information, illustrations, or photos for other volumes in the series (Massachusetts, Maine, North Carolina, etc.) would be greatly appreciated. Photos and illustrations will be copied and returned, and credit will be given in the caption.

Table of Contents

The Bell Tolls

BOOK I
chapter one
SHIPWRECKS

But one man of her crew alive,
What put to sea with seventy-five.
—Robert Lewis Stevenson,
Treasure Island

The expansion of speed, capacity, and range of ships, beginning in the 15th century, challenged venturesome mariners to navigate their craft farther from their home ports. They did so with primitive charts or no more knowledge than Columbus had when he headed for America seeking a route to the Orient. Fog, snow, and tempest exacted a heavy toll on unwary navigators. Hidden reefs, turbulent eddies, and deceptive shoals multiplied the danger, and losses to the sea increased. Even in familiar surroundings such as home port, care was needed to avoid hazards that might even sink a local vessel. War added to the toll with naval engagements that left ships of war and commerce at the bottom of the sea.

No ship is more seaworthy than her hull. Until the late 1700s, the hull of any wooden vessel was at the mercy of shipworms. Contrary to the name, a shipworm is not a worm but a bivalve mollusk (such as a clam) that has become adapted for burrowing in wood. The shell is reduced in size, but the two small valves (parts of the shell) at the anterior end of the long, narrow, worm-like body are modified to form rasping structures for drilling cylindrical tunnels in wood. Shipworms and other wood-boring marine animals cause severe damage to wooden ship bottoms and wooden pilings in harbors.

In 1730, shipworms threatened the very existence of Holland by attacking the dikes. They were not identified as mollusks until 1733, when the Dutch zoologist G. Snellius studied the animals causing the damage. During the late 1940s, shipworms disappeared from New York Harbor because pollution had turned the harbor into an unsuitable habitat. That mixed blessing was lost with the 1972 Clean Water Act. By the mid-1980s, the reduced pollution showed positive results. Shipworms were among the various forms of marine life that began to flourish again.

Infestations of the bivalve mollusks below the waterline frequently shortened the life of an otherwise sound wooden-hulled ship. Relief came with the application of steam power to rolling mills. That made copper plating a readily available solution that was quickly adopted to protect hulls against shipworms. The entire British battle fleet was copper sheathed during the American Revolution. Early in the 19th century, better constructed merchant ships were protected in the same manner. When experience proved that copper sheathing in contact with the head of an iron fastening destroyed the iron by electrolysis, copper-zinc alloy fastenings were substituted for iron below the water line.

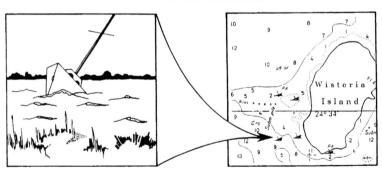

Visible stranded shipwreck as depicted on a nautical chart.
Illustration by Robert C. Hansen.

When a wooden ship sinks, its unprotected structural components are ravaged by shipworms and other marine wood-boring animals causing disintegration. Shipworms pose no problem to iron-hulled ships, but metal plates will break up and slowly disintegrate from electro-chemical action, especially in salt water. Iron corrodes ten times faster in sea water than in air. Given time, it will disappear in a salt water environment.

The coast line of every continent is littered with the remains of ships, some intact, others in stages of disintegration, still others buried in silt or disintegrated beyond recognition. Storm, fire, collision or navigation error account for some shipwrecks, and some were sunk intentionally to encourage the habitation of an artificial reef by marine life. Sport and professional divers are engaged in an endless search for those shipwrecks, some out of interest in maritime history, others for photographs, and still others for treasure, artifacts or salvage. They are guided by accounts of the sinking, maritime records, reports by a survivor, local fishermen whose nets have become entangled in the wreckage, even random debris that has washed ashore.

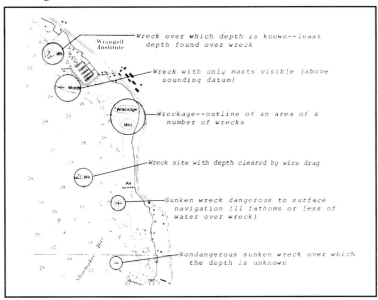

Sunken (submerged) shipwreck symbols on nautical charts.
Illustration by Robert C. Hansen.

One type of debris that is often overlooked is pieces of coal on a beach, washed ashore from a shipwreck off the coast. Thousands of vessels have sunk along America's eastern seaboard since colonial times. The remains of some that are buried in the sand appear and disappear with the wind and tides. They are alternately exposed and buried by the ever-shifting sand. Although some offshore wrecks may extend out of the water at times, most are completely submerged. Only an occasional reminder of their existence washes ashore in the form of a chunk of its coal, a bottle, a coin, or timbers with protruding bronze fastenings. In the hands of a diligent searcher, any of them can launch an all out exploration of the offshore water.

ARTIFICIAL REEFS

It is interesting to note that man, albeit accidentally, has provided the basis for fascinating ecosystems—shipwrecks along shores that are devoid of natural reefs. They provide large areas of hard surface for colonizing marine organisms, and in a few years each is an entire ecosystem. They are not only oases in a desert of sand, but they also increase biologic productivity. The result is an incredible abundance, beauty, and diversity of marine life in or around those sunken ships. On some, the growth of marine organisms is so dense that it completely obscures the details of its host vessel.

Dust on the Sea
by Edward L. Beach

Ashes to ashes, dust to dust—so goes the litany as a mortal body is committed to the ground. When a ship dies there is no grave save the devouring sea. However, for a little while there is always a residue—debris, an oil slick, a streak of coal dust, an accumulation of dust and trash floating on a white canopy of air bubbles. This pattern is extensive if she sank suddenly, if catastrophe shattered her compartments, burst her bunkers open, blew her guts out.

Then the white bubbles dissipate, and for a short time longer there is only the streak of dust and a few items of junk to mark the place. Soon that, too, is gone. The dust on the sea is the grave of a ship. It is only a temporary marker, but it is an indelible one to those who have seen it. And it is forever engraved on the souls of those who have had to be the cause.

SALVAGE
Methought I saw a thousand fearful wrecks;
Ten thousand men that fishes gnawed upon;
Wedges of gold, great anchors, heaps of pearl,
Inestimable stones, unvalued jewels,
All scattered in the bottom of the sea.
—William Shakespeare, *Richard III*

The sea has been a welcome source of unexpected merchandise, building materials, and coal to heat the homes of the residents of Long Island. Surfside residents have looked at anything that washed ashore from a shipwreck as "Finders, keepers; losers, weepers." The government, however, disagreed with that old adage, and from 1787 to 1886 a wreck master was appointed by New York State for each shorefront area. His duty was to protect the owners', insurance companies, and the States' interests. By 1886, the marine insurance underwriters were directing salvage operations and New York State abolished the office of wreck master. Even with wreck masters trying to eliminate pilferage, many homes along the shore contain objects cast up by the sea after a sinking.

Nathaniel S. Prime, in *History of Long Island*, wasted no words in his criticism of the "Finders, keepers" philosophy. "There are men who would scorn the imputation of taking the most trifling article of their neighbor's property, who would not hesitate, under this mistaken notion of right, to appropriate to their own use whatever they might find on the shore, without making the least effort to discover the rightful owner, not to speak of any direct efforts to conceal the fact."

Prime also wrote that a whole house floated across the Sound and grounded on the north shore of Long Island. A farmer found the house and took possession of its entire contents—carpets, beds, and all. Jeannette Edwards Rattray, in *Ship Ashore*, described the cornucopia of treasures recovered by residents of East Hampton Town: "… timber … Spanish gold pieces … coconuts, peanuts, choice liquor from France, trees and shrubs, ostrich eggs, Maltese cats [no falcons], masts that were turned into village flag poles, shoes, and calico. A ship's bell from the tragic *John Milton* wreck at Montauk in 1858 hangs in the belfry of the Presbyterian Session House in East Hampton; the ship's clock from the terrible *Circassian* wreck at Bridgehampton in 1876 keeps good time in the kitchen of J. Howard Hand at Wainscott. Bed quilts lined with 'wreck calico' printed with white circles on red, yellow, or a dismal brown from the *George Appold*, ashore at Montauk in 1889, are still [1955] in use around the Hamptons."

Following a heavy spring storm, the March 13, 1896, issue of *The East Hampton Star* reported on the wide variety of goods that came ashore to the benefit of appreciative eastern Long Island residents. "The gale last week from the northwest brought quantities of drift timber of all kinds on shore here [Montauk]. About 500 chestnut posts were picked up and quantities of good oak plank and some pine…. a horse and wagon, one or two dogs, and several pigs."

David Stick in *Graveyard of the Atlantic* wrote of the Cape Hatteras, North Carolina area that maintenance of law and order at the scene of shipwrecks there has long been a problem for the authorities. "It has been said of the people of Ocracoke Island that they would drop a corpse on the way to burial if they heard the cry of 'Ship ashore!' Many a stranded cargo has brought wealth to the finder, and even today [1952] the person who first locates a cargo drifting on the beach shares in the proceeds at the auction sale … that follows. Houses are built from salvaged lumber—pay checks come from the service of guarding the shores. The rarity of shipwrecks today has depopulated some coastal towns."

Henry Beston in *The Outermost House* describes his year spent on Cape Cod, where conditions parallel those on Eastern Long Island, Block Island, and probably any Atlantic seaboard area that is subject to shipwrecks: "The Cape Codders have often been humorously reproached for their attitude toward wrecks. On this coast, as on every other in the old isolated days, a wreck was treasure trove, a free gift of the sea; even today [1928], the usable parts of a wreck are liable to melt away in a curious manner. There is no real looting; in fact, public opinion on the Cape is decidedly against such a practice, for it offends the local sense of decency…. When men are lost on the beach, the whole Cape takes it very much to heart … when men are saved, there is no place where they are treated with greater hospitality and kindness. Cape folks have never been wreckers in the European sense of that dark word. Their first thought has always been of the shipwrecked men."

Henry Thoreau, in *Cape Cod*, wrote: "We saw this forenoon a part of the wreck of a vessel, probably the *Franklin*, a large piece fifteen feet square and still freshly painted. With a grapple and a line we could have saved it…. It would have been a lucky haul for some poor wrecker, for I have been told that one man who paid three or four dollars for a part of the wreck of that vessel, sold fifty or sixty dollars' worth of iron out of it."

Justified or not, residents of the seashore often have been accused of intentionally luring ships to destruction with false lights, then killing the crew and passengers and plundering the ship's cargo. Many slanderous tales about Block Islanders have been told. The distorted stories may have started with John Greenleaf Whittier's poem "The Palatine". An example is an article by Joseph Mitchell published in the January 11, 1947 issue of *The New Yorker*: "Old Chrissy was an old rascal of a woman that was the head of a gang of wreckers. They lured ships in with false lights, and they killed the sailors and passengers, so there wouldn't be any tales told. Old Chrissy took charge of the killing. She had a big club and she'd hist her skirt and wade out in the surf and clout the people on the head as they swam in or floated in. She called a wreck a wrack, the way the Block Islanders do. That's the way she pronounced it. One night, she and her gang lured a ship up on the reef, and the sailors were floating in, and old Chrissy was out there clouting them on their heads. One poor fellow floated up, and it was one of old Chrissy's sons, who'd left the island and gone to the mainland to be a sailor. He looked up at old Chrissy and said, 'Hello, Ma.' Old Chrissy didn't hesitate. She gave him a clout on the head with her club. 'A son's a son,' she said, 'but a wrack's a wrack.'"

In a letter dated March 11, 1907, Superintendent Knowles, 3rd Life-Saving District, wrote General Superintendent Kimball, U.S. Life-Saving Service, the following about Block Islanders: "In order to illustrate the generosity and hospitality of the inhabitants of the Island, [I] will begin with the first body that was cast upon its shore in 1704. It evidently came from some wreck, although unidentified, and was properly buried like those recovered from other wrecks already mentioned, and also the infant unidentified, that floated from the wreck of the steamer *Metis* (that collided with the schooner *Nettie Cushing*) and was buried in the cemetery near the graves of the *Warrior* victims. In all cases, suitable coffins were made and they were given a proper burial …

"And from personal experience at the time I was keeper of the Point Judith station, when I landed with my full crew with surfboat in a 72-mile gale of wind on Christmas day 1885, after examining the schooners *Mott Haven* and *Willie DeWolfe*, several miles from shore which had collided during the previous night. The number one man … and I were cared for by Hon. J.T. Dodge, then Senator of the island. Other members of the crew, as well as Capt. Ashford and his crew [from one of the schooners] were provided for by other leading families of the Island. While nothing was lacking, their unremitting efforts to do more for us seemed to have no limit."

"The same hospitality and kind treatment was shown to Miss Golub, one of the two survivors of the *Larchmont* disaster. Enough could not be done for her comfort, and when she left the Island she was given a purse of $125 by sympathizing residents of the Island…".

SALVAGE COMPANIES

Captain Thomas A. Scott was born in Snowhill, Maryland, in the 1820s. He went to sea at the age of 15, and was master and owner of the schooner *Thomas Page* soon after.

After his marriage he left the sea and settled in Fort Lee, New Jersey. When a steamer burned and sank nearby, he contracted to raise her cargo. His success led him to start the T.A. Scott Wrecking Company. Later, he moved the company to New London, Connecticut. In addition to ship salvage, the company performed underwater construction work. The underwater foundations of the Race Rock Lighthouse and the Brooklyn Bridge were among the company's achievements.

Scott's only son was lost when he was knocked overboard by a boom during salvage work on a sunken ship. Apparently the boy was knocked unconscious by the blow, because he did not surface after falling into the water. Scott put on his hard-hat diving gear and searched the bottom until his men forcibly brought him to the surface.

When Captain Scott died on February 18, 1907, the *New London Day* wrote that he "was a type of rugged, honest manhood of the highest order.... Not only was he a capable, hardworking and efficient wrecking master, but he was of unquestioned integrity and sterling loyalty to fundamental principles.... There is no maritime company on the Atlantic seaboard that has not had cause to bless Captain Scott and his intrepid crew of workers."

In May 1860, the Port of New York insurance underwriters formed a company, the Coast Wrecking Company, to salvage sunken ships and refloat stranded vessels. They selected Captain Israel J. Merritt, a skilled and responsible captain who had been doing salvage work since 1835, to run the new company. At the age of 15 he starting working aboard a salvage vessel operating off Long Island and Manhattan. In 1880, Merritt bought the salvage company and renamed it the Merritt Wrecking Organization. Five years later he added a second base at Norfolk. Merritt merged with his principal rival, the Chapman Derrick and Wrecking Company of Brooklyn, and in 1922 with the T.A. Scott Wrecking Company. The result was the Merritt-Chapman and Scott Corporation, which by 1958 had diversified its operations and reached a net worth of 142 million dollars.

INSPIRATION

Three hurricanes struck the northeast in December 1839. They sank 121 vessels and many carried their crews to their deaths.

Another 218 vessels were damaged or driven ashore. More than 160 people perished in the three storms. The first struck on December 15, the second on the 22nd, and the third and the worst on the 27th. Although none of the three were the most severe to hit the northeast, their combined effect was very destructive.

Henry Wadsworth Longfellow, 32 years old at the time, witnessed the fury of the "Triple Hurricanes" and their aftermath. That experience moved him to pen his famous poem "The Wreck Of The *Hesperus*." In the poem the mythical schooner *Hesperus* is wrecked on Norman's Woe Reef in Gloucester Harbor, Massachusetts. *Hesperus* is symbolic of all the vessels wrecked in the storms. No vessel by that name was sunk in Gloucester Harbor during that period.

Longfellow's tale is that of the death of a small girl and her father, the captain of *Hesperus*. The poet appears to have been inspired by reports of several ships wrecking on the rocky reef of Norman's Woe during the storms and one woman's body did wash ashore lashed to a piece of wreckage. The following are selected stanzas of Longfellow's poem:

> *It was the schooner* Hesperus,
> *That sailed the wintry sea;*
> *And the skipper had taken his little daughter,*
> *To bear him company.*
> ...
> *The skipper he stood beside the helm,*
> *His pipe was in his mouth,*
> *And he watched how the veering flaw did blow*
> *The smoke now West, now South.*
>
> *Then up and spake an old Sailor,*
> *Had sailed the Spanish Main,*
> *'I pray thee, put into yonder port,*
> *For I fear a hurricane.*
>
> *'Last night the moon had a golden ring,*
> *And to-night no moon we see!'*
> *The skipper he blew a whiff from his pipe,*

And a scornful laugh laughed he.

Colder and louder blew the wind,
A gale from the North-east,
The snow fell hissing in the brine,
And the billows frothed like yeast.
. . .
'Come hither! come hither! my little daughter,
And do not tremble so;
For I can weather the roughest gale
That ever wind did blow.'
. . .
Then the maiden clasped her hands and prayed
That saved she might be;
And she thought of Christ, who stilled the wave
On the lake of Galilee.

And fast through the midnight dark and drear,
Through the whistling sleet and snow,
Like a sheeted ghost the vessel swept
Tow'rds the reef of Norman's Woe.
. . .
She struck where the white and fleecy waves
Looked soft as carded wool,
But the cruel rocks they gored her side
Like the horns of an angry bull.
. . .
At daybreak on the bleak sea-beach
A fisherman stood aghast,
To see the form of a maiden fair
Lashed close to a drifting mast.
. . .
Such was the wreck of the Hesperus,
In the midnight and the snow!
Christ save us all from a death like this,
On the reef of Norman's Woe!

The cry "Ship ashore!" is seldom heard today on Long Island. When it does, few residents have the equipment or the know how to manage a boat through rough surf to aid those in distress. Disasters are now dealt with professionally by the United States Coast Guard.

> *The sea is still and deep;*
> *All things within its bosom sleep;*
> *A single step and all is o'er,*
> *A plunge, a bubble, and no more.*

—Longfellow

chapter two
LIFESAVING

A gun is heard at the dead of night,
"Lifeboat ready!"
And every man to the signal true
Takes his place in the eager crew,
"Now, lads, steady!"
First a glance at the shuddering foam,
Then a look at the loving home,
Then together, with bated breath,
They launch their boats in the gulf of death ...
—J.L. Molloy, *A Race for Life*

There were four occupational heroes in the dime novels and newspapers of 19th century America—cowboys, firemen, railroad engineers, and the men of the United States Life-Saving Service (L.S.S.). Few people today are familiar with that branch of the U.S. Treasury Department or the rugged men who manned the desolate lifesaving stations. They patrolled the storm-swept beaches during harsh winter months and saved the lives of thousands of shipwreck victims. Among the numerous works of late 19th and early 20th century juvenile literature are *Fighting the Sea* (1887), *The Beach Patrol* (1897), and *Heroes of the Storm* (1904). In those books young boys lived through the courageous and dangerous rescues made by lifesavers. The Milton Bradley company produced the board game "Life Saver" to capitalize on the appeal of those hardy heroes.

The U.S. Life-Saving Service grew out of private and local humanitarian efforts to save the lives of shipwrecked passengers and sailors. By the time the L.S.S. merged with the Revenue Cutter Service in 1915 to form the U.S. Coast Guard, there were 279 lifesaving stations covering the Atlantic and Pacific Oceans, Gulf of Mexico, and along the Great Lakes.

Passengers being rescued from the stranded passenger liner *Rusland* off the New Jersey coast in March 1877. The lifesavers on the right are pulling the life-car to shore The enclosed life-car resembled a boat and held several people.   *Harper's Monthly.*

The lifesavers had to work under the most adverse conditions, for ships seldom ran aground on clear, balmy summer days. Shipwreck disasters almost always happened at night, usually in winter and during a raging nor'easter, a blizzard, or in dense fog.

The crew of a lifesaving station usually consisted of a keeper (captain) and six surfmen. The men were numbered in order of seniority. Numbers 4, 5, and 6, the juniors had to patrol the beaches at night. In 1885, a seventh man was added to cover for ill or off-duty men. When a surfman left his station to start on patrol his captain handed him a brass tag. The patrol was usually two or two and one-half miles to a halfway house (a crude shack) between two lifesaving stations. If there was a stove he would build a fire and wait for the surfman from the adjoining lifesaving station to reach the house. The men exchanged tags and returned to their stations. That tag exchange system ensured that the beach was completely patrolled four times between sunset and sunrise.

Two surfmen shortly after exchanging brass tags.
Courtesy of the U.S. Lighthouse Society.

Walking four or five miles in sub-zero temperatures, wind driven spray, sleet, and sand, and during severe storms was not a pleasant stroll. Many surfmen wore home-made face masks of canvas or leather during the winter. The patrol was exhausting and often the men returned soaked to the skin or caked with ice— all for about $50 a month. The following is an account of one patrol during a stormy night on Fire Island, Long Island: "... a patrolman named Allen had to keep behind the dunes, only to surmount them long enough to attempt to observe the fury of wind and sea. When Allen finally arrived at the shack, much later than usual, he found that the lantern, although extinguished, was still a little warm. He surmised that the man he was to have met, had waited and finally left. Exhausted and warmed by the fire, Allen fell asleep, but awakened to what he thought was a cannon shot. Hearing nothing further, he decided to return to his station. He donned his oilskins, backed out into the furious storm, and latched the door shut behind. He paused just long enough to look toward the sky for any sign of a break in the storm. Allen was flabbergasted.

Directly above him and jutting over the shack, was the bowsprit of an enormous, three-masted schooner! A man, still alive, his arms and legs frozen to the bowsprit, stared down at him. Allen rescued him, then clambered onto the ship, which was already breaking up, leaving no time to go for assistance. One by one, he chopped seven more crewmen out of the ice and carried them to safety. At daylight, Allen's captain and two surfmen ... started out to look for him. Halfway to the shelter they met him and the sailors whose lives he had saved. With typical L.S.S. modesty, the unemotional captain made the following brief entry into his logbook: 'Three-masted schooner Beaumont came ashore in heavy gale two miles west of station and crew of eight were assisted ashore by surfman Allen.'"

Disease and disability were hazards of the profession. L.S.S. General Superintendent Sumner Kimball wrote: "The majority of these men enter the vocation of lifesaving at the most vigorous period of their lives. They know that if they continue in the Service—and its efficiency depends upon their retention—they will sooner or later incur disability and be compelled to stand aside. Their incapacity may be the result of injury sustained in the performance of wreck duty, such as broken bones, sprains, hernia, etc., or it may be due to heart trouble, rheumatism, tuberculosis, or several of a dozen others traceable to overstrain or exposure."

Because winter was the stormy season, there were fewer shipwrecks during the summer months. The lifesaving stations were closed from May through August, leaving only the keeper to man a facility. The surfmen were laid off and had to fend for themselves with temporary employment. However, it was surprising how fast the off-duty lifesavers appeared whenever a shipwreck occurred during summer months.

Each station was equipped with a 26-foot surfboat on a cumbersome, four-wheeled carriage that could be dragged, more than rolled, through sand to a wreck site. The surf that met a responding crew was often 12-foot waves. The double-ender (bows fore and aft) boats were propelled by huge oars, with the keeper always commanding, and using an oar mounted aft to steer it.

Launching a surfboat or lifeboat in heavy surf was dangerous and the L.S.S. Regulations stated that the keeper "will not desist from

his efforts until by actual trial the impossibility effecting a rescue is demonstrated. A keeper must test the surf by launching his boat."

Reaching the wreck through storm tossed seas was only the beginning of the danger. Sailors, panicked by waves washing over the ship's deck, often jumped into the surfboat overturning it and drowning them and the surfmen. Some of the Life-Saving Service's most terrible losses resulted from such actions. The surfmen's motto became "You have to go out, but you don't have to come back."

Some lifesaving stations had a completely enclosed, sheet metal lifeboat with a screw-propeller that was turned by hand cranks. Those heavy boats could not be hauled to a shipwreck site, they had to be launched at the station.

Surfboats and lifeboats were part of the lifesaving stations' rescue equipment.

The stations were built to several designs, but usually had a tall square observation tower, but often with modifications. One large room with a set of swinging doors housed the lifeboat and surfboat as well as a wagon loaded with rescue equipment (Lyle gun, breeches buoys, lines, life preservers, etc.). The surfmen harnessed themselves to the heavy wagon like horses and pulled it through the soft sand to the wreck site.

THE GUN THAT SAVED LIVES

Using a mortar to throw a line to a stranded ship (1849).

When rough seas prevented the launching of lifeboats and surfboats, potential survivors of shipwrecks perished, even when they were in view of would-be rescuers. The destruction of *Adventure* on the English coast with a great loss of lives in 1789 prompted corrective action. Three years after the disaster, Sergeant John Bell of the British Royal Artillery developed a method of reaching from shore to ship, using a mortar projectile to carry a line over a stricken vessel. The mortar he used at the time weighed between 500 and 600 pounds, and fired a 60-pound shot. In 1807, Captain George W. Manby saved the crew of the brig *Nancy* at Yarmouth, England by firing a mortar to a stranded ship with a line attached to the projectile. After the successful rescue, Manby improved his line throwing device by using a leather braid to connect the line to the projectile, preventing the line being burnt from the muzzle blast. He also put bright burning fuses in the projectile so people on the stranded ships could spot it in its long arc from shore. The first use of the method in the United States was in 1849 by the Massachusetts Humane Society. Although Manby's device saved hundreds of lives, he died in poverty.

In 1875, the U.S. Secretary of War directed the Board of Experimental Guns to develop a new lifesaving mortar. By 1877, a lighter, 267-pound mortar was in use, but it was still difficult to move about. A report at the time stated: "Either the government must station permanent mortars of large caliber along the coast almost as close to one another as guns are placed in a battery, or someone must invent a mortar that will stand a heavy charge of powder and will, at the same time, be light enough to be portable. As yet no such mortar has been constructed, and unless some other material than iron can be used, it is difficult to see how the problem is to be solved."

Also, in 1877, a 32-year-old West Point graduate Captain David A. Lyle was "specially assigned to this duty in addition to his regular duties" at the Springfield Armory in Springfield, Massachusetts.

The solution came the following year, when Captain Lyle revolutionized the projectile technique with a bronze gun weighing only 163 pounds. It fired a long metal projectile weighing 18 pounds, best described as a "sash-weight-with-eyebolt." The gun's carriage was ironbound oak, with a notched wooden block for elevation settings. The eyebolt on the projectile was connected to a light shot line, and remained outside the mouth of the cannon. When the cannon was fired, the line was pulled out of a wooden faking box and carried above the rigging of a stranded vessel by the projectile.

Inside the box, the line was coiled around a series of vertical wooden pegs. The line was prepared in advance by placing a false bottom, with holes bored in it, over the pegs, then coiling the line over the pegs. Before firing, the box was turned upside down, leaving the line resting on the cover of the box, which was then tilted

45 degrees toward the target vessel. If the line was improperly faked (coiled), the shot line would snarl and break or fall short of the ship.

A hawser was attached to the end of the shot line. The crew of the stranded vessel retrieved the line, hauled the hawser aboard, and tied it to a mast or some other stable projection. The lifesavers tied their end to a sand anchor and positioned an X-shaped wooden support under the hawser, raising it and making it taut. A free-running "traveler block," with a breeches buoy attached, was placed on the hawser. The breeches buoy is a pair of heavy-duty canvas shorts attached to a cork life ring. The shipwrecked person got into the device as if putting on a pair of pants.

Captain Lyle made "no claims of great originality" and acknowledged that his device "is a direct evolution from the system of Captain Manby." However, he was awarded the rank of chevalier in the French Legion of Honor for his work at the Paris Exposition in 1889. Captain Lyle described the development of his gun as "a labor of love. I am deeply interested in anything bearing upon a service so noble and successful" as saving lives.

The U.S. Life-Saving Service issued the following instructions to mariners for their use in case they were wrecked and a Lyle gun fired a shot with a small line attached to the projectile across their vessel:

"Get hold of the line as soon as possible and haul it on board until you get a tail block with a whip or endless line rove through it. This tail block should be hauled on board as quickly as possible to prevent the whip drifting off with the set of the current or fouling with wreckage, etc. Therefore, if you have been driven into the rigging, where but one or two men can work to advantage, cut the shot line and run it through some available block, such as the throat or peak halyards' block, or any block which will afford a clear lead, or even between the rat lines, that as many as possible may assist in hauling.

"Attached to the tail block will be a tally board, with the following directions in English on one side and French on the other: Make the tail of the block fast to the lower mast, well up. If the masts are gone, then to the best place you can. Cast off shot line, see that the rope in the block runs free, and show signal to shore.

"The above instructions being complied with, the result will be as shown in **Figure 1.**

"As soon as your signal is seen a three-inch hawser will be bent on to the whip and hauled off to your ship by the lifesaving crew.

"If circumstances will admit you can assist the lifesaving crew by manning that part of the whip to which the hawser is bent and hauling with them.

"When one end of the hawser is got on board a tally board will be found attached, bearing the following directions in English on one side and French on the other: 'Make this hawser fast about two feet above the tail block; see all clear, and that the rope in the block runs free, and show signal to the shore.'

"These instructions being obeyed, the result will be as shown in **Figure 2**.

"*Take particular care that there are no turns of the whip line round the hawser; to prevent this, take the end of the hawser* **UP BETWEEN** *the parts of the whip before making it fast.*

"When the hawser is made fast, the whip cast off from the hawser, and your signal seen by the lifesaving crew, they will haul the hawser taut and by means of the whip will send off to your ship a breeches buoy suspended from a traveler block ... running on the hawser.

"**Figure 3** represents the apparatus rigged, with the breeches buoy hauled off to the ship.

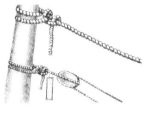

"If the breeches buoy be sent, let one man immediately get into it, thrusting his legs through the breeches.... This operation will be repeated until all are landed.

"In many instances two men can be landed in the breeches buoy at the same time, by each putting a leg through a leg of the breeches and holding on to the lifts of the buoy."

Children, when brought ashore by the buoy, should be in the

arms of elder persons or securely lashed to the buoy. Women and children should be landed first."

From 1878 to 1952, the durable and portable Lyle gun was the official projectile device of the U.S. Life-Saving Service, and around the world. In 1908, Sumner Kimball, General Superintendent of the U.S. Life-Saving Service, said that Lyle guns were used to save over 4,000 lives from shipwrecks to that date worldwide.

EARLY LIFESAVING ORGANIZATIONS

The Massachusetts Humane Society, founded in 1786, was the first organization designed to aid victims of shipwrecks off the U.S. coast. The society constructed a hut for them on Lovell's Island, near Boston. In 1807, it built the first lifeboat station at Cohasset, just south of Boston. By 1845, 18 stations manned by volunteer crews and many huts had been constructed along the Massachusetts coast.

Secretary of the Treasury Alexander Hamilton, in 1790, created the Revenue Cutter Service, and in 1837 Congress directed the cutters to make "seasonal cruises along the coast for the relief of distressed mariners."

Rescue by breeches buoy

In 1847, Congress passed a $10,000 appropriation to construct eight lifesaving stations along the New Jersey coast. Stations were built on the Long Island shore the following year. Each station was supplied with rescue equipment, but no money was appropriated to man any of them. A key to the station and a printed card of instruction on operating the equipment was left with the "nearest responsible person."

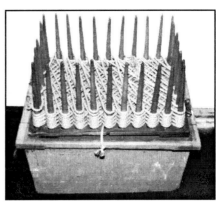

Above left: Bronze tags like this, exchanged by surfmen, ensured that the beach was completely patrolled four times each night. *Photo by H. Keatts.*

Center left: Life-Saving Service surfman.

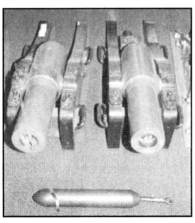

Lyle guns and a projectile (left), and a faking box (top right). The faking box was aimed toward the wreck and the pegs were removed. The shotline was tied to the projectile. The assignment of faking (folding) the rope onto this apparatus was one of the most onerous duties of a surfman. *Photos taken at the Coast Guard Museum by H. Keatts.*

Top Right: The Rocky Point Life-Saving Station (East Marion, Southold Town) became a Coast Guard Station in 1915 (top), and today is a two-family private residence (bottom). The glass-enclosed watchtower has been kept in its original condition. A speaking tube, once used by the watchman to alert the keeper in case of emergency, still rests in one corner. *Courtesy of Van Field.*

Halfway houses such as this were located between lifesaving stations. Patrolling surfmen met there and exchanged tags. *Courtesy of the Quogue Historical Society.*

Ditch Plain Coast Guard Station in 1917. *Courtesy of Albert R. Holden.*

The Life Saving Benevolent Association of New York was founded in 1849 to assist in the organization and maintenance of the lifesaving stations in New York and New Jersey. The Association, with federal funds, constructed additional stations on Long Island. The ten Long Island lifesaving stations were at Eaton's Neck, Fisher's Island, Amagansett, Bridgehampton, Quogue, Moriches, Mastic, Fire Island, Long Beach, and Barren Island. Except for occasional volunteers to man them, the stations were of little value.

The passenger ship *Powhattan* sank off the New Jersey coast in 1854 with the loss of 354 passengers and crew. The tragedy received widespread public attention, and prompted Congress to appropriate money for two superintendents ($1,500 per year each), one to supervise the Long Island stations and one for the New Jersey stations. Money was also appropriated for station keepers, often called "captains," ($200 per year). The same year four more stations were built on Long Island, for a total of 14.

In 1869 Congress, determined to make meaningful use of existing stations, passed a bill to pay for lifesaving crews in alternate stations along the New Jersey coast.

THE LIFESAVING MEDALS

Congress passed the Life-Saving Act of June 30, 1874, to recognize heroic deeds and daring rescues. A First Class Medal was to be awarded for rescues of extreme and heroic daring, a Second Class Medal for those slightly less outstanding.

Eight years later, Congress changed the designations from First and Second Class to Gold and Silver Lifesaving Medals. They were designed by Anthony Paquet and were first struck at the Philadelphia Mint. The Gold Medal is 99.9 percent gold and the Silver Medal is 99 percent silver. Since 1874, more than 600 Gold Lifesaving Medals and more than 1,900 Silver Lifesaving Medals have been awarded.

One of the most celebrated lifesavers, Joshua James, is credited with saving more than 600 lives. He earned two gold medals, three silver, and other awards, including the U.S. Congressional Gold Medal in addition to another gold, three silver, and a bronze from the Massachusetts Humane Society.

His most famous rescue, for which he received one of his two Gold Lifesaving Medals, was during a severe storm in November of 1888. James and his crew, stationed at Hull, Massachusetts, saved 29 people from five different vessels.

The following are examples of 19th century rescues or rescue attempts that resulted in the award of lifesaving medals.

Keeper Silas H. Harding and his crew of the Jerry's Point (New Hampshire) Life-Saving Station received gold medals for a rescue during a winter storm. With the temperature below freezing, the schooner *Oliver Dyer* stranded on a rock ledge about 150 yards from shore. Heavy breakers lifted the schooner off the ledge and moved her to within 75 feet of a large, flat, ice-covered, wave-swept, offshore rock.

When Harding and his crew managed to reach the rock between heavy seas, they saw a man struggling in the breakers. Surfman Hall leaped into the water, but as he dragged the victim out of the water, a wave swept both men off the rock. Fortunately, they were carried to the inshore side of the rock. Hall's hands and arms were cut badly by razor sharp barnacles as he clung to the rock, but when the sea receded for a moment he climbed back up and pulled the sailor after him. Meanwhile, Surfman Randall saved another man just as he was being carried under a second time by undertow. Harding used a heaving-stick to throw a line from the rock to the wreck. The lifesavers carried their end of the line back to shore and ran a pulley and another line between ship and shore. Sailors leaping from the schooner with the line under their arms were hauled ashore.

Gold
Lifesaving
Medal

Harding could not determine if anyone was left on the wreck, because the survivors were too exhausted to answer questions. He sent surfmen Randall and Amazeen back to the rock for a better view of the ship. When they reached the rock a heavy breaker knocked both surfmen off their feet. Amazeen grabbed Randall as the sea receded and held him with one arm while he clung to the rock with the other. Other surfmen of the lifesaving crew dashed out to their rescue. Thus, the lifesavers not only recorded a rescue of *Dyer*'s crew, but each other.

Another example of an entire lifesaving crew receiving gold medals occurred at the station at Evanston, Illinois, on Lake Michigan. With the exception of the keeper, the crew was composed of students from Northwestern University, who, when not on duty at the station were pursuing their studies. One Thanksgiving morning the station received word that a steamer was aground 12 miles up the coast. The surfmen rushed the station's surfboat to a bluff overlooking the site of the disaster. From the bluff they could see the steamer in the breakers, about 1,000 yards from shore. The weather was horrible, with a gale blowing snow and sleet, and the temperature below freezing. An ice-covered, steep ravine in the bluff led down to the shore. It was impossible to take the boat safely down through the ravine until soldiers from Fort Sheridan and civilians, armed with picks and shovels, hewed out steps from its side, and cut a path through the heavy brush.

The surfboat filled with water three times as the lifesavers attempted to launch it. The bluff was lined with spectators, and each held his breath as the frail-looking craft finally maneuvered through the pounding breakers. Once it nearly capsized, then filled with water, but the young men pulled with heart and muscle into the teeth of the gale. The lifesavers' clothing was frozen stiff when they reached the steamer to rescue six half-frozen men. Three trips were made in all. When the lifesavers finally beached their boat, they were almost in as bad condition as those they had saved. Gold medals were awarded to Keeper Lawrence O. Lawson and Northwestern University students George Crosby, William M. Ewing, Jacob Loining, Edson B. Fowler, William L. Wilson, and Frank M. Kindig.

Not all recipients of the gold medal were successful in their rescue attempts. Keeper Jerome G. Kiah of the Point aux Barques Life-Saving Station on Lake Huron received his for one of the most daring attempts at rescue and one of the greatest tragedies of the Life-Saving Service—a tragedy that wiped out an entire crew, except for Kiah.

A ship grounded too far out to be reached with the Lyle gun. Kiah and his crew realized the risk of attempting a rescue with the surfboat, but they managed to make the launch. Their strength and skill enabled them to push through the tumultuous seas between shore and the sandbar but, the real danger began beyond the sandbar, where the storm-driven seas were huge. The surfboat capsized several times and was righted, but the last time the crew was too exhausted. They clung to the side of the up-ended boat until, one by one, they let go and vanished beneath the waves. When the boat was flung ashore, Kiah was on the beach muttering "Poor boys! Poor boys! They are all gone—all gone!" He was awarded the gold medal but his health was shattered by the tragedy and he resigned from the Service. Later he was appointed district superintendent, but never attempted another rescue.

One winter night the Barnegat, New Jersey lifesavers launched their surfboat in a rescue attempt during a severe storm. They disappeared and were never seen again.

UNITED STATES LIFE-SAVING SERVICE

Secretary of the Treasury George S. Boutwell, in 1875, placed the revenue cutters and lifesaving stations under one administration, the Revenue-Marine Bureau. Three years later the Life-Saving Service was separated from the Bureau, and Congress established the United States Life-Saving Service (L.S.S.) as a separate branch of the Treasury Department.

By 1893 there were 243 lifesaving stations: 182 on the Atlantic and Gulf of Mexico coasts, 12 on the Pacific coast, 48 along the coast of the Great Lakes, and one at the falls of the Ohio River, Louisville, Kentucky. The L.S.S. was divided into 12 districts. The Third District included the coasts of Rhode Island and Long Island.

During 1893, a total of 427 disasters struck documented vessels within the 12 districts, but the toll in

lives was remarkably low. Only 23 of 3,565 aboard were lost, even though 88 of the vessels were a total loss. Thirty-five of the

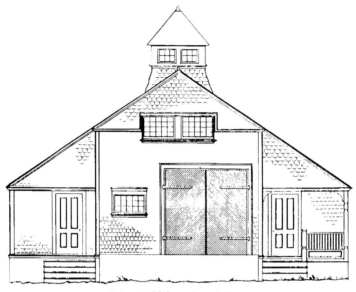

A typical lifesaving station.

disasters occurred in the Third District, with the loss of nine vessels and five lives. Five men from a Massachusetts lifesaving crew paid a penalty for that record on February 24, of the same year, when they lost their lives attempting to rescue the crew of *Aquatic*.

By 1914, shortly before the L.S.S. was absorbed into the Coast Guard, there were 30 lifesaving stations along the shore of Long Island. Only two of them were on the north shore, because the Atlantic is more dangerous than Long Island Sound. The 28 stations on the south side averaged four miles apart.

Wages, especially for the surfmen, were never high. They were paid $40 per month, and only for the eight months they worked. Their salaries increased to $50 in the 1880s. A common day laborer at that time earned only 41 cents less a day than a surfman whose life was at risk whenever he responded to a call for help. By 1895 surfmen received $60 per month. The keeper's salary was $700 per year in 1881, not bad for the time. By 1911, it was $1,000 per year.

Maybe even worse than the low wage scale of surfmen was the lack of pension or disability pay. Members of the L.S.S. who retired before their merger into the Coast Guard did not receive a pension.

WOMEN'S NATIONAL RELIEF ASSOCIATION
The Women's National Relief Association, with headquarters in New York City, was founded in 1880. Members of the Association realized the need of shipwreck survivors for clean clothing and other articles, and were aware that poorly paid surfmen at the lifesaving stations could no longer afford to clothe and supply the survivors that had lost all their personal belongings when their ship sank. Association members gathered clothing and other items and shipped them to the stations where cold and wet survivors were able to put on warm-dry clothing before resuming their journey. President James A. Garfield's wife, Lucretia, was very active in the Association. The Women's National Relief Association later became the Blue Anchor Society.

COAST GUARD
By Act of Congress on January 30, 1915, the Revenue Cutter Service and the Life-Saving Service were combined into a single unit, the Coast Guard Service. Later, it became the United States Coast Guard. By then, the lonely, towered stations and halfway houses manned by the daring surfmen were as obsolete as the graceful sailing ships that had brought them into existence.

Official records noted: "The value of the Life-Saving Establishment may ... be comprehended when it is stated that out of the multitude of persons imperiled in all the shipwrecks that have occurred within its scope during the 43 years (1871-1914) since the present system was inaugurated a smaller number has been lost than perished on the *Titanic*.... The value of property saved by the crews from year to year invariably exceeds the cost of maintaining the Service."

The history of lifesaving in America is captured in an interesting collection of U.S. Life-Saving Service memorabilia that is on exhibit at the U.S. Coast Guard Academy Library and Museum at New London, Connecticut.

The drama's done. Why then here does anyone step forth? – Because one did survive the wreck.

– Herman Melville
Moby-Dick or the Whale

The Bell Tolls

chapter three
LIGHTHOUSES

*I*ndividual states maintained their own lighthouses until 1789, when Congress created the United States Lighthouse Service to take over responsibility for the new nation's 12 lighthouses and:

> ... support, maintain, and repair the lighthouses, fog signals, beacons, and buoys on the bays, inlets, and harbors of the United States for the purpose of assisting the navigation and safety of marine traffic.

The new service was under the direction of the Undersecretary of the Treasury until Congress created the Treasury Department Lighthouse Board in 1852 to control all U.S. lighthouses. In 1903, the Lighthouse Board was transferred to the Department of Commerce, and in 1910 was re-named the Bureau of Lighthouses. In 1939, responsibility for the operation of lighthouses and other aids to navigation was assumed by the U.S. Coast Guard. As technology and cost control made them obsolete, manned lighthouses were abandoned or automated with no permanent personnel. Technology and economics have virtually banished the professional lighthouse keeper from lighthouses, now run by battery or solar power and requiring only periodic maintenance.

Charles Dickens, in his *Pickwick Papers*, chose Sam Weller, Mr. Pickwick's witty servant, to utter the words, "Anythin' for a quiet life, as the man said wen he took the situation at the lighthouse." Nineteenth century American surfmen serving as lifeguards for only $480 a year fully supported that opinion in their protest that they were paid less than lighthouse keepers who only had to tend a light in a home furnished by the government. They, on the other hand, faced life-threatening situations when they rescued shipwrecked crews and passengers. Their petition bore fruit in the form of a $300 increase for them.

Despite Dickens' wit and the surfmen's low regard for the role of lighthouse keepers, lighthouses have, for centuries, provided ships with a navigational point of reference and an indication of dangerous rocks or shoals by day and by night. Their role was served in ancient times by beach or hilltop fires. Today, modern masonry or steel-frame towers capable of resisting the severest storms are equipped with optical and sound signaling systems.

CONSTRUCTION

Lighthouses are unique because each site demands individual consideration. They range in form and size from a towering, tapered structure of reinforced concrete hundreds of feet high to a stubby extension rising above the roof of a traditional house. Illumination might be from a source of wood, coal, candle, kerosene, oil (whale, lard, or colza), or electricity, depending on when it was built or last upgraded. They were built on land or surrounded by the water that threatened safe navigation. When maintaining a wave-washed lighthouse was too difficult, a lightship was anchored at the site. No matter how they differ, each is a symbol of survival of those spared by its guidance or diligent warning of danger.

The earliest lighthouse for which a detailed account exists was the Pharos of Alexandria, one of the "Seven Wonders of The World." The rectangular, tiered stone tower crowned with fire was built on the island of Pharos c.280 B.C. It lasted until its destruction by earthquake in the 14th century. Its actual height has been lost in antiquity, but estimates range from 200 to 600 feet. Other ancient lighthouses include those built by the Romans; one still stands inside the walls of Dover Castle, England. Navigational guidance was provided by open buckets of burning coal hung from a tall pole or by burning tar or pitch on poles or in open towers. In time, the towers were protected from the elements by glass enclosures and candles replaced the burning buckets of fuel, until they were replaced by wick lanterns. The first lighthouse built in the English colonies was Boston Lighthouse on Little Brewster Island, constructed in 1716.

The Eddystone Lighthouse, off Plymouth, England was an example of a 17th century wooden tower completely exposed to the sea. It stood 120 feet (37 m) high, with its solid base anchored to rock by 12 iron stanchions. It was built in 1696-1699 by Henry Winstanley, and lasted only until its destruction by a November 1703 storm. In 1708 it was rebuilt by John Rudyerd, in the form of a slender, tapering wooden tower around a central timber mast. When it burned down in 1755, it was replaced by John Smeaton, using dovetailed masonry blocks in a curved profile for wind and wave resistance. That design dominated future lighthouse construction, with the exception of low-profile lighthouses with elaborate Gothic or Roman architecture. Rapid advances in construction and equipment occurred at the end of the 18th century. After 127 years, Smeaton's lighthouse was replaced in 1882 by the one that still stands. Nearly twice as high as Smeaton's, it rests on a solid masonry base, with foundation stones dovetailed into each other and into the reef.

In the 1880s, the sinking of steel caissons underwater was first used to support the foundation of the Rothersand Shoal Lighthouse in the Weser Estuary in Germany. A major advance, using prefabricated cement, was introduced in Sweden in the 1930s. Twenty years later, that technique led to the telescopic construction method in which two or more sections of closed-bottom caissons, one inside the other, are floated to the site and sunk. The outer section forms the foundation of the lighthouse and the inner telescopic sections are then raised by hydraulic jacks and locked in position to form the tower.

In the 1960s, the U.S. Coast Guard erected a number of lighthouses that resembled oil rigs. They consisted of a tubular steel-braced framework with hollow legs. After the structure was positioned on the sea bed, piles were driven through the hollow legs into the bedrock and concrete was poured into the legs.

By 1880, no fewer than 3,500 light stations were in operation throughout the world. A history of lighthouses written by Patrick Beaver in 1971 estimated that more than 50,000 were in existence, with the likelihood that 10,000 more were on inland waters of countries like Russia and the United States. Along the Atlantic coast alone, from Maine to Florida, 413 lighthouses were built at one time or another.

In addition to warning ships away from rocks or shoals, a lighthouse must tell a navigator where he is. That is accomplished during daylight with the architecture, bright colors, and bold design that distinguish one lighthouse from another. A mariner sighting one of the three lighthouses in the illustration on the right would recognize: Cape Hatteras Lighthouse on Hatteras Island (left), with its spiral black stripe from Bodie Island Lighthouse (right) with two circular black stripes, a few miles to the north, or Ocracoke Lighthouse, (center), broader and without stripes, a few miles south. Such a visual identification is called a "daymaric."

Courtesy of the National Park Service.

FUEL

Bales of oil-soaked cotton or oakum and pitch provided fuel for early lighthouses. Coal followed sometime before the mid-900s, then wood in the 1500s. The use of wood gave way to other fuels, but coal remained in some European lighthouses until 1858.

Candles were first used to illuminate lighthouses in the 1600s. Those in use at the Caistor, England lighthouse in 1628 weighed one-third pound each. Candles weighing one pound each lighted Harwich Lighthouse in 1676. Sixty of that size went into the first Eddystone Lighthouse. One deterrent to using tallow or beeswax candles was that keepers prized them for cooking, or eating if food stores were scarce.

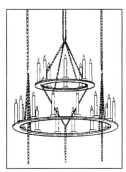

Until the first enclosed lantern room was installed at Eddystone in 1699, the open fires of lighthouses were more productive of smoke than light, particularly under wet, windy conditions.

Solid wick oil lamps came into use, but they were so inefficient and sooty that in 1796 the inspector of the Boston Lighthouse condemned the 16 solid-wick lamp of the lighthouse ineffective because "the lantern became in a short time full of smoak." In 1782, a Swiss scientist, Aime Argand,

A two-tier, 24 candle chandelier used in a British lighthouse.
Courtesy of the U.S. Lighthouse Society.

invented an oil lamp with a circular wick protected by a glass chimney. Earlier wicks were solid and either round or flat. The outer edges burned before the center and the center smoldered

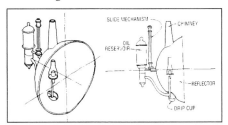

An Argand lamp and parabolic reflector.
Courtesy of the U.S. Lighthouse Society.

instead of burning. Argand positioned a metal tube inside a slightly larger tube, with just enough clearance for a circular wick and a small screw adjustment to move the wick up and down. The result was better combustion, with a light that was bright and steady, and with a minimum of unburned carbon soot. In a fortunate accident, his brother lowered a hipped glass, narrowed at top, over the burning wick. The result was increased power of the light.

A further advance was made in the 1860s with development by the Austrian chemist Carl von Welsbach of the gas-mantle lamp. Welsbach's lamp burned coal gas, although electric carbon-arc lamps had already been installed in 1858 in the South Forelands on the English Channel. An unheralded American experiment in lighthouse illumination that might have altered the direction of 19th century lighthouse development was conducted in 1817. For one year David Melville, a Newport, Rhode Island resident illuminated the Beavertail Lighthouse with gas. He manufactured the gas on site by heating rosin and tar, then passing it through water into copper pipes to the light tower. Although it was praised for cleanliness, brilliance, and simplifying the keeper's duties, Melville's contract was not renewed. It was suggested that the continued use of whale oil was favored by the Federal Government because the whaling industry served as a training school for the United States Navy.

In 1886, an electric arc lamp was installed in the Statue of Liberty, and before the end of the century the Sandy Hook beacon at the entrance to New York Harbor was electrified. Electricity was not always available at a lighthouse site, although an electric generator was installed at the 1858 South Foreland Lighthouse. Despite the introduction of electricity, a new lantern using vaporized kerosene to heat an incandescent mantle was introduced by Arthur Kitson in 1901. In 1921, David Hood modified Kitson's lamp to use petroleum.

Swedish engineer Niles Gustav Dalen introduced an acetylene burner in 1906 as a more efficient, cost-saving alternative to petroleum. He overcame the explosive danger of acetylene's high volatility with a sponge-like mass, primarily of asbestos and charcoal, to hold the gas in its shipping container. It proved far more effective than the existing French "Dissous" porous mass method. Although flashlight apparatus to create a flash of light, already existed, Dalen developed one that reduced the length of flash to about three-tenths of a second. Between flashes, only a small amount of gas was used to feed a very small pilot light.

As a further fuel economy measure and to reduce maintenance, Dalen eliminated the need for turning lighthouse beacons off during daylight hours with his invention of a sun valve that turned off the burner when exposed to light. To increase light intensity, several lenses rotated around the burner. In addition, the Dalen mixer provided an optimum ratio of nine parts of air to one of acetylene. Dalen also designed a metal net incandescent mantle that provided a brighter and more even flame. However, despite Dalen's accomplishments with acetylene, David Hood's vaporized kerosene lamp continued in use at some lighthouses.

In recognition of Dalen's contribution to navigation, he received the Nobel Prize in Physics, but King Gustav V presented the medal and diploma on December 12, 1912, to his brother, Professor Albin Dalen. Niles Gustav was still recovering from a terrible explosion two months earlier, an accident that ironically blinded the man who contributed so much to visual navigation.

In 1917, five years after he lost his eyesight, Dalen developed an elevator mechanism to automatically replace a broken incandescent mantle, eliminating the need to visit beacon sites only to replace mantles.

The incandescent lamp came into use in the 1920s and became standard equipment in lighthouses with electricity. The most recent innovation is the xenon high-pressure arc lamp, which provides a powerful electric arc in a quartz bulb filled with the inert gas xenon.

LIGHT

Brilliance of the beam from a lighthouse has multiplied with the evolution of today's lamps, but the light source is only part of the picture. When hilltop fires were used to guide navigators, as much light was directed inland as to sea. Even lanterns, protected from the elements by glass, lost much of their efficiency behind, above, and below the source of light. Successful efforts to collect and concentrate those errant light beams have magnified their intensity toward the target area at sea.

First, a tiny reflector positioned behind the flame of a lantern reversed the direction of its light rays to reinforce those directed to sea. Late in the 1800s, hundreds of silver-coated, copper reflectors shaped into cone or parabolic form behind the light directed otherwise wasted beams into streams of light headed toward the target area. That technique, referred to as the *Catoptric* method, was an improvement over a single reflector, but much

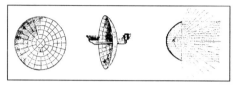

light still escaped to the top, bottom, and sides of the lamp. Still, the resulting beam was so concentrated that it had to be rotated to serve more than a single position at sea. The first revolving light was installed in 1781 at Carlsten, Sweden. Early

A parabolic reflector formed of small facets of slivered glass. Reflectors directed otherwise wasted beams into streams of light headed toward the target area, but much light still escaped to the top, bottom, and side of the lamp.

lenses revolved on metal wheels about three inches in diameter, operated by a clockwork mechanism.

A method for rotating lights by floating them on a bath of mercury was invented in 1890. It minimized friction and permitted revolutions as low as 15 seconds. That led to the identification of a lighthouse by its pattern of intervals of light and darkness. Although colored lenses could signal identity or specific hazards, they are not widely used. A red or green lens loses 70% of the strength of a light. However, color panels over every second or third panel of a light provides an effective pattern of long range white flashes to capture attention, followed by a less intense color signal.

FRESNEL LENS

In the 1820s, the French physicist Augustin Fresnel designed the *Dioptric* system, an improvement on the Catoptric reflector. He installed a curtain of prisms around a bulls-eye lens, to bend or refract light into narrow, horizontal beams. Fresnel later added prisms above and below to reflect and refract errant light into beams parallel to the main beam. The result was a beehive-like design that captured about 85% of the light produced for projection to the target area. That method, the *Catadioptric* system, is the basis of all Fresnel lens lighthouse optical systems still in use.

Six major sizes of Fresnel lenses, referred to as Orders, were established, with the 1st Order being the largest. It is over six feet in diameter and its array of prisms is about ten feet high. It stands about 19 feet high with its pedestal and clockworks. The smallest is the 6th Order lens, with a diameter of 12 inches and only 18 inches high. Three additional Orders of Fresnel

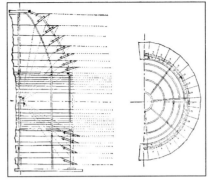

Fresnel's catadioptic system

lenses to satisfy specific needs included 3 ½, meso-radial, and hyper-radial 8 ½ feet in diameter.

A lighthouse may serve several purposes, sometimes to show danger, at other times to invite entry. In some instances, they may serve multiple purposes. The size Fresnel lens required is generally determined by the range needed. Where the distance is 8 to 12 miles, 4th and 5th Order lenses are used. Other factors include the purpose of the light:

> Landfall, or Making Lights (what a mariner first sights approaching a country from overseas)—1st or 2nd Order
>
> Warning Lights (reef, shoal, or coastal harbor entrance)—3rd or 4th Order
>
> Coasting lights (fix position along coast - usually situated so mariner may take a bearing on two or three at a time)— individually dependent on range requirements, but probably 4th or 5th Order
>
> Leading Lights (showing entry to harbor or channel - usually range lights, lined up one behind and taller than the other)-- 4th and 5th Order
>
> Port or Entrance Lights (marking ends of piers)—5th and 6th Order

It took the United States 30 years to follow the lead of European countries in adapting the single lamp Fresnel system because one man thought they were too costly. He was Stephen Pleasontson, Auditor of the Treasury, who headed the United States Lighthouse Service. He insisted that multiple Argand lamps backed by reflectors were satisfactory and less expensive. American mariners returning from European waters cited the brilliance of the Fresnel-equipped lighthouses, but Pleasonton was adamant.

The demand for improvement finally resulted in Congress appointing the United States Lighthouse Board to serve as an ad hoc committee in a one-year investigation of U.S. lighthouses and world-wide navigation systems. The study revealed glaring administrative problems in Pleasonton's Lighthouse Service and confirmed the

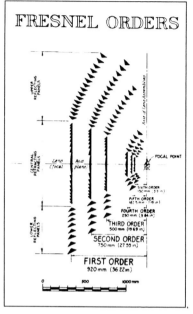

Lens sections are superimposed at the same scale for comparative purposes only. No lens was constructed with all orders combined.
Courtesy of the Historic American Engineering Record,
Mabel A, Baiges delineator, 1988

superiority of the Fresnel system. In 1852 Pleasonton was removed and the Lighthouse Board was appointed to head the Lighthouse Service. The Fresnel system was adopted, and only nine years later all American lighthouses were equipped with Fresnel lenses.

SOUND

Of his five senses, sight and hearing are the two used by a helmsman trying to maneuver his vessel to safety through dangerous waters. Under a blanket of fog, or blinded by snow or tempest, he gains nothing from a warning light he cannot see. Unless he depends on intuition or telepathy, hearing is his salvation, and when that sound is the crashing of surf on rocks, it is usually too late. Lighthouses experimented with cannon, bells, steam whistles, sirens, reed trumpets, diaphones, and diaphragm horns before settling on variations of the siren. Its mournful wail, caused by jets of compressed air forced into a plate revolving around another similarly slotted plate, howls like a fire engine or police car.

Rockets and canons provided navigational warnings in Europe during the 18th century. Although cannons were employed in a few American locations, the first sound signal used on a regular basis was the bell. Caladon Daboll of New London, Connecticut pioneered the development of an automatic bell striker. He also developed the first practical power operated successor to the bell, the compressed air fog trumpet. It was powered by horses walking on a ramp or in a circle to pump air into a compressed air holding tank. Alternatively, air could be pumped into the tank manually. A valve released the air through a locomotive whistle or reed trumpet. The first installation was a manual system aboard the Bartlett Reef Lightship off New London. Its performance led to a horse-powered system at the Beavertail, Rhode Island lighthouse.

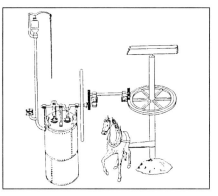

Horse-powered fog signal.
Courtesy of the U.S. Lighthouse Society.

Success of the Beavertail experiment was attested to by mariners and the Collector of Customs at Newport. Many stated they could hear the signal six miles from the source. Other installations followed. By 1852 the Light List carried bells and trumpets as aids to navigation for the first time.

Although the trumpet program was successful in its performance, horse maintenance was costly and inconvenient. Introduction of the caloric steam engine by John Ericsson in 1833 overcame that shortcoming, extending the useful life of Daboll's signal. The designation caloric distinguished the engine from earlier, hot air engines. It was powered by the expansion of air heated by a coal-fueled fire or gas flame driving a piston-like canister up and down.

In 1857, a 5-inch steam-powered whistle was installed at the Beavertail station. Nine years later it was replaced by a caloric engine driving a reed horn signal, reflecting the emphasis on experimentation to improve American aids to navigation. But the age of steam had arrived and steam powered a 10-inch locomotive or ship's whistle at Maine's West Quoddy Head and Cape Elizabeth stations in 1869.

Technology advances in sound signals were so rapid that the whistle was being driven into obscurity even before the 1869 Maine installations. The siren was tested in 1867, and was installed in 1868 at the Sandy Hook East Beacon. It was a slotted revolving disc on a fixed, slotted disc. About 70 pounds of steam forced through the discs produced the siren tone.

By 1898 oil engines had already begun to replace coal-fired caloric engines. Two events about the beginning of the 20th century further advanced the technology of maritime sound signals. Electricity provided instantaneous power without the maintenance of a steam plant, and the diaphone was developed in Canada to replace the siren. The diaphone produced a single or two-tone signal with slotted cylinders that moved rapidly forward and backward instead of spinning. Its vibrating tone is known to shake buildings and set off landslides.

The diaphone was not introduced in the United States until 1914, and fifteen years later it was replaced by the diaphragm horn because of its initial cost and high maintenance. Its sound, somewhat like a diaphone, was produced by passing air between two $1/16$-inch thick metal discs. One disc was solid and $5\frac{7}{8}$ inches in diameter. The other was $6\frac{1}{4}$ inches in diameter with a 3-inch hole in the center.

Over the years, a variety of other sound signals provided guidance for mariners. At the West Point Lighthouse on the Hudson River, an approaching ship's whistle automatically activated the signal. Another system, "Echo Boards", usually installed at bends of a channel or at the junction of waterways, reflected an approaching ship's whistle. But the most unusual was the 1859 installation of a blowhole-activated trumpet on the rugged coast of California's Farallon Islands. The wilder the weather, the more it blew. Unfortunately, it blew not at all at low tide or when the sea was calm and foggy. An 1863 storm tore the whistle loose, and in 1880 a steam-powered siren replaced it.

Today, only a few diaphragms and "pure tone" electronic signals remain in operation, and the electronic signals are so damaging to hearing that the Coast Guard has discontinued their use when the sound encroaches on residential areas.

ELECTRONICS

Radio came into maritime use in the early 1900s, but though it provided communication between ships and shore stations, it was of no help in fixing a vessel's position. The radio compass and direction finder allowed a ship to follow a beam to its source, but with no indication of its distance. What did work was to combine a radio signal with a diaphone sound signal sent from the lighthouse at the same instant. Radio beams travel at 186,000 miles per second (instantaneous for the purpose) and sound at only one mile in five seconds, That permits a navigator with a stop watch to measure the time difference between the signals in seconds and divide the result by five to determine distance to the lighthouse. With a time difference of fifteen seconds, the distance would be three miles.

RADAR and SONAR, both products of World War II, emitted signals that were reflected back to a ship, where they registered a blip on a screen in the case of radar or sounded a ping to a sonar operator, who could also measure distance by elapsed time between emission and reception.

Those developments contributed to the safety of navigation, but the Second World War also produced a remarkable system called LORAN A and LORAN C, with a useful range of about 1,400 miles by night and about 750 miles by day. Signals emitted by a master (primary) station on shore are repeated by a slave (secondary) station hundreds of miles away, under radio control by the master station. Both signals were received aboard ship by a TV-like machine that displayed them on a screen as small waves or irregularities. The distance between the waves reflected the difference in arrival time of the signals. An electronic timing device measured the time difference in microseconds (millionths of a second) and showed all positions with the same arrival time in the form of a curve. By referring to a map showing curves for each time interval, called LORAN lines of position, the navigator could identify the one corresponding to the machines' reading. Repeating the procedure, but selecting LORAN transmitters at a different location, the navigator pinpointed the ship's position as the point where the two loran lines of position intersected.

That post-World War II state-of-the-art LORAN system has since been upgraded to eliminate the intermediate manual steps, and provide a navigator with direct output that tells him where he is with remarkable precision. However, LORAN is slowly becoming obsolete. Its replacement is Global Positioning Satellite navigation or GPS. GPS is a system that can establish the position of any object on earth using the principle of triangulation. Precise atomic clocks aboard GPS satellites are used to measure the time it takes an encoded radio signal to travel from the satellite to a GPS receiver. When signal travel times are calculated from orbiting satellites whose positions are precisely known, the position of the receiver becomes known. Originally developed by the U.S. Department of Defense, the unprecedented accuracy of GPS is now available for commercial use.

LIGHTHOUSE KEEPERS

There is no longer room in the lighthouse for Dickens' Sam Weller, but if there were, he might not find the daily routine as easy as he expected. In an environment of close quarters, solitary existence, and constant exposure to danger, some early lightkeepers were called on to pilot ships into port and serve as health inspectors. Others, with the unofficial duty of lifesaving, made heroic rescues at sea or were lost when their lighthouse toppled into the sea. And dispelling the impression of a quiet, easy life, the following duties of a lightkeeper appeared in an undated (circa 1915) issue of *The Lightkeeper*, journal of the Literature to Lighthouses Mission. "The most important are the night duties, which commence at lighting time (sunset), when the lamps are lit and must be kept burning brightly till sunrise the following morning. The night is divided into watches of about three to four hours, according to the number of men at the station. Most lighthouses are of a revolving character. At a lens station the lamp is fixed on a table in the centre of the lens, which revolves round the lamp by means of a machine. The lens apparatus are differently constructed so as to distinguish the character of the lights in the same district.

"The kind of machine used is just clockwork on a large scale; sometimes the weight is five cwt. A similar small machine is used for pumping the oil up to the lamp. This machine pumps up far more oil than the lamp consumes, but the overflow runs back to the fountain again. Both machines run for about one hour, when the Keeper on watch must wind them up again, and so on through the night. He has also to keep the lantern clear of sweat inside, and of snow on the outside whenever snow falls; and perhaps the most arduous job a lightkeeper has to do is to go outside the lantern in a gale of wind to clean the snow off. Sometimes he has to hold on with both hands for fear of being thrown off; and he may not be a quarter of an hour in when he has to go out again. He has also to keep constant lookout, especially in rough weather, for any vessel which may be in distress. Whenever such occurs it must be immediately reported to the nearest Coast Guard or lifeboat station. A number of lighthouses are now connected by telephone for this purpose, which can be used day or night. Rockets are kept at some others for summoning lifeboats, and the International Code of Signals for using through the day, but only for reporting casualties at sea.

"The Keeper on duty has to make readings of the barometer and thermometer, and to mark down the state of the weather and different directions of the wind, which must be written in a book for the purpose, returns of which are sent to the Office and Meteorological Society monthly. He has also to note every light in the district, and to write it in another book, whether seen or not seen as the case may be. If a lightkeeper, through his negligence, allows a light to become extinguished, or a revolving light to become stationary, he is dismissed the service, and forfeits all claim to pension, however long he may have served.

"A lightkeeper's daily routine commences at 9 a.m. in the light room, trimming the lamps and cleaning the lens and prisms; the reflectors (the face of which is of finely polished silver) must be particularly cleaned and polished by commencing in the centre and working with a circular motion outwards. A little rouge is used on the chamois skins for the reflectors. Visitors to a lighthouse often wonder at their brightness and beauty, and ask what they are cleaned with. Then the machines have to be rubbed and oiled, brass work polished, and the whole place dusted down. These duties usually occupy both Keepers from an hour to three hours daily in the light room. The outside premises have also to be kept in order. All woodwork and ironwork is painted every summer; lighthouses are so exposed to sea-spray that this is absolutely necessary. Tower dwelling-houses and boundary walls are lime-washed annually. Besides a little gardening, the above duties roughly forms the Lighthouse Keeper's daily routine."

Dr. Robert Scheina included the following selected stanzas from a poem by Cliff Morena in *Coast Guard History*:

ON BRASSWORK

Oh, what is the bane of a lightkeeper's life,
That cause him worry and struggle and strife,
That makes him use cuss words and beat up his wife?
It's brasswork.

The lamp in the tower, reflector and shade,
The tools and accessories pass in parade,
As a matter of fact the whole outfit is made,
Of brasswork.

I dig, scrub and polish, and work with a might.
And just when I get it all shining and bright,
In comes the fog like a thief in the night.
Goodnight brasswork.

And when I have polished until I am cold,
And I'm taken aloft to the heavenly fold,
Will my harp and crown be made of pure gold?
No. Brasswork!

In addition to the tedious work of lighthouse keeping, danger lurked everywhere. In addition to the obvious danger of the sea, many lighthouses were outposts of civilization. John W.B. Thompson, assistant keeper at Cape Florida Lighthouse, wrote in his log on July 23, 1836:

"As I was going ... to the dwelling house, I discovered a large body of Indians within 20 yards of me ... I ran for the lighthouse ... At that moment they discharged a volley of rifle balls, which cut my clothes and hat and perforated the door ... As I was turning the key the savages had hold of the door ... I kept them from the [light]house until dark.

"... They poured in a heavy fire ... to the door and to the window even with the ground.... Their balls had perforated the tin tanks of oil, consisting of 225 gallons. My bedding, clothing, and in fact everything I had was soaked in oil .... I retreated to the top of the [lighthouse] .... At last the awful moment arrived, the crackling flames burst around me.

"The savages at the same time began their hellish yells.... The lantern was now full of flame, the lamps and glasses bursting and flying in all directions, my clothes on fire, and to move from the place where I was, would be instant death from their rifles. My flesh was roasting, and to put an end to my horrible suffering I got up and threw the keg of gunpowder down the scuttle. Instantly, it exploded and shook the tower from top to bottom.

"It had not the desired effect of blowing me to eternity ..."

The Indians left after the fire died down, believing that Thompson was dead and the keeper was rescued the following day.

The great gale of April 1851 washed the newly constructed Minots Ledge Lighthouse into the sea and drowned two keepers. In 1893, three lighthouses in Chesapeake Bay, Solomons Lamp, Wolf Trap, and Smiths Point, were swept away by ice floes.

In 1906, a hurricane destroyed 23 lighthouses along the Gulf of

Mexico. Sand Island and the lighthouse on it disappeared, along with the keepers. The Horn Island keeper and his wife and daughter drowned in the same storm.

HEROISM

Heroic acts were not uncommon in the U.S. Lighthouse Service and they were not isolated to the grizzled male prototype clenching a pipe in his teeth. Women often served as light keepers. Most were wives and daughters of Revolutionary War and Civil War veterans who were incapacitated by war wounds. A Rhode Island woman, Ida Lewis, was the most famous of the female light keepers. She was only 15 years old when her father suffered a stroke and she took over, initially as assistant to her mother, then as keeper of Lime Rock Lighthouse in Newport Harbor. In addition to caring for her father and the lighthouse, Ida rowed her younger brothers and sisters to the mainland so they could attend school. She developed into such a skilled boat handler that in her first year at the lighthouse she single-handedly saved four young men from a capsized sailboat in rough water, where they were clinging to the craft.

Ida became a celebrity as several other rescues quickly followed. She received numerous medals and awards, and in 1869 was featured on the cover of *Harper's Weekly* magazine. The state of Rhode Island proclaimed an Ida Lewis Day, children wore scarves like hers, and girls wore their hair "Ida Lewis Style."

President Ulysses S. Grant visited Ida at the lighthouse. During her 39 years as keeper of Lime Rock Lighthouse, she was credited with saving 18 lives, but the total may have been as high as 24. She made her last rescue at age 65, pulling a drowning woman from the harbor. After Ida's death four years later, the lighthouse was renamed the Ida Lewis Lighthouse, the only such honor afforded a keeper.

On July 2, 1906, the fog machinery at Angel Island Light in San Francisco Bay broke down. Juliet Nichols, the female keeper, "struck the bell by hand for 20 hours and 35 minutes, until the fog lifted...." A few months later, it failed again, and she "stood all night on the platform outside and struck the bell with a nail hammer with all her might."

At dawn on September 7, 1838, 22-year-old Grace Darling and her father, the keeper of Longstone Lighthouse off England's Northumberland Coast, awoke to the sight of the steamship Forfarshire on Big Harcar Rock. The wreck was almost a mile away but, Grace and her father could see survivors in the steamer's rigging, using the station's spyglass.

They lowered the lighthouse's 21 1/2-foot long, flat-bottomed boat. The huge waves and violent current, it required about an hour to row to the wreck. They only could take five of the nine survivors and had to make a second trip for the remaining four.

The casualties of the disaster have been estimated to be between 42 and 64. The following is an excerpt from _The Grace Darling Song_, author unknown:

> *Twas on the Longstone Lighthouse,*
> *There dwelt an English Maid:*
> *Pure as the air around her,*
> *Of danger ne'er afraid.*
> *One morning just at daybreak,*
> *A storm-toss'd wreck she spied;*
> *And tho' to try seemed madness,*
> *I'll save the crew!' she cried.*

The role of lightkeeper flourished until automation virtually eliminated the need for lighthouse attendance. By the end of the 1980s, the last U.S. manned lighthouses, the Ambrose Beacon in New York City's harbor and several on the Maine coast were completely automated. Their keepers are gone, but the sturdy towers, supported by new technology, still signal salvation to mariners in distress.

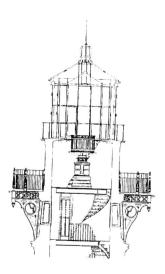

BOOK II

EASTERN LONG ISLAND

*L*ong Island, New York stretches 118 miles northeast from the mouth of the Hudson River to the tip of the southernmost fluke of the two peninsulas that make up much of Eastern Long Island. Great and Little Peconic Bays, and Gardiners Bay separate the two, but they share the same heritage. Both are composed of the terminal moraine of retreating glaciers. Unlike New York City and the suburban communities between, the "East End" is thinly settled and is known for its beaches, fishing, agriculture, and the rural charm of its old villages and hamlets.

The 27-mile northern fluke (North Fork) extends from Riverhead to Orient Point. The longer, 43-mile, southern fluke (South Fork) ends at Montauk Point. It is bordered on the south by the open Atlantic, except for a stretch of barrier beach that extends from the west, part way along the fork. Long Island Sound separates the North Fork from Connecticut.

The first English settlement on Long Island was a result of the "Pequot War" of 1636-37, a conflict between the Pequot Indians of Connecticut and the English and their Indian allies, Mohegans and Narragansetts. An Englishmen named Lion Gardiner who had served in the British Army, crossed the Atlantic in 1635 with his Dutch-born wife Mary. The following year he built a fort at the mouth of the Connecticut River. His son David, born while the fort was being constructed, was the first white child born in what is now the state of Connecticut.

During the Pequot War, Wyandanch, an Indian from a group of Algonquin Indians on Long Island the English called Montauketts, crossed the Sound in his canoe and Gardiner recorded the event in 1660 in his written account of the Pequot War: "Waiandance [sic], next brother to the old Sachem [chief] of Long Island ... He came to know if we were angry with all Indians. I answered No, but only with such as had killed Englishmen. He asked whether they that lived upon Long Island might come to trade with us."

The Montauketts had been paying tribute (to be left alone) to the powerful Pequots. Wyandanch told Gardiner that if the Indians could trade with the English, they would make tribute payments to him. After the English massacred hundreds of Pequots at the Indian fort near today's Mystic, Connecticut, the Montauketts realized they were the new power and could dominate them the way the Pequots had.

Gardiner also wrote that he told Wyandanch that they would trade with him, "if you will kill all the Pequots that come to you, and send me their heads." He continued, "so he went away and did as I said, and sent me five heads ..."

In 1639, after the Pequots were vanquished, Gardiner purchased the island off East Hampton, that stills bears his family name, with Wyandanch's help (see Gardiners Island Lighthouse). Gardiner's daughter, Elizabeth, was the first English child born in what is now New York State.

Gardiner and Wyandanch, who eventually became sachem of the Montauketts, became good friends. When a war party of Niantic Indians attacked the Montaukett village in 1653, and kidnapped Wyandanch's daughter, Gardiner went to Rhode Island and ransomed her back for his friend. He purchased about 100,000 acres of Long Island from Wyandanch, including much that Wyandanch probably did not own, including ten square miles of what is today Smithtown and Setauket. On one of the deeds Wyandanch drew stick figures of two men, one an European, the other an Indian, and they are holding hands. Steve Wick wrote in the November 10, issue of *Newsday*: "Last summer, on a day rich in history, descendants of both men met. Robert David Lion Gardiner and Robert Cooper, a descendant of Wyandanch who lives in East Hampton, traveled together to Gardiner's Island. There, they talked about the friendship of their ancestors.... 'When Wyandanch died, Lion wrote a letter to a friend in Connecticut and said his heart was broken, his best friend was dead.' Gardiner said."

When Lion Gardiner died in 1663, he was buried in his British Army uniform, a steel corset, a steel helmet, and with his sword attached to his belt. In 1888, Sarah Gardiner, a descendant noticed that his tombstone, near the center of East Hampton's Old Cemetery, was badly eroded and ordered a new one. She commissioned James Renwick, the designer of St. Patrick's Cathedral, to design a Gothic granite tombstone. His design is cathedral-shaped and under its roof is a sarcophagus with a recumbent knight in steel hat and corset on top.

By 1640, other English colonists had followed Gardiner and sailed from Connecticut to settle both forks of Eastern Long Island. Southold, named for the English village of Southwold, on the North Fork; Southampton on the South Fork. Both villages claim to have been settled first.

Early English settlers of the "East End" chose it for fishing or agriculture. The rich soil and bountiful sea attracted immigrants from Poland and other European countries. The population grew, but generations kept family traditions alive. Produce and poultry farms expanded and fishing flourished. Long Island ducks, oysters, and potatoes were demanded by discriminating diners. Beautiful beaches eventually attracted vacationers and tourists from less idyllic communities.

Today, large potato farms have given way to vineyards, shellfish have diminished from over harvesting, and duck farms are disappearing (to the delight of nearby residents). Service industries have taken root to accommodate the needs of retirees who now compose a large part of the "East End" population. The sea is now a source of recreation instead of a means of survival, but ships are still lost in the waters off the east end of Long Island.

New York City owes its beginnings to its waterfront, its harbor, and the trade enterprise of the Dutch. Their founding of New Amsterdam in 1624 led to a steady growth of sea commerce until New York became the commercial capital of the New World, then the entire world. A continuing flow of merchant vessels linked metropolitan New York with trade centers along the Atlantic seaboard and exotic ports of call around the globe.

Prior to the Civil War all great American fortunes stemmed from the sea. Ships and shipping were the most conspicuous features of New York business life, with the waterfront the city's focal point of interest and activity. Trade routes developed to the north, south, and east. Traffic to the north and east traveled through Long Island Sound or along the south shore of Long Island. Storm, fog, shoals, boulders, military conflict, and navigation errors exacted a toll of shipwrecks that now litter the bottom of Eastern Long Island shores.

Residents and tourists of Eastern Long Island have ready access to history under the sea in the many ships of war, commerce, and transportation that lie on the bottom of waters off Long Island. Some have been there since before the Pilgrims set foot on Plymouth Rock. The first recorded Long Island shipwreck was Adriaen Block's *Tiger* in 1613. The Dutch ship caught fire while at anchor off the southern tip of modern-day Manhattan Island. The ship was beached in a small cove on the west side of what is now Greenwich Street where it burned to the waterline. Timbers of Block's burned ship were found in 1916 during a subway excavation. They now hang in the Museum of the City of New York.

Tiger's crew cut down trees and hewed them into planks and beams with tools salvaged from the wreck. With nails and other fastenings recovered from the wreck, they built a 44-foot long ship they christened *Restless*, a name that probably reflected their mood. The following year Block rediscovered the island Verrazano had named Louise in 1524. Thereafter the island appeared on Dutch maps as "Adriaen Block's Eylant."

Block's ship was not lost off Eastern Long Island, but hundreds of other vessels of all types have sunk off Eastern Long Island since then. During both world wars German U-boats crossed the Atlantic to prey upon merchant and naval vessels in American waters. One ship, the tanker *Coimbra*, covered in this book, was sunk by a U-boat.

Montauk Point, Long Island's lands end, reaches into the Atlantic, probing for victims to add to its toll of shipwrecks that line its shores. Orient, too, is littered with the remains of ships that failed to successfully navigate its coast. One, an unnamed sloop that sank on December 12, 1800, inspired poetry by an anonymous author. The poem, published in *Sporting Scenes and Sundry Sketches, Volume I*, 1842, reflects the empathy of local residents of the seafaring community for the victims and those left behind by such tragedy. The original spelling has been retained.

OYSTERPOND POINT DISASTER
December 12, 1800

Come all ye good people of every degree
come listen awhile with attention to me
a sorrowful story i am going to relate
a mournful disaster that hapened of late

O Oyster Pond tremble at that awful stroke
remember the voice that Jehovah has spoke
to teach us we are mortals exposed to death
and subject each moment to yield up our breath

on Monday the 12th of december so cold
in the year 18 hundred as i have been told
the winds blowing high and the rains beating down
when a vessel arived at Oyster-Pond town

their anchors being cast their ships tore away
all hands for the shore were preparring straitway
down into the boat soon they did repair
and on to the shore was praying to steer
But mark their hard fortune it is mournful indeed

yet no one can hinder what God has decread
the council of heaven on that fatal day
by death in an instant calld numbers away

A number of men in their halth and their prime
called out of this world in an instant of time
the boat turning plunge them all into the deep
and 5 out of 7 in death fell asleep

the sorrowful tidings were caried straitway
to friends and relations without more delay
but o their lamentins no launge can express
nore point out of joy, great grief and distress

the widows are breaved in sorrow to mourn
the loss of their husbands no more to return
besides a great number of orphans we hear
lamenting the loss of their parents so dear

Also a young damsel a making great mourn
for the untimely death of her lover that gone
for the day of their nuptials apointed had been
and the land of sweet wedlock those lovers to join

Alas all their lamenting are all but in vain
they can't come again
o friends and relations lament not to late
the council of heaven has sealed their fate

their bodies when found were all conveyed home
on the sabbath day following prepared for the tomb
their bodies in their coffin being all laid aside
in Oyster Pond meeting house ally so wide.

EASTERN LONG ISLAND SHIPWRECKS

The Bell Tolls

COMMODORE—DISREGARD FOR SAFETY

Type of vessel: side-wheel passenger liner
Where built: Bishop & Simonson, New York
Launched: 1848
Length/beam: 275' / 32'
Gross tons: 984
Sunk: December 27, 1866
Cause of sinking: storm / intentionally beached
Location: about one mile west of Horton Point Lighthouse
Approximate depth of water: an anchor was recovered in 11 feet of water

DURING THE MID-1800s, an unwritten Long Island law decreed that everything that washed ashore from shipwrecks belonged to the resident of that property. Halsey Haynes owned a farm of 110 acres in Southold Town, with frontage on Long Island Sound. His granddaughter, Mrs. Eva Gordon Statebeck wrote: "... a good Presbyterian though he was. Sunday or weekday he paced the beach for trophies. Thus on December 26, 1866, he saw the wreck of the steamer *Commodore* with 100 passengers [actually 92] and a variety of merchandise. A beautiful purple and gold carpet came ashore which later adorned the new home which Grandpa Halsey was building across the street. The heavy front-door of this new domicile also came from the *Commodore*'s remains, and also a very beautiful mahogany stair-railing. The door had a massive lock and key ..."

The side-wheel *Commodore* carried passengers between New York City and Stonington, Connecticut. The wooden-hulled, 275-foot-long steamer, with a beam of 32 feet, displaced 984 tons. She was built in 1848 by Bishop & Simonson in New York for the Stonington Line.

COLLISION

On the morning of August 6, 1851, *Commodore* cautiously felt her way through dense fog on Long Island Sound, en route to New York. Her fog whistle was in use and a lookout was posted in her bow. Suddenly, the massive shape of another steamer, the eastbound *Connecticut*, emerged from the fog and cut into *Commodore*'s hull, destroying her wheelhouse. The other steamer's stem raked *Commodore* from the point of impact all the way to her stern. *Commodore*'s boiler was punctured and driven off its mounting by the force of the blow that almost capsized her, spreading a panic among the passengers.

Connecticut continued on her course after the collision. Although *Commodore* was badly damaged in her upper works, she was not in danger of sinking; she hove to, and awaited help.

About two hours after the accident, *Knickerbocker*, coming out of Norwich, took off *Commodore*'s passengers and towed the disabled steamer to Rikers' Island. Two tugs later towed her to the East River dry-dock for repairs.

Commodore's captain placed blame for the accident on *Connecticut* for not blowing her whistle in the heavy fog.

In 1863, the side-wheeler was sold to the Merchants Navigation and Transportation Company. Three years later, after 18 years of transporting passengers across Long Island Sound, *Commodore* was condemned as unseaworthy. Captain William Bradford, district supervisor of the U.S. Treasury Department's steamship inspection service, found many of her wooden beams and planking rotten and in need of replacement. The owners sent the steamer to New Haven, Connecticut for repairs. The overhaul, including replacement of rotten wood, cost $10,000. That failed to satisfy Captain Bradford; he still considered the ship unsafe for the winter ice of Long Island Sound. The local steamship inspectors agreed with Bradford and refused to issue a conditional certificate for her to transport passengers unless her hull received additional repairs.

Commodore returned to New York without further repairs or certification. The lack of a certificate and the possibility of a fine had no influence on the Merchants Navigation & Transportation Company's decision to send its ship from New York to Stonington, carrying 92 passengers, many of whom were immigrants.

STRANDING

December 27, 1866, was not a pleasant day for steaming or sailing. The wind blew hard all day, but around 4:00 p.m. its intensity decreased. *Commodore*'s captain, M.H. Gregory, either ignored his barometer or was pressured by his employer, because the steamer left her dock at about 4:10 p.m. and proceeded east through the Sound. At 8:00 p.m., the wind freshened so severely from the west-northwest that a violent gale developed with heavy seas. By 10:30 p.m. the rough seas and the wind, nearly aft, made steering very difficult. About ten miles east of New Haven, a tremendous wave damaged the steamer's rudder and the helmsman lost control of the wheel. The side-wheeler almost capsized—almost, but not quite. She rolled onto her side and remained there. Her smokestacks were torn off and water poured into the engine rooms. The boilers fires went out, leaving *Commodore* at the mercy of the heavy seas. She was still on her side, while the wind blew her across the sound. Near the Long Island shore, about one-mile west of the Horton Point Lighthouse, two anchors were dropped to hold her offshore near Peconic (Goldsmith's) Inlet.

Anchored with her keel to the wind, the steamer did not seem to be taking on water. However, when the crew managed to right the vessel by use of the anchor cables, the severe strain on her hull opened seams. *Commodore* was taking on water faster than her crew could pump it out, so Captain Gregory released the anchor cables and beached her on a sandbar, 300 feet offshore with her deck awash.

Commodore aground and breaking up.
Courtesy of the Southold Historical Society.

One newspaper reported that the crew landed the passengers in the lifeboats, although some seemed to be totally unfamiliar with their operation. Another account stated that, "the crew broke into the liquor locker and became insubordinate.... They lowered the one lifeboat and left everyone else out there."

The following morning the miller at the Peconic Inlet grist mill, Gilbert Terry, who, like Halsey Haynes, was a beachcomber, brought his wagon to the beach with him. The newspaper report continued: "Terry was picking up pieces of things from the *Commodore*, not knowing from where they came, when the fog parted and there's a big boat sitting there. There was a line washed ashore from the ship, so he went down the beach with his wagon and dragged the lifeboat back and tied it to the line and the people onboard pulled the boat back out and got themselves ashore. They were pretty well frozen and wet ... Terry ended up with two wagon loads full of life preservers."

No matter how the steamer's passengers reached shore, everyone survived the harrowing experience. After almost capsizing in the middle of the Sound, the steamer went ashore in a sandy spot with few boulders. A newspaper reported that had *Commodore* beached anywhere five miles east or west of where she did, the sea probably would have pounded her to pieces on the many large boulders. None would have survived. It was also fortunate that she grounded at a spot of low shore elevation. To the east or west there are steep, precipitous, sandy cliffs and no houses within a mile of the beach. Local residents, including Terry whose home was just back of the mill, took the survivors into their homes until they could return to New York by train.

The beach from Southold to Cutchogue was strewn with cargo and debris. *The Brooklyn Daily Eagle* on October 15, 1900 reported that much of the flotsam was "stolen before the arrival of the wreck master from Mattituck."

Commodore was not worth the salvage price to refloat her, so the owners decided to sell her where she lay. Haynes and Terry were not the only Southold residents to end up with pieces of the steamer. Terry reported that the beach provided a variety of goods to the Islanders. He said that one man salvaged a package of gold leaf paper and each Christmas he decorated his tree with gold paper chains, reminding him of *Commodore*'s destruction. A wreck master was appointed to protect what was left until the wreck could be auctioned off. The winning bid, from *Commodore*'s Captain Gregory, was $8,050, about 80% of what the steamship line paid for her repairs. After the ship was stripped by Gregory's salvors, heavy storms broke up the remains. The boilers and walking beam engine were visible above water until the early 1890s.

OWNERS AT FAULT

The U.S. Treasury Department was upset by the owner's disregard of the need for a certificate to transport passengers. The Treasury Department noted: "The loss of this vessel affords another commentary on the necessity for additional and effective legislation. The law, as it now stands, is totally inadequate to the enforcement of the moral obligation of owners and others toward those who place their lives in their hands. Happily there are exceptions to this necessity, for there are many honorable and high-minded owners of vessels whose constant desire is to obey the law in all its provisions, and provide their passengers and crews with adequate protection to the best of their ability, and regardless of exposure. But, on the other hand, there is a class of owners (far too numerous for the public welfare) who can be reached at once by the most stringent enactments, and made to fear the consequences of defying the laws and regulations by the certainty of a swift appropriate penalty; and such enactment's must be made as soon as practicable, and such rigorous enforcement thereof prevail, embracing in their scope every obligation which a shipowner owes to the people whom he serves, and providing a punishment for reckless offenders inaccessible to higher motives, which shall be severe enough to deter them from periling human life and property."

One of the anchors that had stopped *Commodore*'s wild ride across the Sound, and then was used to right her, was recovered in the net of fisherman Leonard Knotoff of Hampton Bays in 1996, 130 years after it was lost. Knotoff said: "We knew the anchor was there because other guys have caught their nets on it in the past. I figured I would either free the net or rip it off and try to salvage part of it. All of a sudden I heard this banging noise on the bottom of the boat and there was the anchor."

The 3,000-pound anchor measures 9 feet in length, 9½ feet across the stock and 5½ feet fluke to fluke. It was sold to the Horton Point Lighthouse Nautical Museum in Southold for "under $5,000." The museum placed the anchor on the lawn in front of the lighthouse. Cliff Benfield, the museum's curator, said: "The stock is unusual because there's no wooden stock of that age that has survived the Sound as far as we know. It's oak; it's very hard and it survived very well. The bottom is in excellent shape because it was buried. On top it's a little spongy, but we'll fix it up. What we have to do is replace the moisture in the wood with polypropylene glycol."

Benfield declared that the anchor is "a nice addition to the lighthouse." It was recovered from 11 feet of water. The second anchor and the chain for both anchors, are still on the bottom awaiting recovery. The ship's boilers and her walking beam steam engine are believed to be covered by sand.

Benfield hopes that other town residents will donate *Commodore* artifacts in their possession. He said: "What I'm finding now is that people still have stuff that came off the boat in their houses. A woman has an antique chair in her living room ... There's a house that has a door ... and another house that has a banister from the wreck. In the newspapers of the time they said everyone around had purple and gold rugs that had washed ashore. There's a lot of things around."

It is reassuring that although Long Island museums are denied 19th century relics by the unwritten decree of coastal property rights, Long Island homes have ensured their preservation.

TURTLE—SEMI-SUBMERSIBLE OR SUBMARINE

Type of vessel: semisubmersible or submarine
Where built: New York City
Launched: 1813
Length/beam: 23' / 10'
Gross tons: unknown
Sunk: June 20, 1814
Cause of sinking: stranded / explosion
Location: Hashamomuck Beach,
            near Horton's Point, Southold Town
Approximate depth of water: wreckage has not been located

AMERICA'S ROBERT FULTON, widely acclaimed for his commercial success with the steamship *North River Steam Boat*, better known as *Clermont*, also designed and built submarines. He built the four-man submarine *Nautilus*, with financial support from the French government. She was 21 feet 4 inches long with a 6-foot 4-inch beam. Her noteworthy features were separate propulsion for surface and submerged cruising, horizontal hydroplanes for depth control, surface-floated hose for underwater air supply, anchor gear release from the interior, and a copper hull over iron framework.

Sails provided surface propulsion with a mast that was hinged and stowed in a deck groove while the boat was submerged. A hand-driven screw propelled the submarine underwater and a rudder provided maneuverability. The vessel's hollow keel served as a ballast tank, taking in water to submerge and pumping it out to resurface. The detachable keel was designed to be dropped for rapid surfacing in an emergency. Submerged runs at Paris, Brest, and Le Havre demonstrated that the submarine could be navigated successfully underwater. It was claimed that a four-man crew could remain submerged for one hour. Fulton did submerge *Nautilus* to a depth of 25 feet on July 9, 1800, and remained down for 17 minutes.

Fulton added several offensive weapons that carried 80 to 100 pounds of gunpowder. They were not torpedoes, but they served the same purpose in a uniquely different manner. Unlike the self-propelled torpedoes of today's navies, Fulton's were towed under a target vessel, like underwater kites. When the trailing explosives reached the hull of the intended victim, towline slack was taken up and the explosion was triggered by a gunlock. The device was demonstrated successfully in Brest Harbor, where an old 40-foot sloop was demolished. Napoleon missed a wonderful opportunity to command the seas with an exclusive, proven naval advantage when he refused to finance the construction of larger versions of *Nautilus* to attack British ships. He may have been influenced by the prevalent attitude of most French naval officers; they termed underwater warfare "unworthy, ungallant, and fit only for Algerians and pirates."

Fulton protested the moral objection in a letter to a French government official: "If at first glance, the means I propose seem revolting, it is only because they are extraordinary. They are anything but inhuman ..."

Fulton had gone as far as he could with the French. He then persuaded England's Prime Minister William Pitt to let him try his torpedoes against the French. Not one to play favorites, all he wanted was some nation to adopt his invention, with only one reservation. His methods of destruction were never to be used against his own nation, the United States, unless she used them first.

On the night of October 2, 1805, several of Fulton's 18-foot torpedoes were towed by British ships into Boulogne Harbor. But instead of towing them underwater as designed by Fulton, they were set loose and allowed to drift with the tide to explode on contact. It is a wonder that even one small French vessel with a crew of 21 was destroyed by such primitive mine-laying tactics. The experience did little to prove the worth of Fulton's armament towing concept.

The British lost interest in Fulton's invention when the French fleet was destroyed by conventional naval conflict at Trafalger on October 21, 1805. First Lord of the Admiralty, Earl St. Vincent, remarked that, "Pitt was the greatest fool that ever existed, to encourage a mode of war which they who commanded the seas did not want, and which, if successful, would deprive them of it."

Britain's naval leaders persisted in St. Vincent's attitude for the next hundred years.

MUTE

Fulton returned to the United States, determined to continue his experiments. During the War of 1812, he designed a submarine for use against the British squadron based at New London, Connecticut. He attributed America's second-rate status to the superiority of European Navies and, "How then is America to prevent this? Certainly not by attempting to build a fleet to cope with the fleets of Europe but if possible by rendering the European fleets useless." His solution was a new submarine, *Mute*, 80 feet long, with a beam of 21 feet. Manpower provided surface propulsion so quiet that it led to the vessel's name. The crew, rowing like galley slaves, turned a paddle wheel mounted aft amidships. The system produced a speed of about four knots submerged. The hull and top hatch were constructed of eight-inch planking covered with a half-inch of iron armor plating. The hull resembled a conventional boat but the top arched down the sides like a turtle shell, leading the British to dub her a "turtle boat."

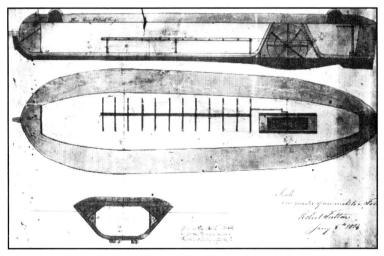

Mute was built for the U.S. by Noah Brown under Fulton's direction.
Courtesy of the Submarine Force Library and Museum, Groton, CT.

The submarine, built in New York City by Noah Brown, was designed to tow five of Fulton's torpedoes. One destroyed a vessel of 200 tons during a test in New York Harbor, assuring Fulton that both boat and armament were effective. Also, the submarine proved that the compass was unaffected under water, whether at rest or when in motion. However, Fulton died in 1815, before *Mute*'s trials were completed.

TURTLE

While Fulton's submarine was being constructed and tested, the Common Council, an association of New York City business leaders, provided several hundred dollars to a Mr. Berrian to construct another vessel to break the British blockade at the eastern end of Long Island Sound. British spies, aware that the vessel was being constructed in New York, led British naval officers to believe that it was being built by Fulton.

Berrian named his vessel *Turtle* in honor of David Bushnell's Revolutionary War submarine that unsuccessfully attacked H.M.S. *Eagle* in New York Harbor. Berrian tested *Turtle* in a trial run in Long Island Sound at the end of the summer of 1813, but the records do not state whether the vessel was a semi-submersible or submarine. A journalist described the vessel as she left New York in June 1814 to break the blockade: "A new invented torpedo boat resembling a turtle floating just above the surface of the water, and sufficiently roomy to carry nine passengers within, having on her back a coat of mail ... so as to bid defiance to any attack ... left this city ... to blow up some of the enemy's ships off New London. At one end of the boat projected a long pole, underwater, with a torpedo fastened to it, which as she approached the enemy at night, was to be poked under the bottom of a seventy-four [ship-of-the-line], and then let off...."

Turtle left New York on June 19, 1814, under the command of Captain Penny, and headed down Long Island Sound toward the British ships at New London. Unfortunately, an unpredicted northwest gale blew in the next day. It battered the small vessel, and grounded her at Long Island's Hashamomuck Beach, northwest of Greenport and northeast of Southold. One crew member drowned while attempting to swim ashore before the vessel stranded. Unable to refloat the craft, the crew removed the spiral wheel that propelled her, as well as her crank and rudder, leaving a hastily-assembled group of American militiamen to protect the helpless craft.

On June 26, two British warships, the frigate *Maidstone* and the sloop-of-war *Sylph*, located the stranded American vessel in the wash of the beach in a small bay. The British raked the beach with cannon fire, dispersing the militia. One shot hit the Abraham Mulford house on the bluff high above the stranded vessel. British Royal Marines commanded by Lieutenant John Bowen of *Maidstone*, stripped *Turtle* and set charges that blew her to pieces. Seven months later, *Sylph* was lost when she ran aground near Southhampton with the loss of 115 men (see index).

Before ordering his men to destroy *Turtle*, Lieutenant Bowen sketched the new craft and measured her dimensions. She was only 23 feet long with a beam of 10 feet. Her top was arched and she had the supports of a 100-ton ship, with eight-inch thick wooden planks covered with half-inch plate iron. Drawing six feet of water, only one foot of boat was exposed above the surface. Lieutenant Bowen wrote that she was "so strongly and well constructed that a shot cannot penetrate, or can anything grapple with it." The ironclads of the Civil War would be very much like her.

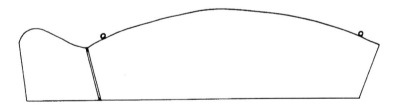

This sketch is based on Lieutenant Bowen's rendering of *Turtle*.

The semi-submersible "Davids" produced by the Confederacy during the Civil War carried spar torpedoes like *Turtle*'s. However, Lieutenant Bowen wrote that *Turtle* was also designed to tow five floating torpedoes, "each on its own lead," like Fulton's submarine.

Captain Burdett of *Maidstone* credited Lieutenant Bowen's action in the warship's log: "To Lieutenant Bowen I am again indebted for the very skillful manner in which he performed this most desirable piece of service, which probably has saved the lives of many gallant and valuable subjects of His Majesty in this treacherous mode of warfare."

Captain Penny, commander of *Turtle*, was from Northwest, near Sag Harbor. The British captured him at his home and shipped him to Halifax where he was held until the end of the war.

The British newspapers called the American's attempt at underwater warfare "cowardly," "barbarous," and "inhuman." How quickly they forgot Fulton's efforts on their behalf. American newspapers, however, lost no time reminding them. Although Fulton expected his submarine to win him fame, he is still best known for the commercial success of his steamboat, not his contribution to underwater warfare.

U.S.S. *OHIO*—POWER, GRACE, AND SPEED

Type of vessel: ship-of-the-line
Where built: New York Navy Yard (later Brooklyn Navy Yard)
Launched: May 20, 1820
Length/beam: 208' / 53'10"
Gross tons: 2,757
Sunk: April 1884
Cause of sinking: storm / stranded
Location: Greenport Harbor
Approximate depth of water: 20'

> *Come, let our hearts and hands unite, and let us sing a glee,*
> *Concerning one of the finest ships that ever swam the sea;*
> *She was modelled by Eckford, a builder of great note;*
> *She is a wooden wall pronounced by all, the finest ship afloat.*
>
> ...
>
> *As to her sailing qualities, all hands they say it is fine,*
> *Amongst your gallant Navy like a diamond she shall shine;*
> *May God protect the Ohio, and all her gallant crew,*
> *She is a specimen of beauty for all the world to view.*
>
> *May the figure bold of Hercules preclude all danger that may be*
> *Before the bold Ohio, whilst she sails upon the sea.*
> *Now I hope, my tars, that these few lines will suit ye,*
> *But here is health to one and all,*
> *and success to the New York beauty.*
>
> —F.P. Torrey,
> *Journal of the Cruise of the United States Ship Ohio*

THE STATUE OF Liberty vies with the stars and stripes as the symbol of Americanism. Known throughout the world as a shrine of freedom, that "Green Lady" has extended her welcome at the entrance to New York Harbor since 1886. The citizens of France, in an unprecedented demonstration of international friendship, presented the statue as a gift to commemorate 100 years of United States independence. The magnificent gesture might better have been reversed. The coast of France should be adorned with a memorial—an American one dedicated to the decisive role of the French Navy in this country's successful Revolution.

The impoverished Colonists stood impotent against the impressive sea power of Great Britain. They were defiant and determined—but they had no navy. The British advantage of sea-borne commerce threatened early defeat for the insurgents until France intervened in 1778. The move was not without self-interest; the cautious French had been waiting for the right moment to enter the conflict and settle their own score with the British. The formidable French fleet filled the void for the Colonists. It provided time for the new country to develop some semblance of a navy, to gradually improve it—and ultimately, to survive as an independent nation.

A COUNTRY IS BORN

The Declaration of Independence introduced a new country to the world in 1776. It would require a substantial navy—not only to survive the war, but also to protect future commerce and what was even then an extensive coastline.

Military spending faced stern opposition after the Revolution. The new government was so desperately short of funds that fiscal-minded leaders found a ready audience for their proposal to eliminate the small navy. Two of the young nation's most prominent patriots expressed shocked opposition to such ill-conceived action. George Washington cautioned that if the nation wanted its neutral flag to be respected, an organized naval force must be ready to protect it from insult or aggression. In his words: "This may even prevent the necessity of going to war by discouraging belligerent powers from committing such violations of the rights of the neutral party as may, first or last, leave no other option."

Alexander Hamilton asserted: "With a navy, a price would be set, not only on our friendship, but upon our neutrality."

The sage advice of those eminent leaders went unheeded, overwhelmed by arguments for austerity; the Navy's last vessel was sold in 1785. The decision to terminate the short-lived navy was founded on trust by naive individuals that good will and amity of the world powers would prevail. They managed to persuade the country that an American Navy and its attendant cost were an unneeded luxury. International contempt, indignities, and humiliation followed.

The French Revolution of 1789 led to Franco-British hostilities that continued until 1802. The navies of both belligerents freely preyed on American merchant ships, ignoring claims of neutrality. American vessels were attacked and captured, even within their own waters; cargoes were confiscated, and crews were impressed into foreign service. It took such events to prove the wisdom of Washington's and Hamilton's words of caution.

NEW NAVY

The United States was left with no option but to build a navy capable of protecting the country's interests on the high seas. Congress acted on March 27, 1794, authorizing the construction of 6 frigates, carrying 24 to 50 guns—the nucleus of the new United States Navy. One, *Constitution* (Old Ironsides), is still afloat and celebrated her 200th birthday on July 21, 1997.

Financial problems and public apathy continued to hamper naval build-up until British squadrons committed the major sea provocations that led to the War of 1812. Britain confronted the United States with more than 100 first-class warships while the Americans could muster only slightly more than a dozen fighting vessels, other than gunboats. In *The History of the American Sailing Navy*, Howard I. Chapelle wrote: "There was widespread doubt that Americans could possibly cope with the British Navy at sea ... There was no reserve of trained naval seamen, and naval funds were lacking. One thing alone the navy possessed, a fine officers' corps, well disciplined and trained, spirited, and aggressive."

Constitution received her nickname "Old Ironsides" during the War of 1812, when H.M.S. *Guerriere*, a British warship, fired a cannonball at her. When it bounced off, a sailor reportedly said, "Her sides are made of iron!" The 54-gun *Constitution* defeated *Guerriere* and in her 84-year career she destroyed or captured 32 enemy ships.

SHIPS-OF-THE-LINE

The Act of Congress of January 2, 1813 ordered construction to begin on the U.S. Navy's first ships-of-the-line. These magnificent warships were the battleships of the age of sail, with armament that qualified them for position in the first line of a sea battle. Carrying from 64 to more than 120 heavy guns, they were floating fortresses, the nation's most tangible symbol of seapower throughout the 1700s—until they were outdated by steam power and iron hulls in the mid 1800s. The square-rigged, three-masted vessels bristled with guns from two or three enclosed decks and from the upper spar deck. The Naval History Division of the Navy Department, in *American Ships Of The Line*, pays tribute to those heavily armed Goliaths: "In the days of sail, this great ship of the battleline sailed nobly for generations as the backbone of fleets. It was the mighty, mobile fortress that could hit the hardest blows and take the most punishment—for in war one must expect to suffer as well as to harm. It was matchless in grace, speed, and beauty. Then when iron and steam replaced wood and sail, the successor that evolved for the sailing ship of the battleline came to be called battleship."

On April 29, 1816, Congress authorized construction of nine more ships-of-the-line, each to have no fewer than 74 guns. One million dollars a year funding for the next eight years was specified to ensure that they would be built. Construction was to be in government yards rather than private shipyards because of the uncertainty of the eight-year funding. The newly formed Board of Navy Commissioners knew that delayed appropriations might keep a ship on the stocks for years. No private builder would accept such an unpredictable program—except on a high rental basis. The Navy's concern proved to be well founded; as early as 1818, seven 74's were on the stocks officially, but construction was underway on only three, *Ohio*, *Delaware*, and *North Carolina*. The other four, *Vermont*, *New York*, *Alabama* (renamed *New Hampshire*), and *Virginia* were at a virtual standstill.

Predictably, economy dictated the completion schedules of the new ships. The powerful 74's would be held in readiness, and were to be launched only as required to protect the nation. Two never reached the water; *New York* was still on the stocks when the Civil War broke out, and was burned when the Norfolk Navy Yard was destroyed; *Virginia* was broken up in 1874, still incomplete at the Boston Navy Yard—58 years after her authorization by Congress.

Ohio was launched in 1820 at the New York Navy Yard, *Delaware* in 1820 at the Norfolk Navy Yard, *North Carolina* in 1821 at Philadelphia, and *Vermont* in 1848 at Boston. *Vermont* was the last ship-of-the-line built for the United States Navy, although *Alabama* was still to be launched.

Alabama was almost completed by 1825, but she remained on the stocks for an additional 39 years, until she was needed for Civil War service, having been "under construction" for 45 years. She was re-named *New Hampshire*, a name more suitable for Federal service during the war with the Confederate States. The obsolete sailing vessel was fitted for wartime use as an administrative receiving ship, not a line-of-battle ship. Her first assignment after commissioning on May 13, 1964 was to relieve *Vermont* as receiving ship at Port Royal, South Carolina. By then, obsolescence had indeed caught up with the once mighty ships-of-the-line.

U.S.S. OHIO

Ohio was first of the 74's to be launched, two and a half years after her keel was laid in November, 1817 at the New York Navy Yard (later Brooklyn Navy Yard). However, after her launching on May 20, 1820, she spent the next 18 years in ordinary, a term that means "moth-balled," with only a skeleton crew aboard.

Ohio, like the other six ships-of-the-line of her class, was based upon the design of the Washington Navy Yard's naval architect, William Doughty. However, she was built in New York by another naval architect, Henry Eckford, with his own substantial modifications that put *Ohio* into a class of her own for size, speed, firepower, and sailing quality. Eckford's design was slightly larger and considerably deeper than Doughty's. Consequently, the decks of *Ohio* rode higher above the water, permitting effective use of lower deck guns, even in rough seas. The specifications of Eckford's final product were impressive:

Currier & Ives lithograph.
Courtesy of The Old Print Shop, 150 Lexington Ave., NY.

Spar Deck length	208'
Between perpendiculars	196'3"
Molded Beam	53'10"
Depth in Hold	14'
Displacement	2,757 tons
Draught	26'
Sail	18,000 yards

Ohio carried a complement of 820, including marines. The ship's armament varied from one command to another—usually 84 guns. Her modest cost of $547,889 permitted very little ornamental work—only a light gallery at the stern and an impressive figurehead of Hercules with a British lion skin and club, on the bow. The figurehead was produced by Wood and Sharpe, New York City woodcarvers. Expense-minded critics could hardly have considered the $1,500 bow decoration essential to defense, but there it remained.

In 1837, Captain L. Kearney sailed the 18-year-old ship-of-the-line to the Boston Navy Yard for fitting out. She was commissioned on October 11, 1838, and placed under command of Captain Joseph Smith.

Like the others of her class, *Ohio* was designed for maximum firepower. She was nominally a 74, but carried anywhere from 84 to 104 guns, depending on the decision of her various captains.

Commodore Issac Hull, a veteran rich in naval experience, selected U.S.S. *Ohio* as his flagship in 1838. The commodore's most famous command was "Old Ironsides," 26 years earlier, at the outbreak of the War of 1812. His standards of performance were high, and he expected much of his new flagship. *Ohio* did not disappoint him. She set sail on December 6, 1838, still under command of Captain Joseph Smith, to join the U.S. Navy Mediterranean Squadron at Gibraltar. The massive warship confirmed the commodore's confidence as she overcame rough Atlantic seas for an average speed of 12 knots. During her career, *Ohio* was acknowledged to be the Navy's fastest ship-of-the-line.

For over two years, *Ohio* patrolled the Mediterranean, leading a U.S. Navy squadron to display the flag and provide protection for American commerce. She returned to Boston on July 17, 1841, to spend the next five years in administrative service as a receiving ship, also known as a floating naval depot.

War with Mexico broke out, and *Ohio* sailed to Vera Cruz under command of Captain Silas H. Stringham in March, 1847. She contributed to the fall of that city—not in a naval engagement, but by landing a contingent of seamen and marines equipped with ten of her guns to participate in the assault.

The large ship-of-the-line drew too much water for effective operation along the shallow coast of the Gulf of Mexico. She left Mexico on May 9, 1847, for return to New York.

When hostilities ended, the gold rush that followed the acquisition of California by the United States generated a boom economy on the West Coast. *Ohio* was called on to provide protection for commerce during that chaotic period. She policed the newly acquired California Territory when the Navy's major problem was to deter U.S. Navy crewmen from deserting to look for gold in the California mountains. One officer was badly mauled during an aborted attempt by two would-be deserters. A

drumhead court-martial found the two guilty and sentenced them to be strung from *Ohio*'s yardarms. The bodies remained there as a grim warning to others who might otherwise have been tempted by gold.

In 1849, the ship-of-the-line returned to Boston, where she was decommissioned on May 3, 1850, and again went into ordinary. A year later, she was recommissioned, and served as a receiving ship for the next 24 years. In 1863, *Ohio* was temporarily rearmed in anticipation of a projected Confederate attack on Boston.

END OF A NAVAL CAREER

In 1875, *Ohio* was once more placed in ordinary, until her 63-year career ended on September 27, 1883, when she was sold to Israel L. Snow of Rockland, Maine for $17,000. The ship-of-the-line cost $547,889 to build. Snow later sold her to Greenport, New York shipyard owners for $20,000. Two tugs, *Luther C. Ward* and *Germania*, towed *Ohio* out of her berth in the Boston Navy Yard's "rotten row" on October 28, 1883. Four days later, they delivered her to Greenport Harbor. While under tow the old ship-of-the-line was under the command of S.T. Preston who established a world-wide recognized ship chandlery, which is still in Greenport today.

Ohio was moored alongside Main Street Wharf—to accommodate the thousands of sightseers who streamed aboard and walked the decks of the old ship-of-the-line for a small fee. But it was for her copper and bronze fastenings, not display, that the warship had been purchased. Dismantling was interrupted in April 1884 by a violent storm that broke the vessel loose of her moorings and stranded her near Fanning Point at the end of Fourth Street in Greenport. She was burned to reduce her obstruction to shipping, but much of the hulk resisted the flames.

Metal fastenings and other salvage were gathered at the site, sometimes with the help of dynamite cartridges that were exploded to facilitate break up of the wreck. On the morning of July 26, 1884, Robert N. Corey of Greenport, a professional wrecker, exploded one of the cartridges in timbers containing prized bronze spikes and pins. He lit the fuse, ran approximately 80 paces and turned away from the blast. A horrified observer later reported watching a 15-inch iron bolt, blown in a high arc above its restraining timbers, plunge into Corey's skull with piledriver impact. Corey died three hours later.

The $1,481 heroic Hercules figurehead was removed from its place on the bow and sold at auction for $10. Later, it was resold to the owners of Canoe Place Inn in Hampton Bays, New York for $15. The legend on the figurehead's pedestal when it stood by the roadside in Canoe Place:

> *The maid who kisses his mighty cheek*
> *Will meet her fate within a week.*
> *The one who presses his forehead*
> *In less than a year will wed.*
> *No maid, nor matron ever taunted*
> *Him with refusing what he wanted.*
> *To whisper what you wish the most.*
> *Fair maid, it's yours ? the cost.*

Edna Yeager in *Around The Forks* wrote: "... so many teenage girls kiss him, that the town-fathers are dismayed, as their lipstick makes a ruddy smear on the classic features ..."

The Canoe Place Inn is now a popular nightclub. In the 1950s, Hercules was transferred to the Village Green, at Stony Brook, New York where it is prominently displayed with *Ohio*'s anchor—vestiges of one of the most magnificent warships of the 19th century U.S. Navy.

REDISCOVERY OF U.S.S. *OHIO*

Almost a century passed before extensive research by the Peconic Bay branch of the British Sub Aqua Club discovered the wreckage of *Ohio*, late in 1973.

The club's objective was to raise the hull for use as the central theme of a planned marine museum. The location of the wreck remained secret until the Mobil Oil Company of Greenport applied for a permit to add clusters of pilings, called dolphins, in their mooring area to improve safety in the unloading of oil barges. The Sub Aqua group contested the permit request because the new dolphins would penetrate the wreck site.

Their determination to preserve the historic relic had forced them to divulge its general location. Ultimately, the dolphins were installed without appreciable damage to the wreck, that lies less than 100 yards from shore in about 20 feet of water. The Mobil Oil Company dolphins that led to disclosure of the wreck site have since been removed, and are no longer marking the location.

With very little wreckage usually exposed, the wreck can be difficult for scuba divers to find. Many brass fastenings have been found close to shore—in only four to six feet of water.

The remains of the old hulk are a memorial to the forerunner of today's battleship. The few fastenings and copper nails now exposed once sailed in glory as the pride of an emerging United States Navy, the grand old ship-of-the-line, U.S.S. *Ohio*.

Left: The old ship-of-the-line *Ohio* at her pier in Greenport, Long Island, after being sold for scrap. In 1884, a storm sank her off Fanning Point. *Courtesy of the Naval Historical Center.*

Carole Keatts beside *Ohio's* Hercules figurehead, now located at the Stony Brook, Long Island village green. *Photo by H. Keatts.*

An East Hampton Town Marine Museum display of the *Culloden* wreck site during mapping, sketching, and excavation of the site by Dr. Moeller. *Photo by H. Keatts.*

The British warship *Culloden* ran aground near Montauk during a storm in 1781. *Courtesy of the Suffolk County Historical Society.*

Above: In 1876, a storm drove *Circassian* ashore at Bridgehampton. The ship was being salvaged when she was destroyed by a fierce storm that killed 24 of the 28 men on board, including 10 Indians from the Shinnecock Reservation. The men in the rigging were visible from shore, but nothing could be done to save them. *Courtesy of the Quogue Historical Society.*

Below: Remains of *Nahum Chapin* and the crew of the Quogue Life-Saving Station. In 1897, the three-masted schooner grounded at Quogue. Huge breakers made it impossible for lifesavers to attempt a rescue. The ship broke up and all on board drowned. *Courtesy of the Quogue Historical Society.*

THAMES—IN "ROTTEN ROW"

Type of vessel: whaler
Where built: Essex, Connecticut
When built: 1818
Length/beam: unknown
Gross tons: 350
Date of sinking: 1838
Cause of sinking: intentionally grounded
Location: west of Conklin's Point, Sag Harbor
Approximate depth of water: unknown

THE EARLY ENGLISH settlers of Long Island's south fork quickly discovered the deep water bay by present day Sag Harbor. Originally, the area was named Sagaponack Harbor, but it was later shortened to Sag Harbor. The ship-building industry in the late 1700s and the whaling industry, especially between 1820 and 1850 accounted for the growth of the village. In 1789, according to Dorothy Zaykowski's *Sag Harbor — The Story of an American Beauty*, the village "had more tons of square-rigged vessels engaged in commerce than even New York City." That year, the U.S. Congress declared Sag Harbor a "port of entry" and established Long Island's first U.S. Customs House there.

Robert Keene, Southampton Town Historian, stated: "In 1843, a history of New York State was published. In the Long Island section, it says there were only two places of any importance — Brooklyn on the west end and Sag Harbor on the east end."

The War of 1812 devastated Sag Harbor's merchant fleet. U.S. Representative Ebenezer Sage wrote: "We formerly had twenty to twenty-five coasting vessels employed in southern trade and in carrying wood to market … Three or four of them remained …"

However, after the war, the need for whale oil to light American homes and lubricate industrial machinery stimulated three decades of intense whaling activity from the port, and Sag Harbor became the first great whaling community on Long Island. The opening two stanzas from William H. Elliston's poem *Captain Henry's Christmas Gift* reflects Sag Harbor's whaling past:

From picturesque Sag Harbor
A quaint village by the sea,
Come historic tales of whaling
That would startle you and me.

This was a famous whaling port
In whaling days gone by;
Exciting tales beyond compare,
And these tales ne'er shall die.

James Fenimore Cooper was born and raised in upstate New York, but his wife's family owned land in Sag Harbor and on Shelter Island. He and his wife came to Sag Harbor in 1819 and he bought shares in the whaling ship *Union*, which sailed from Sag Harbor on her maiden voyage. Cooper also spent time in Orient Point and he based two books, *The Water Witch* and *The Sea Lions*, on his experiences in Long Island's two forks.

THAMES

The 350-ton sailing ship *Thames* was built at Essex, near the mouth of the Connecticut River in 1818, by Captain Noah Scovell. His son was master of the ship for four years as she carried passengers and freight between New London and New York City.

In June 1822, *Thames* was purchased by a newly formed whaling company in New Haven. The ship was extravagantly fitted out as a whaler and in October sailed for the Pacific Ocean in search of sperm whales. Her captain Thomas Clasby and most of the crew were from Nantucket. On her first excursion as a whaler *Thames* also carried 14 passengers, missionaries and their wives, assistants, and domestics, to Honolulu, Oahu, Sandwich Islands (now Hawaii). The ship arrived at Honolulu on April 27, 1823.

In 1825, the whaler returned to New Haven with 1,800 barrels of sperm whale oil, only to find a low market value of 40 to 45 cents per gallon for the oil. Oil prices ranged from a few cents a gallon to more than $2 a gallon depending upon supply. The great expense in refitting *Thames* as a whaler and heavy expenses while she was abroad, generated a considerable loss for her 23 owners.

The ship was sold "for a small price" and sailed to Sag Harbor, to be fitted out. In the summer of 1826 *Thames* set out for the False Banks in search of right whales under the command of Captain Huntting Cooper. He commanded the ship on five successful voyages, returning to Sag Harbor with a total of 137 barrels of sperm oil, 8,708 barrels of whale oil, and 70,198 pounds of whale bone. Whale bone was used to make fertilizers, lime, buttons, canes, fishing rods, corset stays, and many other products.

In 1831, Cooper's first officer, David Hand, took command of the whaler. The following year, Hand returned to Sag Harbor with 30 barrels of sperm oil, 1,846 barrels of whale oil, and 15,000 pounds of whale bone. Captain Barney R. Green of Southampton replaced Captain Hand and sailed to the Indian Ocean in search of whales. He returned to Sag Harbor in March 1834, after an absence of two whaling seasons, with 358 barrels of sperm oil (the fine oil found in a large cavity in the heads of sperm whales was more valuable because it was used to

Broken Mast Monument in Oakland Cemetery, Sag Harbor. The inscription commemorates six whaling ship masters who lost their lives pursuing their profession, three in the Atlantic Ocean, three in the Pacific Ocean.

produce candles and to lubricate industrial machines), 1,800 barrels of whale oil (from other species of whales), and 16,000 pounds of whale bone. Two years later, Green was succeeded by Captain Henry Nickerson who made two voyages in her.

END OF CAREER

On May 20, 1838, the 20-year-old *Thames* was considered unseaworthy and she was intentionally grounded just west of

Conklin's Point, east of the Yacht Club, in what is known as "Rotten Row." *Thames* had spent 12 years as a successful Sag Harbor whaler, and was considered to be "the swiftest sailing sea vessel belonging to this port and District."

In 1860, "a portion of her once proud remains" could still be seen above water.

Dr. Henry W. Moeller and Donald Getz, in *Suffolk County Historical Society Register*, stated, "The late Gene Rhodes, a Sag Harbor resident and a historian, remembers seeing the *Thames* keel among sand and marsh grasses in the 1940's or early 1950's ... he tried to get Sag Harbor residents to save it for future generations. When that failed he and others convinced Mystic Seaport to bring a truck over and transport the keel assembly back to their museum ... conservators at the museum used the keel and the pieces of wood ... to make an exhibit ... the keel assembly is an interesting exhibit. It is unfortunate however that one has to take a ferry ride to Connecicut to observe a part of Long Island's history."

In 1968, while dredging at the water's edge, remains of the old whaler were uncovered.

In 1973, a scuba diver recovered an oak rib with a bronze hand wrought pin from the site; that artifact is now in the Sag Harbor Library.

The remains of two other old whaling ships, *Fair Helen* and *Andes* are embedded in the sand off Conklin's Point. The latter burned to the waterline and sank on the east side of the channel off Long Wharf, where a sandbar known as "Andes Shoal" formed over her.

H.M.S. CULLODEN—PILOT BLUNDER

Type of vessel: ship-of-the-line
Where built: Deptford, England
Launched: May 18, 1776
Length/beam: 170′ / 47′2″
Gross tons: 1,650
Sunk: January 23, 1781
Cause of sinking: storm/stranded
Location: Culloden Point, Montauk
Approximate depth of water: 20′

APRIL 17, 1746, marked the bloody Battle of Culloden—the critical conflict for the throne of England between the royal army of the House of Hanover and the forces of Bonnie Prince Charles, claimant of the throne for the House of Stuart. That claim was forever silenced by the resounding defeat of Charles and his supporters on the Scottish moors of Culloden and Dunmossie, five miles east of Inverness at the head of Loch Ness.

The decisive victory so impressed the British that the following year a new warship was named for the battle site. That first H.M.S. *Culloden* sailed under the British flag for 27 years until she went out of commission in 1770. Six years later, a new *Culloden* was launched at Deptford on May 18, 1776,—only seven weeks before the American colonies declared their independence. The bow of the new 74-gun ship-of-the-line was adorned with a figurehead of Britain's reigning monarch, King George III. The warship, symbol of England's victory over the insurgents of Scotland, was destined to be lost in His Majesty's defeat by ill-equipped but dedicated rebels who had been stung to rebellion by the continuing infringement of their liberties. Thus, *Culloden* forged a historic link between two divergent societies, one dominated by royal decree, the other freed from such domination.

Culloden's specifications were impressive:

Length of Gundeck - 170′	Depth of Hold - 19′ 11″
Beam - 47′ 2″	Tonnage - 1,650

Armament	Number	Pounds
Gun Deck	28	32
Upper Deck	28	18
Quarter Deck	14	9
Forecastle	4	9

WAR SERVICE

The new 74-gun ship-of-the-line carried 650 officers and crew under Captain George Balfour who remained in command for the life of the vessel. She spent her first year intercepting French or Spanish ships supplying the rebellious American Colonists.

French sympathies for the American cause led to an open alliance between the two, and war between England and France. A French fleet of 16 warships sailed from Toulon on April 13, 1778. It's three-fold mission was to deliver the first French minister to the United States, to intercept a British squadron under Admiral Richard Howe, and to keep it blockaded in Delaware Bay. The British countered with a powerful fleet of 14 ships that sailed from England under Vice Admiral John Byron, grandfather of the illustrious poet. *Culloden* was one of Byron's ships.

NATURE INTERVENES

The Atlantic crossing was a disaster for Byron's fleet. It was battered by torrential storms and gale-force winds. Six ships were lost, and the eight that limped into Sandy Hook, New Jersey needed major repairs before they were fit for action. Although ten years would pass before the birth of his poet grandson, Admiral Byron's emotions as he surveyed his decimated fleet were captured in Lord Byron's epic poem, "The Isles of Greece:"

> *A king sate on the rocky brow*
> *Which looks o'er sea-born Salamis;*
> *And ships by thousands lay below.*
> *And men in nations; all were his!*
> *counted them at break of day—*
> *And when the sun set, where were they?*

Byron's objective, the French fleet, was still to be dealt with, but it lay safely anchored in Boston Harbor as the English left the protection of Sandy Hook to fulfill their mission. En route to Boston, a fierce Atlantic gale struck the northeast, and Admiral Byrons' ships were again buffeted and battered by nature. That repeat performance, so soon after his disastrous Atlantic crossing, earned Byron the nickname, "Foul Weather Jack."

Culloden, only two years old, was dismasted and swept to sea, a target for total destruction if another Atlantic storm should strike. Fortunately, the weather held, and she managed to limp home to Milford Haven, England by December 1778 for refitting after six months of furious battle—against neither the French nor the Americans, but the forces of nature.

FRENCH THREAT

The French were active in the American Colonies, where they created a major problem for British interests by establishing a strong base at Newport, Rhode Island. Their seven ships-of-the-line and 6,000 troops posed a constant threat to Admiral Marriot Arbuthnot, Great Britain's Commander-in-Chief of North America. He lacked the naval power to cope with the situation and requested naval reinforcements from Admiral Rodney's Caribbean fleet. The positive response was far more than Arbuthnot expected, or wanted. Admiral Rodney, himself, was in command when the reinforcements (including *Culloden*) arrived on September 13, 1780. Rodney outranked Arbuthnot, and he assumed overall command. Protests were dismissed by Rodney with, "I am convinced no man has His Majesty's service more at heart than yourself;" continuing, perhaps with tongue in cheek, "It was not inclination which brought me ... it was the duty I owed my King and my country."

As relations between the two Admirals worsened, the British cause suffered. Arbuthnot accused Rodney of "partial interfering with the American War." Rodney, in turn, was enraged by Arbuthnot's disregard of his orders, which he reported to the Admiralty as "unprecedented" actions.

That was the political situation when *Culloden*, with three other ships of the same class, *Centaur*, *Shrewsbury*, and *Russel*, sighted the American ship *Washington* on October 18. They were cruising: "between the South End of Nantucker [sic] Shoals and Montock [sic] Point," and chased the enemy vessel for six hours before she was captured and claimed for the Crown. The prize, a 20-gun privateer with a crew of 120, was overwhelmed by the firepower of the four British 74's.

The ruffled feelings between the two Admirals were sorely aggravated when the prize money of 3,000 pounds was awarded to Rodney as senior officer. Arbuthnot's responsibility for the squadron's actions and Rodney's absence in New York at the time were ignored.

British naval dominance left the cause of the Colonists heavily dependent on the French fleet. General Washington wrote to France: "Next to a loan of money, a constant naval superiority on these coasts is the object most interesting. This would instantly reduce the enemy to a difficult defensive ... removing all prospect of extending their acquisitions...."

The selection of Newport as the French base moved Arbuthnot to locate his own headquarters at Gardiner's Bay on Gardiner's Island, New York, close enough to keep track of the French fleet. From there, a spyglass could bring the enemy ships into view on a clear day. Besides, Gardiner's Bay was a perfect haven—with a diameter of six miles and a depth of 3.5 to 7 fathoms—more than adequate to maneuver the largest warships. Plum Gut, between Plum Island and Gardiner's Island, provided entry to Gardiner's Bay for the largest ships in the fleet.

Arbuthnot's headquarters were set up in the island's manor house. The overseer's house, "T'Other House," as it was known, was established as the base hospital. Several reminders of the British presence remain: a checkerboard carved into the upstairs floor of the hospital and the grave sites of several British seamen. The admiral enjoyed a good social relationship with the Gardiner family. He and his higher ranking officers exchanged visits with the Gardiners, entertaining aboard his flagship, *Royal Oak*, and being entertained at Abraham Gardiner's mansion on Main Street, East Hampton.

Arbuthnot had cause to celebrate when Admiral Rodney left New York for the Leeward Islands on November 19th, leaving

Culloden behind to serve in Arbuthnot's fleet. As soon as Rodney left, Arbuthnot headed for New York to replace Rodney's appointments with his own men. That task accomplished, he returned to Gardiner's Island.

DISASTER

On January 20, 1781, the British received word that several French warships at Newport were about to run the British blockade. *Culloden*, *America*, and *Bedford* were ordered to intercept them if such an attempt was made. They rendezvoused in Block Island Sound on the 22nd. The next night, a heavy winter storm struck the area, packing the kind of violence the *Culloden* crew had good cause to remember. She was severely battered, as she had been three years earlier. Gale force winds lashed the three ships with sleet and snow that blinded half-frozen lookouts.

The British ships headed for the open sea to ride out the storm, *Culloden* following *Bedford*'s lights. *Bedford* came about at 12:30 a.m., a change of course that confused Third Lieutenant John Cannon, on watch aboard *Culloden*. He informed Balfour, and the captain decided to maintain *Culloden*'s course on the premise that neither he nor the captain of *Bedford* could be certain of his position. There could be no danger; every half hour, a crewman was taking soundings with a 20-fathoms hand lead without finding bottom.

Fourth Lieutenant Ralph Grey relieved Cannon at 4 a.m., and was instructed to maintain course while the pilot was in the captain's cabin discussing the situation with Balfour. Without warning, pounding surf and coastline loomed directly ahead. Balfour raced on deck and ordered the anchors cut free to keep the vessel offshore. But before the crew could comply, *Culloden* shuddered violently; her copper-clad bottom had run fast aground. Shortly after, her rudder broke in two and was lost.

The shore, barely visible through darkness and foul weather, led the pilot to conclude that the ship had grounded on Block Island. Dawn revealed that it was really Welles Point (known today as Culloden Point), near the northeastern edge of Fort Pond Bay—not far from Montauk Point.

Lieutenant Grey's log entry reads: "... at 8 a.m. we backed her head off shore ... and endeavoured to run her off, but her bow came around to the westward and lay fast ... at 10 the gale increased, also the sea, she laboured and strained much."

Captain Balfour was determined to save his command, if at all possible. He ordered the top and main masts cut away and kept men on the pumps continuously. The water being pumped out was filled with sand and gravel, indicating that the heavy seas had probably split the seams of the ship. The storm ended with *Culloden* still fast into the sand. "We made every effort to get her off at high water," wrote Lieutenant Grey. But every effort was not enough because planking on the starboard bow gave, allowing water to pour into the ship. By 10 a.m., nine feet of seawater had accumulated below decks.

The situation was hopeless, prompting Balfour to order everything possible transferred to shore. Powder, gunner's stores, blocks, sails, carpenter's stores, pitch, and tar were stacked under tents for protection. Even water-soaked bread was laid out to dry. Later in the day, Balfour sent a boat to Gardiner's Island to report the disaster.

Bedford had come close to following *Culloden*'s fatal example—driven toward shore until her forward progress was halted by releasing her anchors. Finally, her masts were cut away to reduce the effect of the heavy winds.

America fared better than either of her sister ships. During the storm, several hull planks loosened, but she reached the open Atlantic afloat and still capable of maneuvering on her own. Even so, the storm carried her down the Atlantic coast to the Virginia Capes; the return voyage took almost two weeks.

The French ships that were reported to be running the blockade were even more fortunate; they returned to their protected harbor the day before the storm. By that action, they gained a total victory over the British who suffered a major defeat—by Mother Nature.

The transport *William* and the brig *Adventure* were ordered from Gardiner's Bay to salvage *Culloden*'s stores and guns, and to ensure that nothing useful would fall into enemy hands. Even Arbuthnot's flagship, *Royal Oak*, moved materials to Gardiner's

Bay and to the dismasted *Bedford* for jury rigging her with *Culloden*'s masts and rigging. By February 5, *Bedford* was again ready for sea duty.

Blocks and tackle removed at least 46 cannon, gun carriages, and anchors from *Culloden*. It took several days of heavy labor to remove the ship's King George figurehead. Intermittent strong gales, driving snow, and pounding breakers delayed salvage completion until March 1. The 28 obsolete 32-pound iron cannon—not worth salvaging—were spiked and pushed overboard; then the hull was set afire. Saddened British seamen watched their proud ship-of-the-line, that had required at least 60 acres of oak forest to build, burn to the water line in less than four hours.

Arbuthnot conducted a preliminary investigation of the *Culloden* disaster. His finding was that the pilot believed his ship had already cleared Montauk Point, and could safely bear due south. On March 28, 1781, a court martial was held in Lynnhaven Bay, Virginia. Admiral Graves, presiding as judge advocate, merely reprimanded the pilot for using the wrong sounding lead; Admiralty regulations called for a heavier (50-lb.) deep sea sounding lead every half hour instead of the hand lead. In what seems like an unusually compassionate verdict, Captain Balfour, his officers and his men were honorably acquitted. Balfour's record remained so unblemished that he was promoted to rear admiral in 1787.

SALVAGE

After the British left the *Culloden* remains, Joseph Woodbridge of Groton, Connecticut salvaged 16 of her 32-pound iron cannon. He offered them to General George Washington on July 24, 1781, adding that he could recover more cannon and a quantity of shot. The Continental Government, always short of funds, probably could not afford the offer.

Another salvage attempt, headed by the caretaker of Gardiner's Island in 1796, removed iron fittings, copper bolts, sheathing and the remaining rigging. An article in the *Long Island Star*, July 26, 1815, describes the only other early salvage operation. Captain Samuel Jeffers, of Sag Harbor, used a diving bell to retrieve twelve tons of pig iron and a 32-pound cannon. That was the last disturbance of the wreck for 158 years. During that time, Welles Point has become known as Culloden Point. The location, mostly covered with underbrush, is now Culloden Shores, a development with only a few scattered homes. *Culloden* lives on in the identity of the historic site.

Mrs. Jeannette Edwards Rattray, editor of *The East Hampton Star*, commented in her 1955 book *Ship Ashore* that renewed interest in many all-but-forgotten shipwrecks around Long Island: "As soon as the book was out, local fishermen told me they had never seen a vestige of the ship supposed to have gone down there. But Emerson Taber, who used to set his lobster pots in Gardiner's Bay, told me that a good deal of the *Culloden*'s skeleton was still visible when the tide was right. I went to look. Sure enough, a ship's ribs were sticking up four to six feet from the sand ...."

In June, 1958, Frederick P. Schmitt and fellow scuba diver, Donald E. Schmid, interviewed Mrs. Rattray in East Hampton. She mentioned that the ribs of the old vessel were still visible when the tide was right.

SEARCH

Schmitt and Schmid were so intrigued by the possibility of locating *Culloden* that they formed one of the area's first scuba diving clubs, the Club Sous-Marin of Long Island, for undersea research and exploration. Late in June they launched an intensive, three-year search for the wreck. A large rib, about 60 feet long, was found on their first trip to the area. The huge, hard oak timber still held wrought iron fasteners and oaken pegs. They thought it might be the wreckage mentioned by Mrs. Rattray. The location was right, but before the artifact could be authenticated it was set afire by picnickers. Two weeks later, one of the divers, Don Hegeman, discovered a large oak beam, water-logged and rotting, about 30 feet long and one foot thick with a wrought iron pin in one end. It was half buried in sand under three feet of water west of Culloden Point.

Schmitt and Schmid obtained a copy of *Culloden*'s log and a complete set of her construction plans from the National

Maritime Museum at Greenwich, England. Through the fall and winter of 1958, they spent weekends at the New York Public Library researching British naval history, but found nothing new on her location. The Public Record Office, in London, was more productive. A microfilm copy of *Culloden*'s officers' court martial transcript revealed that the ship ran aground in sand and gravel, not rocks. Thus, the wreck must be buried in sand—and most of the area around Culloden Point is rocky.

The best instrument to locate a wreck under sand is a sensitive metal detector, but such a costly device was beyond the limited resources of the new diving club. They abandoned the search after hundreds of hours of diving, but their carefully researched material has survived. It exists in Schmitt and Schmid's *H.M.S. Culloden*, published by the Mystic (Connecticut) Historical Association. Frederick Schmitt's ties to the sea remained strong; he became curator of the Cold Spring Harbor (N.Y.) Whaling Museum.

A new personality entered the search for *Culloden* when Carlton Davidson, a Long Island diver from East Moriches, read *H.M.S. Culloden* in 1970. He was so intrigued by the history of the lost shipwreck that he devoted the next three years to research and hundreds of hours underwater to pinpoint *Culloden*'s location.

Davidson gained two important clues—both from the book by Schmitt and Schmid. The first was that *Culloden* stranded in sand and gravel, not a rocky area. A search for old nautical charts revealed that American charts only go back to about 1848, and charts obtained from England failed to show any local areas of sand or gravel. The second clue was that not all 74 cannon had been salvaged.

Davidson's continuing research led him to the Suffolk County Center in Riverhead, where he learned that a 1661 map involved in a lawsuit might include his area of interest. A local justice, Judge Tasker, showed him the map, which included updating with the new designation, Culloden Point, in place of the original Welles Point name. A large sand shoal was clearly outlined off the Point.

Davidson and two friends, Bob Miller and George Olish, searched the sandy area with a small metal detector during the summer of 1970 and intermittently over several years. Their task was made more difficult than it should have been by their primitive metal detector, a hand-held model that can locate lost coins just below the sand, but is unsuited for the kind of search they were conducting.

Meanwhile, others looking for the wreck were getting results. Two scuba divers, David Warsen of Hampton Bays and Bob Miller of Aquebogue, were credited by Mrs. Rattray, as the first to produce positive identification of *Culloden* wreckage. An August 5, 1971 *The East Hampton Star* article reported that she had met with Warsen, an insurance man and Miller, a painter, to hear their story, and view their artifacts. A third diver, Dr. Henry Moeller of Dowling College and the New York Ocean Science Laboratory, worked with Warsen and Miller, but was out of the country when Mrs. Rattray met with the divers.

The three divers, searching from Culloden Point south into Fort Pond Bay, first found only big pieces of timber six or eight feet under the water. In mid-May, in Fort Pond bay, Warsen uncovered a large bronze object. As he fanned the sediment with his hand, the misspelled name *Culoden* appeared. He exposed enough of the find to reveal its outlines, then spent two days at the Smithsonian Institution in Washington, where he identified it as a gudgeon, a pivot attached to the sternpost of a ship to receive the rudder pintle, or pivot pin.

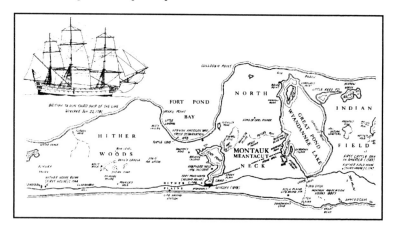

Soon after *Culloden* struck, her rudder broke in two and was lost. The solid brass, 300-pound, 6 ½-foot-long gudgeon Warsen found was broken off, and so was the 40-pound pintle, a big metal pin, about three inches across, attached to a piece of the rudder. The three also recovered a piece of the ship's rudder with a broken bronze pin attached. That pin was a pintle.

Davidson continued his own search, teaming up with Miller and Paul Knight, a fellow member of Miller's 20-man diving club, the Suffolk Sub-mariners, based in Riverhead. The trio launched an intensive scuba and metal detector search that continued for two years. They divided the sandy area into a grid of ten-, five-, and one-foot squares, using a buoy for reference.

Davidson was underwater with George Olish on August 12, 1973, when his primitive metal detector located an iron cannon, 14 inches under sand. He uncovered the find, to reveal the cascabel (a round projection behind the breech) and part of the breech. Davidson's first reaction was that it was a cannon ball, but as more sand was removed he realized that his long search was rewarded.

Two weeks probing with steel rods produced three more cannon projecting out from beneath the sand-covered wooden hull. After they were spiked, then pushed overboard by the British, wreckage settled over them. Heartened, Davidson paid $450 dollars of vacation savings to rent a barge-mounted crane from the Preston company of Greenport.

The 6,328-pound prize was hauled aboard seven weeks after it was uncovered. It was the first cannon retrieved from the wreck since July 14, 1815, when Samuel Jeffers raised a 32-pounder.

PRESERVATION

Davidson knew he must find a chemical process to stop corrosion of *Culloden*'s valuable cannon. While he kept it in freshwater, he obtained a book, *History Under The Sea* by Mendel Peterson, from the Smithsonian Institution. He learned that the *Culloden* cannon had been made in Scotland by Graham and Sons. The National Maritime Museum in England provided information that the Defense Standards Laboratories in Victoria, Australia, had preserved similar iron cannon. The Australians responded to

Davidson with a publication, *Report 508 Restoration of Cannon and Other Relics from H.M.B. Endeavor*, by C. Pearson. *Endeavor*, from which the cannon was jettisoned, was the ship in which Captain James Cook toured the world during the 18th century to chart the transit of Venus.

Davidson had all the information he needed to preserve his cannon—but no funds to do so. He hadn't anticipated the problem of preservation when earlier he announced his intention of donating it to the East Hampton Town Musuem. He searched for any museum that would accept the historic relic—and assure its required treatment.

Mrs. Betty Kuss of East Hampton provided the solution. She arranged through East Hampton Councilwoman Mary Fallon (later Town Supervisor) for the town to accept the cannon on permanent loan.

Scientists from the Ocean Science Laboratory supervised the preservation process with Davidson assisting. Restoration of the cannon and its display became a community-wide Bicentennial project. The exhibit was designed by the Director of the East Hampton Town Marine Museum, Ralph Carpentier. George A. Schutte provided the facilities of his antique-restoration shop to construct an authentic replica of the cannon's gun carriage. Its oak timbers were stripped from a barn that served as George Washington's headquarters while he was in Tarrytown, New York. Sid Cullum and Associates forged the iron work, and the cannon was mounted on a section of typical 18th century gun decking built by local carpentry students.

Funds for the restoration were raised by the East Hampton Historical Society, the Town Baymen's Association, and the Town Bicentennial Committee, chaired by Councilwoman Mary Fallon. The cannon's restoration and display proved to be East Hampton's most impressive and enduring Bicentennial project. The exhibit was opened to the public at the East Hampton Town Marine Museum, Bluff Road, Amagansett, on July 11, 1976.

ARCHEOLOGICAL EXCAVATION

New York State granted Dr. Moeller a permit to perform scientific study, map, photograph, and ultimately perform archaeological excavation of the *Culloden* site. No state or federal funds were allocated for the archaeological excavation, but Dr. Moeller acquired funding from two wealthy patrons.

Dr. Moeller worked the site with students of his underwater archaeology class at the New York Ocean Science Laboratory, from the summer of 1976 through the summer of 1979. They air lifted sand from part of the wreck, and recovered a multitude of artifacts—wood, ballast rock, fire bricks, leather, hemp, glass, pottery shards, cannon balls, a hand grenade, lead shot, pewter spoons, buckles, buttons, copper sheathing, nails and barrel hoops. Their identification, classification and preservation was accomplished at the East Hampton Town Marine Museum—the final resting place for much of the British ship-of-the-line's remains.

PRESENT CONDITION

The remains of *Culloden* lie almost entirely imbedded in the sand shoal to the east of Culloden Point. The site is readily accessible to scuba divers, about 150 feet from shore in approximately 20 feet of water.

From year to year, winter storms expose parts of the wreckage or artifacts, such as the cascabel of a sand-covered cannon, cannon balls, timbers, and planking. They may be observed and photographed, but not removed. The site has been placed under New York State protection, with severe restrictions against the unauthorized removal of artifacts. In 1995, the Town of East Hampton, Suffolk County, and New York State purchased 62 waterfront homesites (14.3 acres) for $2 million at Culloden Point from the developer (511 Equities of Manhattan) to provide shore access to the wreck. The Town of East Hampton and Suffolk County are planning Long Island's first underwater park at Culloden Point that will have facilities for scuba divers and terrestrial visitors.

Hundreds of *Culloden*'s relics have survived recovery from the sea and their transfer to the East Hampton Town Marine Museum, where they were preserved. Thanks are due to many: the Sous-Marin divers; Dave Warsen and Bob Miller; Carlton Davidson, George Olish and Paul Knight; and the divers headed by Dr. Henry Moeller, of the New York Ocean Science Laboratory (the laboratory has since been replaced by condominiums).

Not all the museum's *Culloden* relics came from the divers mentioned above. In addition to the gudgeon and pintles recovered by Dave Warsen and Bob Miller, another gudgeon was found by two boys from Lindenhurst, New York. The youths were guests at a Montauk motel between the entrance to Lake Montauk and Fort Pond Bay when they found the artifact while scuba diving. Unaware of its historic value, they planned to sell it for its value as scrap metal. Fortunately, the motel keeper realized that it might have come from *Culloden*. He informed Ralph Carpentier, director of the museum, of the find, and Carpentier contacted Frank Joseph, father of one of the boys. Mr. Joseph agreed to retrieve the relic and turn it over to the museum, but by that time it had been cut into three pieces—so it could be handled easily by two boys. That is how it is now exhibited, with an explanation of how it came to be in that condition.

The days of H.M.S. *Culloden* as a fighting ship in the cause of King George III ended more than 200 years ago. Her revival as an object of historical interest has generated an entire spectrum of reactions in contemporary Americans. The lure of a lost wreck, self-sacrifice, intensity of the search, persistence, excitement of the find, sharing, frustration, hope, community-wide cooperation, and patriotic fervor were all stimulated by the historic remains of a proud warship of the British Navy, one that grounded on the coast of Long Island in January 1781, H.M.S. *Culloden*.

GREAT EASTERN—"WONDER OF THE SEA"

Type of vessel: passenger liner
Where built: J.S. Russell's Shipyard, Isle of Dogs, England
Launched: January 31, 1858
Length/beam: 693/120
Gross tons: 22,500
Cause of incident: struck a rock, but did not sink
Location: 1.5 nautical miles east of Montauk Point
Approximate depth of water: did not sink

> *Nor forget I to sing of the wonder,*
>   *the ship as she swam up my bay,*
> *Well-shaped and stately the* Great Eastern *swam up my bay,*
>   *she was 600 feet long,*
> *Her moving swiftly surrounded by myriads of small craft*
>   *I forgot not to sing.*
> —Walt Whitman, *The Year of Meteors*

A ROCK PINNACLE off Montauk Point extends off the bottom to within 24 feet of the surface. It is known locally and on nautical charts as the Great Eastern Rock. When the British steamship *Great Eastern* struck the previously unknown rock on August 27, 1862, she made a lasting contribution to American geography.

MAMMOTH STEAMER

The iron-hulled *Great Eastern* was five times the size of the biggest vessel then afloat when she was launched in 1858. The steamer was designed to carry 4,000 passengers, almost twice as many as *Queen Mary*, launched 77 years later.

> *Sublime in its enormous bulk*
> *Loomed aloft the shadowy hulk.*
> —Longfellow

The 22,500-ton "Wonder of the Sea" was 693 feet long, with a beam of 120 feet, too broad for the Panama Canal which opened a half-century later. *Great Eastern*'s displacement was not exceeded until *Lusitania* was launched 49 years later. Her massive iron hull was constructed of 30,000 iron plates, seven-eighths of an inch thick and averaging a third of a ton. She had a double hull, one inside the other, three feet apart and heavily braced, extending to six feet above the waterline. Three million rivets, each an inch thick, were used to fasten the plates. The rivets were hand-driven by 400 workers. Half of them worked by candle light inside the dark, cramped space between the hulls, to the tune of a hellish reverberation of 400 hammers. They worked 12-hours a day, six days a week.

There were many injuries, some fatal, to workmen and the young boys who were their helpers. One man fell to his death, another died between the hulls, and an outside riveter fell off the scaffold onto a man on the ground, killing him. One young boy fell off the hull and was impaled on a standing iron bar. "After he was dead, his body quivered for some time," stated a witness. Even a visitor was killed when he bent over to look at the top of a pile and the pile driver flattened his head. Two workers simply disappeared. It was rumored among the workers that a riveter was sealed up alive in one of the hull cells, but his screams could not be heard over the din of hammering. His ghost was said to haunt the ship.

Great Eastern had six masts and five funnels, more than any ship has carried before or since. The steamer had two engines, one to turn her two 58-foot side paddle wheels and the other to power the 24 feet in diameter, 36-ton, cast-iron screw-propeller.

The ship's 836-ton paddle wheel engine was powered by steam from four boilers containing 160 tons of water. During her trials in 1859, *Great Eastern* made eight knots using only her paddle wheels.

The screw-propeller engine had four cylinders, paired on both sides of the 60-ton, 150-foot long crankshaft. During trials the steam engine, connected to six boilers with a 270-ton capacity, produced a speed of nine knots, using only her screw-propeller. Later, using both paddle wheels and screw-propeller, she reached 15 knots.

Great Eastern could carry 15,000 tons of coal, bunkered around and over her ten boilers, and her crew passed fore and aft through a six-foot iron tube buried under coal. Fully coaled, she was an ocean-borne coal mine.

Compared to boiler pressures of the time, the huge ship was under-powered for her size. She probably never exceeded 5,000 of her 11,000 horsepower potential. The steam turbines of *Independence*, launched in 1951, almost a century after *Great Eastern* was launched, produced seven times the cruising power of the old steamer and could make twice her speed, even though she was about the same length, beam, and tonnage. The main difference was boiler pressure: *Great Eastern*'s was 25 pounds per square inch compared to 620 for *Independence*. *Great Eastern*'s designer, I.K. Brunel, and builder John Scott Russel produced their mammoth steamer before there was technology to adequately power her. Brunel also designed *Great Britain*, launched in 1843, the first major iron-hulled vessel and the first such ship to be propeller-driven.

The directors of the Great Eastern Steam Navigation Company selected the name *Leviathan* for the steamer, but no one else ever called her that. The ship was always *Great Eastern*.

It required three months of trial and error and two fatalities to launch the huge vessel. On one of the many futile attempts to move the massive hull, a 60-ton windlass spun in reverse and the huge handlebars struck a dozen workers, killing two and severely injuring three. Outside, but overlooking the shipyard, an enterprising individual erected a sightseer gallery between two housetops. The overloaded platform collapsed, and crashed to the ground with 100 people. Many were injured, but there were no fatalities.

During the six years of her construction *Great Eastern* cost her shareholders four million dollars. Once afloat, she still needed funnels and masts, of which the mizzen mast was to be a 115-foot pine from Desperation Pass, Oregon. The steamer also needed lifeboats and furnishings for saloons and staterooms to accommodate 4,000 passengers. It would require $600,000 to complete her, but the Great Eastern Steam Navigation Company could not raise the money and went bankrupt. Brunel, the designer, helped found the Great Ship Company that bought the steamer for $800,000. The new company finished the grand saloon which was 62 feet long, 36 feet wide, and 12 feet high. The decor was predominately white and gilt, with silver-oxidized ornamental ironwork. A funnel that passed through it was encased in mirrors. Only staterooms for 300 first-class passengers were furnished; second- and third-class accommodations were not installed for several years after the fitting out was completed in August 1859.

The three-month ordeal of launching, and then trying to finish the ship changed the 53-year-old Brunel, from tough, energetic, and tanned, into a faltering, pale-faced, quaking ancient who was too ill to be aboard on her maiden voyage.

EXPLOSION

Brunel would not have enjoyed that first voyage. The forward funnel blew out of the ship, shattering the mirrors in the grand saloon "into 10,000 fragments." The oak stairways leading into the grand saloon were broken "into splinters." Fortunately, the passengers had just left the saloon and none were injured. There were no paying passengers; all were guests or shareholders of the company. A fireman in the boiler room escaped an exploding boiler by diving down a coal-ash chute designed to carry coal-ash outside the hull and into the water. It dropped him in front of one of the huge paddle wheels that chewed him up and left him in its wake as a broken corpse. Another fireman staggered up from the boiler room. According to a witness, "the flesh of his thighs was burnt to deep holes." The fireman said, "I am all right. There are others worse than me, so look after them." He was far from all right; he died, and so did three others still below.

The cause of the explosion was steam buildup in the funnel's steam jacket. Someone had closed the escape cock on the jacket. News of the tragic accident killed Brunel.

In January 1860, *Great Eastern*'s captain went ashore in the ship's small boat with the steamer's surgeon, seven crew members, and the nine-year-old son of the chief purser. A squall struck, capsizing the boat and drowning the captain, a crew member, and the boy.

By that time, the Great Ship Company was in financial trouble and the directors were forced to resign. A third group of shareholders took control, before *Great Eastern* had carried a single paying passenger.

Great Eastern left Southampton, England on June 17, 1860 for her first transatlantic passage with only 35 paying passengers and 418 crew members. On her second voyage to America, in 1861, she had 100 passengers on board at fares of $130 for first-class and $75 for "very superior accommodations" in second-class.

RECORD CROSSING

The following year *Great Eastern* was chartered by the British War Office to carry 2,144 officers and men, 473 women and children, and 122 horses to Canada. With her crew of 400, the vessel would carry twice as many people as had ever sailed on a ship. Not until the troop transports of World War I, over a half-century later, were so many carried on a ship.

Great Eastern won the coveted Blue Riband, the British maritime award for fastest passage across the Atlantic with her crossing of eight days and six hours. It required two days for the Quebec ferries to take off the 2,617 passengers and 122 horses.

Great Eastern carried 356 passengers back to England. When she left Liverpool for New York on September 10, 1861, she carried 400 paying passengers, still far short of her 4,000 passenger design. The ship could have filled to capacity, but management saw "no profit in emigrants," despite the fact that 800,000 came to the U.S. during the Civil War alone. Refusal to carry emigrants was a major reason why the steamer did not turn a profit. The directors were obsessed with first-class passenger fares. Another factor was that the ship could not cross the Atlantic during the winter; her cavernous spaces were too cold.

UNCHARTED ROCK

On August 17, 1862, *Great Eastern* left Liverpool for New York with 820 passengers. She also carried so much cargo that she drew 30 feet. On August 27, she was off Montauk Point and with her deep draught her captain did not want to risk the sandbar at the entrance to New York Harbor. He preferred to pass through Long Island Sound to Flushing Bay, where he would moor his ship. However, two miles northeast of Montauk Point lay the Endeavor Shoals that came within 19 feet of the surface, and the steamer drew 30 feet. *Great Eastern*'s captain, Walter Paton, waited for a Long Island Sound pilot to guide his ship past the shoals and through the Sound.

At 1:30 a.m. the pilot came aboard and started around Montauk Point. At 2:00 a.m., 1.5 nautical miles off the Point, there was a "dull rumble." The steamer heeled a few degrees to port, and continued on her way. The pilot thought they might have struck a sand shoal, so Captain Paton sent an officer below to check the bilge for water, but there was none. By the time the ship moored in Flushing Bay she was listing to starboard. Paton hired a hard-hat diver to inspect the steamer's bottom.

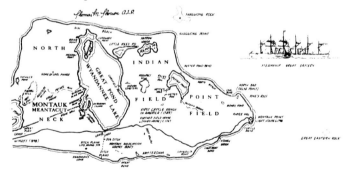

Map showing the location of Great Eastern rock, off Montauk Point. *Courtesy of East Hampton Town*

It took days of moving the diver's tender from spot to spot to permit the diver to survey the huge expanse of hull. He found that the ship had a gash in her bottom 83 feet long and 9 feet wide. The tear, however, was only in the outer hull, the inner hull was intact. No other ship of that time would have survived the incident. When soundings were made off Montauk Point, a rock was found within 24 feet of the surface. It was close enough to the surface to have penetrated both hulls, but the transverse braces between the hulls had apparently protected the inner hull from damage. The rock, christened Great Eastern Rock, is still known by that name.

The very large gash in her bottom required dry-dock repairs for *Great Eastern*, but there was no dry-dock in the world large enough to hold her. Often, ships with round bottoms and pronounced keels were careened on beaches with extreme tides, depending on low tide to expose their bottoms. However, *Great Eastern*, like Brunel's other designed ship *Great Britain*, was flat-bottomed. They were the only flat-bottomed ocean going ships in the world. Many believed that *Great Eastern*, the world's heaviest man-made object, would have to be scrapped.

PROBLEM SOLVED

One day in September the steamer's New York agent was approached by a consulting engineer named Edward Renwick. Renwick, who was almost blind, claimed that he and his brother Henry could repair the ship where she lay in Flushing Bay under the salvor's "no cure, no pay." If they failed, the Great Ship Company would owe them nothing. Henry was blind in one eye, so the two men had the sight of slightly more than one eye between them. The skeptical agent introduced them to Captain Paton, who decided to pin his hopes on the dim-sighted brothers; his only risk was time.

A manuscript by Edward Renwick describing the problem was discovered by his granddaughter-in-law in a Washington, Connecticut barn in 1953. "The whole space between the two skins at one side of the ship, three feet in breadth and 680 feet in length became filled with water ... The first thing to be ascertained was the form of the exterior of the ship. This was done by making templates on the inner skin, and when these were laid down on the moulding floor, and the breadth of the space between the two skins, three feet, was added to the curved lines of the templates, and the form of the exterior was determined."

The two brothers built a cofferdam of heavy wood, 102 feet long and 16 feet wide, with gunwales curved to fit the ship's hull. The large cofferdam was built in a shipyard, launched like a ship, and towed to Flushing Bay. The wooden structure was ballasted and sunk beside the ship. Large chains were wrapped around the steamer, fastening the cofferdam to the ship. Carpets were placed between the edges of the gunwales and the hull as a watertight seal. A powerful pump sucked water from the double hull spaces and the cofferdam. The ship's officers joked that the pump was strong enough to suck the skeletal remains of the lost riveter from his ghostly tomb in the double hull.

The carpets, however, did not seal well and water flowed into the cofferdam about as fast as it was pumped out. Edward had the cofferdam unchained and refloated. Then he had carpenters hollow out a groove in the gunwales. A heavy fire hose was laid in the groove and padded with carpeting. The cofferdam was sunk and chained to the hull, and the fire hose was inflated with water. The seal worked and the pump emptied the cofferdam.

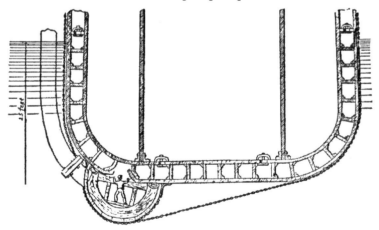

Sectional diagram of Renwick's cofferdam. *Scientific American.*

The Great Eastern Rock had turned the torn hull plates inward, giving the drillers a smooth surface to make rivet holes. Another problem arose when the drillers were ready to drill; iron plates to repair the hole were not available—there was a war on. In the spring, the armored U.S.S. *Monitor* had fought to a draw with the armored C.S.S. *Virginia* in Hampton Roads and the U.S. Navy was armoring more of its ships.

The Renwick brothers found a rolling mill to produce five-eighth-inch boiler plate. They were not the seven-eighth-inch thickness of the steamer's original plates, but they would have to do. It required three months to produce the needed plates without interrupting the mill's orders from the War Department.

Periodically, as new plates were added, a diver descended to inspect the cofferdam. On one inspection after the riveters stopped work for the day, he tugged four times on his air hose, the emergency signal to haul him up. When the tenders removed his helmet the white-faced diver gasped, "The ghost is hammering inside the hull!"

The following day, when the workers who heard the story would not enter the cofferdam, Captain Paton did. When he returned, he told Edward Renwick, "I heard it. Something is pounding on the hull." The ship was searched, and no one was found hammering on the inside of the hull, but there was the sound "of banging on plate." Paton rowed around the ship in a skiff and found one of the cofferdam's heavy swivels hitting the hull as the swells from boat traffic moved it back and forth. He unfastened the swivel and showed it to the workers. They returned to the cofferdam and all plates were installed by the end of December. The Renwick brothers' bill was $350,000.

Lloyd's insurance company refused to allow a claim for damage and the Great Ship Company could not sue the United States for lack of knowledge of the Great Eastern Rock, so the company was $350,000 deeper in debt.

Captain Paton faced a board of inquiry by the Great Ship Company when he returned to England. The verdict was: "Having fully investigated all circumstances, the directors have arrived at the conclusion that no blame whatsoever attaches to you or any of your officers, but the accident is solely attributable to the ship striking on a sunken rock in the fairway channel, which is not laid down in the charts."

In 1863, *Great Eastern* made two trips to New York at a loss of $100,000, and the Great Ship Company went bankrupt. Her total bankruptcy score was $5,000,000. Three of the company's directors bought the ship at auction for $125,000. For the next few years the steamer was used to lay the first telegraph cable across the Atlantic, her most important contribution.

In March 1867, *Great Eastern* was again ready for a transatlantic passage, leaving from France. Among her 123 passengers was the French science fiction writer Jules Verne. Verne interrupted work on his new novel, *Twenty Thousand Leagues under the Sea*, to make the passage and report on his experiences for a French newspaper. On sailing day, crew members on the capstan bars were helping two auxiliary steam engines weigh the anchor. One engine failed when the ten-ton anchor was part way up, and the men could not hold the weight. The anchor dropped, spinning the capstan like a top. The capstan bars struck and killed four men. Verne later wrote, "This event made very little impression on board ... These unhappy men killed and wounded, were only tools, which could be replaced at very little expense."

SOLD FOR SCRAP

By the time the once grand steamer was sold at auction in 1887 for $80,000, seven companies had operated *Great Eastern* at a loss. The stockholders of the last company were paid off at 14 cents on the dollar.

Her new company, Henry Bath and Sons, started scrapping the ship in May 1889, 31 years and three months after she was launched. The new owners had to invent the heavy, iron wrecker's ball to break the steel plates apart. It required 18 months and about $100,000 to break up the massive iron hull, but the company was the only owner to make a profit from *Great Eastern*.

James Dugan, in *The Great Iron Ship*, wrote that workers who broke open one of the hull compartments found the skeletons of the missing riveter and his young helper who were lost during

Great Eastern's construction. The "Wonder of the Sea" left her mark on the geography of Long Island, but although every fisherman on Eastern Long Island refers to the hazard struck by the steamer as Great Eastern Rock, not all know why it was so named.

Bow of *Great Eastern* showing the massive paddle boxes, sketched by Frank Braynard.

The Bell Tolls

ONTARIO—CAPTAIN'S WIFE A "HOODOO"

Type of vessel: passenger/freighter
Where built: New York Shipbuilding Co., Camden, New Jersey
Launched: 1904
Length/beam: 292'/42'
Gross tons: 1,987
Stranded: April 8, 1912
Cause of incident: fire/ran aground
Location: near Montauk Point
Approximate depth of water: refloated

EARLY MONDAY MORNING, April 8, 1912, an urgent wireless call for help jolted the receiving station operator at Point Judith, Rhode Island into action. It was a terse message, "*Ontario*, big fire below," followed by the ship's position. Nothing is more terrifying for those aboard a threatened ship than fire at sea. Such an emergency called for control of the blaze and control of passenger panic, but always with an early call for help.

Ontario was a 292-foot coastal steamer operated by the Merchants' and Miners' Line. The 1,987-ton passenger/freighter was en route from Baltimore to Boston with Captain J.F. Bond in command when, at about 1:30 a.m, fire was discovered in the forward hold. The ship was about ten miles south of Shinnecock Inlet when the captain learned of the danger. While his 31 passengers slumbered, he quietly organized the 50-man crew and struggled to save the steamer without alarming them.

The crew chopped large holes through the wooden deck, then pumped tons of water on the flames below, but the fire gained headway. The prospects of survival were bleak.

CALL FOR HELP

Only 12 years earlier, Captain Bond would have had no resource to call on for help other than a nearby ship in view. That changed in 1900, when the Italian physicist Guglielmo Marconi set up a transmitting station in a small hut on Long Island, in Babylon. From there, he transmitted the world's first shore-to-ship wireless telegraph message. That led to the installation of wireless sets aboard ships at sea, initially staffed by Marconi employees.

The sinking of the White Star liner *Republic* in 1909, south of Nantucket Island, was the first maritime disaster in which wireless telegraphy played an important part in rescue at sea. It led to United States legislation that mandated wireless sets and operators for every ship carrying 50 or more passengers. In 1910, the first weather reports were sent to sea from the naval wireless station at Newport, Rhode Island. That information was picked up by the Nantucket Shoals lightship and relayed to other ships in the area that, in turn, passed on the vital information.

Ontario's wireless operator Hubert Ingalls, a young man in his teens, sent out Captain Bond's initial call for help, and continued sending out the "S.O.S." signals that were certified for general use as distress calls only four years earlier.

The raging fire in her hold convinced the captain that his ship would have to be beached. Later he said: "Owing to the direction of the wind, I was unable to make a straight northerly course, since to do that would have driven the fire aft, and consequently my only alternative was to set a course northeast for Montauk Point ..."

Ingalls transmitted: "uncontrollable fire, southwest gale, heading for Montauk Point" to alert the local lifesaving stations. Newport, Boston, and Norfolk stations received the message and relayed it to the Long Island lifesaving stations. Within an hour, tugboats, revenue cutters, and a U.S. Navy destroyer headed for Montauk. Ingall's wireless house was on the deck, almost directly over the fire, and the heat was intense. He later stated that the temperature was so high that he feared his equipment would stop functioning, but he continued sending out distress signals from the smoke-filled wireless house until fire destroyed his equipment.

BEACHED

Captain Bond beached *Ontario* near Montauk Point at about 3:00 a.m. Five hours later, the tugboat *Tasco* arrived from New

London. By then the fire had progressed from the bow to midships. Passengers huddled aft, watching the crew battle the blaze until lifeboats transferred them to the tugboat; by 9:00 a.m., all 31, including Captain Bond's wife, were safe on board.

Mr. H.W. Sanborn, a passenger, observed: "The women behaved better than the men.... Of course we all got a little excited, but who wouldn't. I was sleeping in the stateroom next to that of the wireless operator, and right on the other side the fire was raging. About 2 o'clock ... I awoke and looked out at the weather and saw people running on deck, crying 'The ship is afire!' I thought it was a fire drill, but the next minute the smoke enveloped us and I realized it was no joke."

Another passenger saw stevedores smoking while they stowed bales of cotton in the forward hold and he believed a smoldering match or cigarette started a blaze before the steamer left port. An editorial in *The New York Times* responded: "So well known is the possibility of spontaneous combustion when baled cotton is stored in a tightly closed place like a ship's hold that it seems hardly necessary to accuse some careless stevedore." The editorial added: "As usual, nowadays, wireless telegraphy played its beneficent role in sending promptly and far the news that life and property were in desperate danger, and the needed help thus summoned, immediately came from many directions.... Probably any reference to 'heroism' will be only embarrassing to the men who fought the fire ... there should be no lack of recognition of the fact that, thanks to them, the episode was made one to reassure ocean travelers rather than to increase apprehension."

The tugboat *Tasco* carried the passengers to New London, where most took the train to Boston.

Captain Bond and his crew fought the fire all that day and through the night, but despite their efforts they could not get it under control. Captain Bond and his crew were taken off by breeches buoy and surfboat by the Ditch Plain and Hither Plain lifesaving crews—none too soon! A few minutes later, an explosion blew off *Ontario*'s deck. The following day, the captain, his face still black with soot, said: "We had 31 passengers on board, of whom about 15 were women. They of course were uppermost in my mind. They accepted the situation with surprising calmness, and at no time was there a semblance of a panic. And I may add that we did not awaken the passengers until after we had beached the ship. By then the fire had eaten up through the forward deck and to the pilot house and wireless house, where Ingalls did such gallant work."

Captain Bond failed to mention his and First Officer Harding's heroic work during the run to Montauk. They remained in the smoke-filled pilothouse to man the helm. The heat became so intense that they took turns at the wheel because it was impossible to hold it for more than a few seconds at a time.

WIFE A "HOODOO"

The day after *Ontario* beached, Captain Bond's daughter, in Baltimore, stated that something always happens when her mother decides to take a trip on her father's ship. She said: "I was down at the slip when they sailed ... We looked at the barometer, and my father said: 'Well if your mother wasn't along, I should say we ought to have a right safe trip; but you can never tell when she is aboard.'"

Captain Bond's daughter recounted several mishaps to vessels her father commanded when her mother was on board, including a fire on the steamer *Kershaw* in 1905. She recalled still another fire that occurred when her mother was along, but that one didn't amount to much. *The New York Times* considered Mrs. Bond a jinx and labeled her a "Hoodoo."

SALVAGE

To lighten the steamer, all of her cargo that had not been consumed by flames, was thrown overboard. Whiskey, tobacco, bales of cotton, shoes, and peanuts were gathered up by the locals. The lightened, burned out hulk was pulled off the sandbar by Scott Wrecking Company salvage tugs, then was scrapped.

Mrs. Bond's spell was particularly effective on *Ontario*'s final voyage.

U.S.S. *BALDWIN*—COSTLY SALVAGE

Type of vessel: destroyer
Where built: Seattle, Washington
Launched: 1943
Length/beam: 348'3" / 36'1"
Gross tons: 1,630
Stranded: April 16, 1961
Cause of incident: towline parted and drifted aground
Location: between Coconuts and the Caswell's, Montauk Point
Approximate depth of water: refloated and scuttled in 1,200 feet

THE JUNE 22, 1961 issue of *The East Hampton Star* reported: "The East End of Long Island has a fascination with shipwrecks, those disasters of the sea which become rarer year by year. On April 16 there was a wreck at Montauk, the wreck of an unmanned ship. It might have been a perfect stranding, since there was no one around to be hurt, except for two acts: A man was killed 13 days after the wreck, and the Navy pulled the ship ... off the beach."

The unmanned U.S. Navy destroyer *Baldwin* (DD-624) was being towed from Boston, Massachusetts to Philadelphia, Pennsylvania by the fleet tug *Keywadin* (ATA-213) when the tow line parted in heavy seas on Sunday, April 16, 1961. The decommissioned 1,630-ton, 348-foot-long destroyer was headed for the mothball fleet. The turbulent seas foiled attempts by the tow vessel to get another line on her. Wind and waves carried the 18-year-old destroyer 23 miles before she grounded west of Montauk Point in five feet of water. The location is just east of the area known as Coconuts, where the schooner *Elsie Fay* went to pieces in 1893, scattering her cargo of coconuts along the shore and naming that section of beach.

SALVAGE ATTEMPTS

The following day the fleet tug *Luiseno* (ATF-156) out of Newport, Rhode Island joined *Keywadin* to attempt salvage. On Tuesday, the Navy salvage vessels *Hoist* (ARS-40) and *Windlass* (ARSD-4) from Norfolk, Virginia, joined the tugs, with Navy scuba divers aboard.

To respond immediately, *Hoist* had to get underway with less than half of her crew aboard. *Windlass* had just returned to her home port from a previous assignment and was duty salvage ship; thus, most of her crew was on board when the call for assistance was received early Sunday evening. Lieutenant Commander Frank Kalasinsky, Salvage Officer on the Service Force Staff, was flown from Norfolk to New York to take charge of the salvage operation.

The destroyer leaked oil as she rocked back and forth in the waves, proof that her hull was holed. For several days, the surf was too strong for the divers to assess the damage with a hull inspection. When the weather allowed them in the water, they found that Montauk's rocks had punctured about 25 holes in the destroyer's thin, steel hull plating. Water was within three feet of the main deck in the engine rooms. It was flowing into the destroyer faster than six pumps with a capacity of 9,000 gallons a minute could remove it. Additional pumps were brought aboard to keep her afloat if she could be pulled off.

The Navy salvage ship *Salvager* (ARSD-3) steamed up from Bermuda and the salvage barge YFNB-17 arrived from Norfolk to help.

Small boats assisted the tugs and salvage vessels to transfer towing cables to the destroyer. Navy seamen took over the destroyer's deck to get the hawsers aboard. Without power, there was no way for *Baldwin* to help haul the 1,000 yards or so of two-inch wire on board. The wire tow lines were shackled to great loops of wire cable laid around the destroyer's number one five-inch gun mount on the forecastle, and the number four mount on her fantail.

Each day at high tide the salvage vessels, one, two, or three at a time, slowly took a strain on the tow lines, pulling intermittently with their main engines and deck winches. Several times, *Baldwin* lurched visibly from a starboard to port list, but moved only a few inches offshore. Each time the destroyer moved slightly, new holes were poked in her hull, or patches placed by the divers were pulled off.

The men aboard *Baldwin* worked day and night; one night,

heavy seas prevented salvage vessels from reaching the stranded destroyer. Navy divers on board swam ashore and picked up food from the Coast Guard at Montauk and carried it back to the destroyer.

KILLED INSTANTLY

On April 29, a seaman was killed during the salvage operation when he was struck by heavy steel cable that snapped and backlashed. The 20-year-old sailor was Tommy J. King of Norfolk, electrician's mate on *Windlass*. A less serious casualty was Charles McCoy of Philadelphia, a medical corpsman on *Windlass*, who suffered a broken leg and other injuries in the same accident and was taken to Southampton Hospital.

The accident occurred as *Windlass* attempted to pull *Baldwin* free. A heavy steel cable, running from the salvage vessel to the destroyer parted. It whipped back and struck King, the cable winch operator, killing him instantly. McCoy was standing nearby when the accident occurred.

By May 1, the six U.S. Navy vessels, divers, portable pumps, and several hundred men were at the wreck site. Spectators swarmed over Montauk's high bluffs watching the formidable team try to refloat the destroyer.

Fog and heavy seas impeded the salvage, but by May 14, *Baldwin* was 160 feet to seaward of her grounding, and her bow was in 18 feet of water, pointed toward the open sea. Lt. Cmdr. Kalasinsky, the officer in command, estimated that another 120 feet would float the 348-foot-long warship.

NEW APPROACH

Patches torn loose during the operation continued to slow progress, and pumping could not empty the water from the destroyer's hull. On May 22, Lt. Cmdr. Kalasinsky chose a new approach. The topside of *Baldwin* was made airtight, and air compressors were brought aboard to pump air below to force water out through the holes in her bottom. Heavy seas again delayed the salvage operation but at 5:23 p.m. on June 4, work resumed. The same day, six weeks after stranding, *Baldwin* was pulled off the beach, with the air compressors keeping her afloat, finally.

Baldwin was built in Seattle and commissioned in 1943. She served as an escort for three transatlantic convoys during World War II and sustained slight damage from shellfire from German shore batteries during D-Day landings at Normandy. The destroyer was nicknamed "the Lucky B" and "Old Baldy" by her crew. She earned three battle stars before her decommissioning in 1946. Even before the World War II veteran was refloated, the Navy realized that the damage she sustained was too extensive to repair. There was another problem. The destroyer might sink while under tow to a shipyard and become a hazard to navigation.

The day after *Baldwin* was refloated at the expense of one death, four injured seamen, great cost, and six weeks of effort, the destroyer was taken under tow by the tug *Luiseno* for scuttling about 95 miles southeast of Montauk in more than 1,200 feet of water. It was a bitter pill to swallow for the Navy officers and seamen who worked 10 to 17 hours a day to refloat the destroyer so she could be sunk.

It must have been especially difficult for the men of *Windlass* who lost a shipmate, then wondered, "Why?"

CHIPPEWA—ALLIGATORS AND OSTRICHES

Type of vessel: freighter
Where built: Philadelphia, Pennsylvania
Launched: 1905
Length/beam: 275' / 40'
Gross tons: 2,155
Stranded: June 23, 1908
Cause of incident: fog
Location: east of Ditch Plains

"BLASTED FOG!" CAPTAIN Macbeth squinted and leaned forward at the wheel as though the additional inches would pierce the thick mist that blanketed his ship. The fog that embraced the freighter was like a silky cocoon, protecting the pupal stage of an insect. But the 275-foot *Chippewa* was no insect and the fog was doing its best to contribute to her destruction. Lookouts were posted, but they served no use in the thick haze. Helpless was a condition Macbeth would never acknowledge, but he felt close to that, with the bow of his ship out of sight. Stripped of vision, he had only dead reckoning and years of experience to guide him along the eastern end of Long Island. Believing he was beyond the end of the island, he changed course veering north to skirt the shore of Rhode Island for Boston, but the murky fog betrayed him. Instead of open sea, the south shore of the island's South Fork lay dead ahead.

GROUNDING

The 2,155-ton Clyde Line freighter *Chippewa* was en route from Jacksonville, Florida to Boston, Massachusetts. Shortly after midnight on June 23, 1908, she drove hard aground on rocks, east of the Ditch Plain Life-Saving Station, near the end of the South Fork of Long Island. There were no casualties, but without help there was nothing the crew could do to refloat their ship.

The following morning, Carl Hedges, captain of the Ditch Plains Life-Saving Station, discovered the distressed ship on the rocky point off his shore. He was alone. Shipwrecks generally occurred in the winter, and his surfmen were all on mandatory vacation. "Gotta' get 'em off," he muttered, but help was needed. He quickly mustered a crew of his furloughed surfmen who lived nearby and local volunteers. In anticipation of such a crisis, everyone was required by law to help in response to a call for lifesaving assistance.

The hastily assembled crew rowed the station's surfboat through heavy surf to the stranded *Chippewa*. The crew greeted them with a hearty welcome, but with no intention of being saved. They intended to stay aboard because there seemed to be no danger of the ship shifting into deeper water and sinking. In appreciation of their readiness to help, Captain Macbeth invited the volunteer lifesavers to breakfast in his cabin the next morning. The guests wolfed down heaps of ham and eggs, fresh baked bread, and coffee while the captain entertained with sea stories.

Laughter and loud voices drowned out increased wind and wave action outside. Perched on her rock, *Chippewa* was spared much of the surge until a tremendous wave struck the ship and the cabin door blew open with a blast that lifted the diners off their seats. Coffee spewed from Hedges' mouth and Macbeth choked on his mouthful of ham. Dishes crashed to the cabin floor and a surfman choked on his scrambled eggs. The orderly meal became a rush to be first to view the damage and prepare to abandon ship if a worse wave followed. Captain Macbeth was first on deck, still clutching a meaty ham bone, and said, "Sturdy, that's what she is. Not a sign of damage—and that was a mighty heavy ripple."

One of the surfmen surveyed the coffee on his shirt and agreed. "Yep, she held up real well, but there's more to come. Look at that sky; this is no time to work on refloating her." With the likelihood of even fouler weather to come, the crew had nothing to gain by staying aboard. The lifesaving team ferried everyone ashore, to wait for better weather.

After the storm passed, the crew and volunteers, 24 in all, returned to refloat the ship. She was only three years old and her owner wanted to save his investment. The steamer was impaled on a large rock with a hole in her bottom and 18 feet of water in her hold. The hole could be patched, but the ship had to be lightened before salvage tugs could pull her free. *Chippewa*'s mixed cargo included an assortment of 39,000 watermelons, yellow pine lumber, and a live consignment of seven ostriches and a number of alligators. The watermelons and lumber were jettisoned, to the delight of local residents who patrolled the beach, scooping up the green fruit filled with juicy red pulp.

Edna Yeager, in *Around The Forks*, wrote that dead alligators and ostriches washed ashore and for days people came to the beach not only to view those victims, but to search for artifacts that washed ashore. She added, "The strangest find of all was one perfect ostrich egg. How had it withstood its violent journey?" She continued that the egg became the prized possession of Captain Carl Hedges of the Ditch Plains Life-Saving Station.

FREED

The crewmen and salvors worked aboard, preparing the ship for removal by salvage tugs. On July 18, the towering waves of a new storm drove them all into the ship's rigging. All were removed by breeches buoy and the work was temporarily abandoned. They returned after the storm and on August 4 *Chippewa* slid free of her perch, ending her 42-day stay. After repairs, in New York City, she returned to service for the Clyde Line.

Stranding, even with a hull torn open, does not always doom a ship. *Chippewa* is one example. Another was the graceful, four-masted Norwegian bark *Clan Galbraith*. Eight years later she ran aground on July 22, 1916, near Flying Point (south of Water Mill). The beautiful vessel, stranded on the beach, became a favorite of sightseers until the iron-hulled ship was pulled off several weeks later. The Long Island Railroad even ran a special train for the occasion. *Clan Galbraith*'s fate was not to be lost by stranding, but by a German U-boat attack later in the First World War.

MADONNA V—RUMRUNNER

Type of vessel: schooner
Where built: unknown
Launched: about 1892
Length/beam: unknown
Gross tons: 7
Sunk: December 21, 1922
Cause of sinking: storm / ran aground
Location: east of the Napeague Coast Guard station
Approximate depth of water: wreckage has not been located

> *Oh, we don't give a damn for our old Uncle Sam*
> *Way-o, whiskey and gin!*
> *Lend us a hand when we stand in to land*
> *Just give us time to run the rum in.*
> —*The Smugglers' Chantey*
> Joseph Chase Allen, 1921

THE SMALL SCHOONER *Madonna V* sailed from the Bahamas in November 1922, when the 18th Amendment (Prohibition) was almost three years old and bootleg booze was big business. The Atlantic Ocean south of Long Island was known as "Rum Row." That was where "hootch"-laden ships from Canada and the Caribbean would anchor, just beyond U.S. territorial waters. Under cover of darkness, small vessels from Long Island ports received their illegal cargo and ran it into some secluded shore. There, it was transferred to trucks that carried it to New York City.

PROHIBITION

Like no other era in American history, Prohibition was colorful and controversial. The 18th Amendment that went into effect on January 17, 1920, prohibited the sale of all liquors containing more than 0.5 per cent alcohol. The period from then until repeal of the amendment on December 5, 1933, is termed Prohibition. Many considered rum running an almost respectable form of protest against Prohibition.

Andrew Sinclair wrote, "The prohibitionists looked forward to a world free from alcohol and, by that magic panacea, free also from want and crime and sin." Prohibition, however, created more problems than it solved. The saloons of New York City and elsewhere went underground to become known as "speakeasies." A person wanting to gain entrance would knock on the door and whisper a name or password. The number of establishments selling liquor in New York City more than doubled, with an estimated 32,000 illegal speakeasies replacing 15,000 legal saloons. Before Prohibition, women seldom entered saloons, but during Prohibition, they flocked to speakeasies.

The wooden-hulled *Madonna V* stranded east of the Napeague Coast Guard station, driven ashore on December 21, 1922, by gale force winds. The small schooner carried a cargo of several hundred cases of wine and whiskey when the Coast Guard came upon her. The rumrunner's crew protested that the approximately 30-year-old schooner, owned by a resident of Halifax, Nova Scotia, was bound for Canada, en route from the Bahamas to St. Pierre in the Gulf of St. Lawrence. The skeptical coast guardsmen found that hard to believe. They held the captain and his eight-man crew for interview by custom officials from New York City.

By nightfall, the rumrunner began to break up in the heavy surf; but not before as much of the wine and whiskey cargo as possible was salvaged by the willing hands of local volunteers. Jeannette Edwards Rattray, in *Ship Ashore*, described the event: "Lifelong teetotalers and even deacons of the church risked pneumonia in the December surf to bring it [whiskey and wine] ashore, prompted no doubt by the inherited custom of "wrecking" and old New England principles against waste of any kind."

That night the storm surge scattered the wreckage and its unsalvaged whiskey along the beach for miles to the west of the wreck site. *Madonna V* was a total loss.

Some bottles from the wreck of the lost rumrunner are on display at the East Hampton Town Marine Museum, in Amagansett.

CATHERINE—IRISH IMMIGRANTS

Type of vessel: brig
Where built: unknown
Launched: unknown
Length/beam: unknown
Gross tons: unknown
Sunk: August 25, 1851
Cause of sinking: ran aground
Location: Amagansett
Approximate depth of water: when exposed, about two feet

IN 1845, DISASTER struck Ireland in the form of a fungus, a potato blight. Potato was the staple food for at least half the country's population and the blight lasted from 1845 to 1849. "Black '47" was the worst year of the five-year Irish potato famine. It was so severe that trap-door coffins were used to accommodate the large numbers of dead; over a million Irish died of starvation and disease. Hundreds of thousands more left Ireland to escape the famine and came to America, seeking a better way of life.

The impact on life in Ireland was so devastating that it became a lasting segment of the country's history. In 1994, the Famine Museum opened in Ireland, and in the United States, Governor George Pataki signed a law in 1996 including the Irish potato famine in the curriculum of New York State schools. The governor, who is of Irish descent, blamed the British more than the fungus for the impact of the blight when he signed the law. They, he said, mounted "a deliberate campaign ... to deny the Irish people the food they needed to survive." The famine served to unite many Irish in their resentment toward the British government because it did little to help its people survive the famine. Those who emigrated to America carried that resentment with them as they boarded ship.

The passenger ship *Susan*, packed with Irish immigrants headed for New York, ran aground off the village of Southampton on Tuesday, March 17, 1846—ironically St. Patrick's Day. The passengers reached shore without loss of life or injury and continued their journey to New York by stagecoach.

The same year, or the following year, the passenger ship *Ashland*, headed from Ireland to Boston, ran aground at Flying Point, Water Mill. There was no loss of life and the wooden-hulled, square-rigged ship was refloated.

CATHERINE

The British brig *Catherine*, en route from Dublin, Ireland to New York, ran aground at 1:00 a.m. August 25, 1851, off Amagansett. The 300 passengers, mostly Irish immigrants, were safely landed together with most of their luggage. The wooden-hulled ship filled with water and her cargo of 200 tons of iron bars, 200 tons of salt, 10 tons of sheet iron, and 10 tons of soap was a total loss. Some of the poorest passengers lost everything but what they were wearing at the time of the grounding because their baggage was stowed below.

Four days after the stranding, the steamer *Achilles* arrived from New York and carried most of the passengers to that city. The steamer also towed the barge *Martha Stuart* laden with *Catherine*'s sails, rigging, chains, and anchors.

In 1896, the *Brooklyn Eagle* printed a story on Amagansett, which included the following: "A little farther down the beach lies the wrecked *Catherine*, the waters rushing forever back and forth between her ribs with splash and gurgle. An old man leading a gray horse which drags behind a wrecked ship's topmasts halts abreast of it to talk of her. 'Aye, the old *Catherine*. I remember the night ... Everyone got safe ashore with only a little wetting, for at low tide her bows were high and dry. I laugh when I think of it. I can see it as though it were yesterday, the people jumping off and dashing right through ... sea ... to shore, when by walking around a short distance they might have got off dry shod.... she was loaded with iron bar and so far up we couldn't get her off.... When Cap'n Jed [Jeremiah Conkling] was wreck master he offered $10 reward to anyone who would just bring him news of a ship ashore. I was paintin' house in East Hampton one morning away up in the gable when I saw above the land fog that hugged the ground, a vessel's topmasts. Blamed! I says, but that's a ship ashore, and I got down and streaked it for Cap'n

Jed's. He was off to the Harbor and I got his boy Ted, on a spare hoss and sent him a-kitin for Cap'n Jed. Meantime Cap'n Hedges from the lookout on his housetop, a-sweepin the ocean with his glass for whales, sighted the wreck, and he started a man post haste for Cap'n Jed; so there was two on the road at onst. My man reached him first, but the money was divided betwixt Cap'n Hedges and me. By and by Cap'n Jed arrived post haste at the wreck. Everybody in the village was there before him and it was a pretty sizable crowd on the beach."

The salvors and ship's crew set anchors offshore and hove the cables taut. Two steam pumps went to work clearing water from the ship's hold. The salvors were confident that they could refloat the ship. However, a storm struck, further damaging her wooden hull, and the ship was declared a total loss.

The brig's master Captain Heselton and his sick wife remained in the area to protect the owner's interests during the salvage operation. They boarded at Henry Conklin's home, where the captain's wife died only a few days after the stranding.

Captain Heselton wrote the following letter to the editor of the Sag Harbor *Corrector*: "Mr. Editor-Sir: Capt. Heselton, late of the British ship *Catherine*, wrecked on Amagansett beach, returns, through the medium of your press, his most sincere thanks to Mrs. Conklin and family, also to Dr. Van Scoy for their unremitting attention and sympathy to his much lamented wife, during her long and fatal illness. He also returns many thanks to the inhabitants of Amagansett for their kindness and sympathy ..."

Patrick Lynch and another passenger from *Catherine* remained in East Hampton Town for the rest of their lives. Lynch, originally bound for the California gold fields, settled for Long Island potatoes instead of gold nuggets, and his descendents still live in East Hampton Town.

PRESENT CONDITION

The lower portion of the hull is covered by sand in the surf at Amagansett. Once or twice a year, usually after a severe storm, shifting sand exposes her shipworm-eaten ribs.

The Bell Tolls

U.S.S. *EAGLE 17*—NEW TECHNIQUE

Type of vessel: antisubmarine patrol
Where built: Ford Plant, outskirts of Detroit
Launched: 1919
Length/beam: 200'9" / 33'1"
Gross tons: 615
Sunk: May 22, 1922
Cause of sinking: ran aground
Location: Egypt Beach, between East Hampton & Amagansett
Approximate depth of water: wreckage has not been located

DURING WORLD WAR I, the United States Navy urgently needed warships, not giant battleships or cruisers, not even destroyers, but small, steel craft for antisubmarine patrol. However, established shipyards were totally engaged in the construction of destroyers, larger warships, and merchant shipping. President Woodrow Wilson addressed the problem on November 7, 1917, with the appointment of Henry Ford to the U.S. Shipping Board. He had confidence that the auto builder's knowledge of mass production would produce large quantities of the boats quickly.

PRODUCTION

The Bureau of Construction and Repair produced a simplified design to permit speedy construction of the miniature warships. Ford approved the plan, with one exception. He recommended that all hull plates be flat to facilitate quick production in quantity. The design was modified, and construction began on the vessels that the Navy called "Eagle" boats. The term stemmed from a wartime *Washington Post* editorial which called for "... an eagle to scour the seas and pounce upon and destroy every German submarine." Some civilians referred to the patrol vessels as "tin Lizzies of the sea," a reference to Ford's automobiles.

Ford built a new plant on property he owned on Rouge River, outside Detroit. Its assembly line followed the continuous flow pattern he used for automobile production. The machinery and fittings were largely produced at Ford's Highland Park plant in

Detroit. The plant went into operation in five months, and on May 7, 1918, the first keel was laid. Only eight weeks later, on July 11 it was launched and others followed close behind. "An Eagle a Day Keeps the Kaiser Away," proclaimed banners waved by celebrating Ford workers. "Warships While You Wait," exclaimed *The New York Times.*

Ford was disappointed that the boats could not move along a continuously-moving assembly line like the automobiles at his Highland Park plant. They were too large, and a "step-by-step" movement was instituted on the 1,700-foot line.

PEACE

Seven patrol craft were completed by December 1, but that was 1918, and the world was at peace. The November 11 armistice that ended hostilities reduced the Navy's original contract from 100 (increased to 112) to 60 Eagle boats. The last 53 were commissioned in 1919.

The Eagle boats never saw service in the First World War, but seven did serve during World War II. *Eagle 56* was a victim of that war, sunk off the southern New England coast by the German submarine *U-853* in April 1945.

The 18-knot, 615-ton vessels were armed with a four-inch gun, a three-inch gun, two machine guns, and 12 depth charges. A crew of 61 was the normal complement. Reports on performance at sea was mixed. Ford's insistence on flanged plates instead of rolled plates did speed production, but at the expense of speed and shiphandling.

The entire Eagle boat operation was briefly challenged by Senator Henry Cabot Lodge of Massachusetts in December 1918. At the ensuing Congressional hearings, Navy officials successfully defended the program as a necessary experiment and attested that the boats were well made. Ford profits were proved to be modest. The naval contract, however, gave Ford the rare opportunity to improve his Rouge River property at government expense. American taxpayers provided $3.5 million to build the plant, deepen the river, and drain marshes. Ford's new plant was immense, more than half a mile long, with steel-framed 100-foot-tall walls and immense expanses of glass. Building B, as it became known, made architectural history and eventually produced Mustang automobiles for Ford Motor Company.

STRANDED

Early Friday morning, May 22, 1922, *Eagle 17* (PE-17) stranded on Long Island at Egypt Beach (Two Mile Hollow), near the polo grounds between East Hampton and Amagansett. She was en route from Norfolk, Virginia to New London, Connecticut when she ran aground. There were no casualties; the entire crew was removed by breeches buoy without incident. The uncomplicated rescue was highlighted the following day when the captain's personal automobile slid down two skids from deck to shore.

Two days later a storm pushed the vessel onto shore until she was high and dry. An estimated 3,500 Long Islanders viewed the stranded patrol craft on one day. Fresh water was pumped into *Eagle 17*'s boilers on June 2, so her engine could be run. That was to assist two tugs from the W.G. Scott Wrecking Company of New London, Connecticut, in an unsuccessful attempt to pull her off at high tide.

All movable materials were removed to lighten the vessel. On January 5, 1923, salvage tugs pulled the warship several feet offshore until a northeaster interrupted the salvage effort. Another storm struck on January 26, turning the boat onto her starboard side, with her masts pointing to sea and her bottom protruding about eight or ten feet above the breakers. *The East Hampton Star* reported that "... the two guns were still aboard and are now under water.... no doubt the *Eagle boat No. 17* will remain where she now lies for years to come."

The patrol craft was declared a total loss and stricken from the Navy list. Later, *Eagle 17* was heavily salvaged and much material was removed, including large steel plates. By January 1923, the wreck was several hundred yards west of its original site, moved there by storms. The boilers of the Eagle boat were visible at low tide for decades.

The Bell Tolls

MARS—CHURLISH CAPTAIN

Type of vessel: brig
Where built: unknown
Launched: unknown
Length/beam: unknown
Gross tons: unknown
Sunk: 1828
Cause of sinking: ran aground
Location: just west of Lily Pond Lane,
Georgica Beach, East Hampton
Approximate depth of water: when exposed, a couple of feet

INSHORE WATERS RESPOND to currents and changing tides with a restless action that transports sand from one place to another. The process results in a continuing cycle of beach erosion and buildup that devastates the residents of as many seashore communities as it elates others. Many inshore shipwrecks, once visible underwater, are now completely covered. Others, earlier buried under sand, are exposed. Severe storms accelerate the transformation, then tides, currents, and gentler seas gradually restore the undersea landscape. When a shipwreck is exposed by such action, it is only temporary. In an area like Long Island's south shore, it is quickly covered again. The British brig *Mars* is a prime example. In 1828 she ran aground just west of Lily Pond Lane, Georgica Beach, East Hampton. Normally, no one would suspect that she was there, but about every 20 years her ribs are exposed.

The wooden ribs of *Catherine*, another sand covered wreck, are visible in the surf off Amagansett once or twice a year, usually after a severe storm. She went aground in 1851 with 300 Irish immigrants aboard; all landed safely with most of their luggage. The brig and her cargo of molasses, iron bar, salt, and soap were a total loss.

STRANDING

Mars' grounding occurred on a voyage from the West Indies in

1828, with a cargo of molasses for New England delivery. She was under the command of very-British Captain Ring, whose poise was severely shattered by the accident. Ships usually run aground because of gale, heavy seas, strong currents and tides, mechanical failure, or navigation error. Running aground at Georgica Beach, East Hampton in foul weather would be no surprise—but the weather was clear when the brig struck.

Curiosity and the prospect of salvage washed ashore drew throngs of residents to view the disabled vessel and her fuming captain. One of the onlookers was Jonathan Osborn, a retired whale ship captain from Wainscott, Long Island. He cocked his head and squinted, with his battered fisherman's cap pushed back off his forehead. First he examined the sky, then the stranded ship, and finally her captain, standing helpless on the beach. What, he wondered, could account for losing so sturdy a brig under such ideal conditions. He scratched his whiskered chin and shook his head, "How did it happen?" he asked.

The haughty Englishman turned away, ignoring the questioner. His stomach churned from his shattered ego and humiliation, and now, questioning from a scruffy old man. Captain Osborn persisted, "Did the crew take frequent soundings?"

Sounding was accomplished with a piece of lead shaped like a window sash-weight attached to a line held by a crew member called a leadsman. The line, marked at six-foot intervals with strips of leather and colored cloth, indicated fathoms of depth. The hand-lead for a line of about 20 fathoms (120 feet) weighed from six to nine pounds. Its hollow base, filled with tallow, picked up sand, shell, gravel, and pebbles to indicate the type of bottom under the ship's hull. That alerted a navigator to what dangers might lie ahead. The leadsman, threw the lead far enough forward of a ship under way so

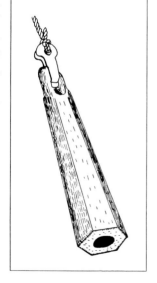

that the line would be vertical when the lead reached bottom. Its reading of a shallow depth or sediment that indicated danger ahead dictated changes of a ship's course to a prudent captain.

Captain Ring fumed at the insolence of the unkempt oaf who had nothing better to do than intrude on a certified British captain's affairs. Instead of ignoring him a second time, the haughty Britisher elevated his chin to stare down the length of his nose and responded, "Old fellow, what do you know about a ship? If I should tell you, do you think you would know any more than you do now?"

The story makes no mention of Captain Osborn's response, but no ex-captain of a whaler would tolerate that kind of arrogance from anyone, particularly someone who was incapable of safe sailing on a clear day. Captain Ring later learned that the "unkempt loafer" had years of experience commanding larger ships than his around the world in search of whales—with never a wreck or stranding. There is no record of an apology.

SALVAGE

Mars was reported to be a fairly new ship with copper fastenings, but the brig could not be refloated. Two young men, Stephen Sherrill and John Osborn (probably related to the old whaling captain), paid $100 for the wreck. They removed the furniture and trim from her cabin, the spars, sails, and much of her copper. Before the remaining copper fastenings were removed from the hull, a severe storm broke up the wreck and covered it with sand.

The wreck's hull ribs are an excellent example of how shifting sands cover and uncover some shallow wrecks. There is no record that *Mars* was ever seen for more than 100 years after she sank, but in 1931 a violent storm exposed the ribs of her hull. The storm surge was so heavy that it eroded the shore close to the wreck, almost toppling the homes of sportswriter Grantland Rice and journalist-author Ring Lardner. That warning prompted both to move their houses back from the water.

The remains of the wrecked brig *Mars* has reappeared several times since 1931. The ship's ribs were last visible in March of 1976.

CIRCASSIAN—TRIBAL LINK

Type of vessel: passenger-freighter
Where built: Robert Hickson & Co., Belfast, Ireland
Launched: 1856
Length/beam: 254'/39'
Gross tons: 1,742
Sunk: December 11, 1876
Cause of sinking: storm/ran aground
Location: off Bridgehampton
Approximate depth of water: wreckage has not been located

THE CIRCASSIANS MAY sound like American Indians, but they are a people who inhabit the mountains of the northwestern Caucasus region near the Black Sea. That area, once part of the Soviet Union is now the separate republic of Georgia. A Shinnecock is an American Indian from eastern Suffolk County. Circassian and Shinnecock share no common culture, but they are linked by a 19th century tragedy that cost the Shinnecock community dearly.

Circassian is an unlikely name for a passenger and cargo ship that was built in 1856 at Belfast, Ireland to sail the Irish Sea. She was an experimental, twin-screw steamer, equipped with double beam engines and auxiliary sail, built for S.S. De Wolf Company. The ship's Indian-sounding name forged a link between those for whom she was named and the far-distant American Indians who were lost when she sank.

CIVIL WAR

The iron-hulled, 1,742-ton ship was modified to sail under British registry as a blockade-runner in the American Civil War. She had three iron masts, was 254 feet long, and had a beam of 39 feet. She transported supplies to the Confederacy in exchange for cotton cargo until her capture in the Gulf of Mexico by the Union Navy's *Somerset*, a converted Robert Fulton ferryboat. She was renamed U.S.S. *Circassian*, and was refitted as a Union troop and supply ship, complete with heavy cannon for use along the

Atlantic and Gulf coasts. When the war ended she was sold as surplus.

In 1864, while operating on the New York to Quebec run, she went aground on Sable Island, Nova Scotia, and was taken off by the Colombian Wrecking Company, under the charge of Captain John Lewis, whose destiny was to be closely linked to the former British ship. A New York firm then purchased the recovered vessel and placed her on the New Orleans route.

In December 1869, en route from New Orleans to New York, she ran ashore for the second time, at Manasquan, New Jersey. Captain Edward Perry freed her, and he too would meet up again with *Circassian*. The vessel was freed in only five days, but she was then kept in dry-dock for three years pending bitter international litigation over her ownership. Eventually she was returned to her original owners, S.S. De Wolf Company of Liverpool, England.

ALL-SAIL

The company decided to convert *Circassian* for exclusive use as a cargo vessel. That added value to space in her hold, space occupied by poorly maintained, outdated engines, boilers, and fuel bunkers. All were removed, the smokestack disappeared, and sails and a new deck were added to make her an all-sail merchant vessel. It was a step back in technology, but was justified by economic considerations. When the new *Circassian* set sail for New York on November 6, 1876, her specifications were: 1,741 tons, 254 feet long, 39 feet beam, 19-3/4 feet draft, and 3 masts, all iron, carrying full sail. She was the largest ship built in Ireland up to that time.

A 35-year-old Welshman, Captain Richard Williams, was in command of the converted vessel and her 34-man crew on her first voyage. Her 1,400-ton industrial cargo, consigned to Snow & Burgess, 66 South Street, New York, was insured for $90,000 by New York insurance companies. The bill of lading included:

> 44 tons of dyewood
> 41,000 bath bricks in 600 boxes
> 332 tierces of soda ash (1 tierce = 42 gallons)

105 hogsheads of soda ash (1 hogshead = 63 gallons)
15 cases of matches, made to order
471 bales of old rags

Circassian was very sound and in excellent condition when she left England. The Liverpool Maritime Exchange rated her A-1, a first-class ship, and the Liverpool companies insured the vessel itself for $100,000 on her first transatlantic crossing since renovations.

The early part of the trip went well; the November weather was favorable and progress was good. The only problem was discovery of a stowaway, John McDermott, who must have been born under an unlucky star in his choice of a vehicle for free transportation. He was put to work to earn passage, bringing the crew total, including the captain, to 36.

Circassian was spotted on November 11, 1876, by an eastbound passing ship, about 900 miles due south of Mt. Kekla on the south central coast of Iceland. It was customary for passing ships to exchange information concerning weather and sea conditions. If such information was relayed, Captain Williams should have been prepared for the heavy storms that lay ahead.

The weather became more and more unpredictable; storms struck with increasing intensity; the crew fought against heavy winds and a stormy sea as gale upon gale assaulted the ship. There was no way to determine location. Celestial navigation was impossible, and the compass was out of order because of the severity of the storms. The vessel lost her top gallant masts and was off course—but she was still afloat.

Heath Park, an English bark bound from Perth Amboy, New Jersey to London with a cargo of slate was less fortunate. On November 30, her distress flag was sighted about 500 miles off Montauk Point. Two lifeboats of 11 survivors, including her entire crew and commanding officer, Captain Smith, were hauled aboard *Circassian*, even while she battled another storm, her deck and rigging frozen in ice.

Ten days after the rescue, weather conditions improved and the ship resumed making good progress. She was running in a good wind, with most sails set, when a small 70-ton schooner appeared on the horizon. It was a New York-Sandy Hook pilot vessel, one that regularly sailed several hundred miles out into the Atlantic searching for ships to assist. When they found one headed for harbor, they would transfer one of their skilled pilots aboard to guide her into port.

Captain Williams took Captain James Sullivan on board to pilot the ship along the dangerous shores of Long Island into the safety of New York Harbor. A ship's captain was allowed to sail her into port alone, but that was deemed foolhardy. Navigation had already been specialized into two categories, navigation on the high seas and coastal navigation. Captain Sullivan's job was to be aware of any dangers and to take all precautions; the coast of Long Island had already proven disastrous to countless ships because of shifting sandbars, dangerous currents and Montauk Point's rocky shoreline.

Until *Circassian's* location could be confirmed by sightings, she was still considered to be on the high seas, with Captain Williams in command. Captain Sullivan was under no obligation to take charge until a lighthouse or other clear landmark of the Long Island shore was identified. On Monday, December 11, all sails were set, trying to make up for lost time; the voyage had already taken over five weeks. However, as darkness fell the weather changed, and the ship was buffeted by heavy gale winds, freezing temperatures, snow and sleet. By 8:00 p.m. the deck and rigging were again coated with ice and snow. Visibility was nil.

GROUNDED AGAIN

By 10:30 p.m., both Captain Williams, still in charge, and Captain Sullivan were concerned that the gale winds would blow the ship onto shore. Captain Williams ordered sails altered and the ship slowly turned windward, with crewmen prepared to throw a lead line for depth soundings. The order came too late. The ship struck hard on a sandbar off Bridgehampton and stayed there. Jib and head sails were hauled down, and all yards were braced to starboard in a fruitless attempt to throw the ship off the bar and head her back to sea.

Distress flares shot into the night sky, answered in moments by a red Coston flare from shore, an indication to those on the ship that their signal had been seen by the local lifesavers. A blue flare followed, signifying that help was at hand. The crew jettisoned some of the freight on board, hoping to free the stranded vessel instead of abandoning her, but the severe weather soon discouraged their efforts.

It took more than an hour to rig tackle and remove only one cask of soda ash and a bale of rags from the hold. Those aboard resigned themselves to wait out the night as the storm raged over and around them. They were stranded only about 400 yards from shore, a little west of the Mecox Life-Saving Station.

Surfman Samuel H. Howell of the United States Life-Saving Service was on patrol along the Bridgehampton beach when he sighted *Circassian*, moments before she struck the bar. It was he who had responded to the ship's distress signal. He headed back to the Mecox barracks to inform the station keeper, Captain Baldwin Cook, of the ship's plight. Additional help was summoned from neighboring stations, Georgica to the east and Southampton to the west, while rescue gear was being readied. The seas were too rough to launch a lifeboat for rescue that night. No attempt would be made until first light of the next day, December 12, 1876.

By dawn the weather had improved, with the storm tide dropping. Attempts were made to launch the lifesaving station's lifeboat into the heavy surf, but each time the breakers threw them back.

RESCUE

By 10:30 a.m. the surf calmed, and another try at launching the lifeboat succeeded. One hour later, the first group of six seamen touched shore. One *Circassian* crewman immediately headed for the nearest telegraph station to inform the ship's agents in New York City of the situation.

All hands were rescued after seven round trips between beach and ship. The 48 saved included 36 from *Circassian*, 11 from *Heath Park* and the harbor pilot, Captain Sullivan. The seas were so rough that the lifesaving crew broke five oars in the heavy surf, not a bad price to pay for no lives lost. Many of the severely frostbitten survivors were taken to the Mecox station for first aid and questioning.

Captain Williams' official statement, recorded in the Mecox

journal, was that the ship ran aground in the heavy blow because of an error of the ship's compass. He attributed it to the intense storms the ship encountered on her crossing. Speculation focused on whether the grounding might instead reflect negligence or error on the part of her captain or the pilot.

SALVAGE

The day after the sinking, New York insurance companies, anxious to limit their losses, engaged the Coast Wrecking Company of New York to save the cargo and get *Circassian* off the bar. One day later, a schooner with a salvage crew and the company's largest tug began work. Two of the salvage crew knew the ship well, each having freed her from earlier groundings. Captain Edward Perry, in overall charge of the salvage, took the ship off at Manasquan, New Jersey seven years earlier. Captain John Lewis, in charge of the vessel itself and all work on board, took her off when she grounded at Sable Island, Nova Scotia five years before that.

On December 13, the ship seemed to be in good condition and stable, broadside to the beach with her bow headed eastnortheast. Company engineers concluded that she was just on the inside edge of a bar, in about 20 feet of water, down in the sand. Although filled with water by the storm, she was structurally sound and had no leaks.

Circassian's cargo had to be removed from the hold to lighten her, if she was to be freed. That required additional manpower. Captain Lewis hired one of the lifesavers, Captain Luther D. Burnett, as his ferryman, to transport men and supplies from shore to the ship and back. Captain Perry stayed with the crew of the salvage tug *Cyclops*, to pull *Circassian* off the bar and into deeper water when the time was right. That would be on a high tide such as the spring tide which was due on December 29, with the full moon. Captain Lewis and four engineers stayed aboard *Circassian* full-time, but more hands were needed to remove the cargo.

Captain Lewis learned that the best men for the task were Indians from the nearby Shinnecock Reservation. Men were needed who were physically strong, had some knowledge of wrecking, and were capable seamen. The Shinnecocks were more than capable; they were excellent seamen and whalers. They were tall, strong, and vigorous, and had volunteered many times over the years in maritime emergencies along the Long Island shore.

At about the same time the call went out for help aboard *Circassian*, a whaler shipping out of New Bedford needed men. Some of the Shinnecocks chose to sign on the whaler. The remaining 11 agreed to work aboard the stranded ship 24 hours a day until it reached New York. That left only women, children and the aged on the reservation.

Salvage work started on Friday, December 15, after steam pumps emptied half the hold, leaving only four feet of water. The ship did not take on any new water, and hopes were high that she would be saved. Two large anchors were placed off the ship's bow to start turning her seaward.

On December 16, she rode through another storm without incident, but it delayed the lightening operations. However, aided by the storm swells, efforts to turn the ship seaward by taking in the anchor lines were more successful. Her bow shifted onto the bar, facing the open sea. The two large bow anchors and several smaller stern anchors kept her safely pointed southeast at an angle to the bar and shore. Her position was secure.

By December 28, almost 400 tons of cargo were removed from the vessel. Pumped dry, she rested facing seaward, with her bow on the bar and her stern floating inside the bar. Most of the salvaged cargo had been removed from midships. That required redistribution of the remainder for better balance. Before that could be accomplished, Captain Lewis decided that he could get *Circassian* hauled over the bar on the next day's 6:00 p.m. high tide.

Ignoring warnings, Lewis ordered the breeches buoy lines removed from the masthead thinking they would interfere with moving the ship across the bar. Captain Huntting, Superintendent of the Life-Saving District, alerted him that the weather was again turning foul, the barometer was gradually falling and the air felt more and more like snow. By 9:00 a.m., the wind picked up and large swells forced the salvage schooners to pull away from their positions alongside the ship.

Captain Luther Burnett rowed out to *Circassian* at about 10:00

a.m. to persuade Captain Lewis to evacuate his ship, and leave a line on shore. Lewis remained confident that he would float the vessel clear. He refused to leave her, and insisted that the crew remain aboard to handle the sails when she rode clear of the beach. Captain Burnett brought ashore with him Charles Pierson, the company's local agent; Mr. Estabrook, the Customs Officer; and any of the cargo crew who wanted to leave. Only one Indian, Alfonzo Eleazer, agreed to return. The others were threatened by Captain Lewis that they would not be paid for the job if they left, and would never get another day's work with a wrecking crew.

Captain Burnett returned once more in a final effort to get the regular crew to shore. He warned, "This is your last chance, for no vessel can withstand the coming storm, and my boat will be the last to come out here." Captain Lewis rejected his warning, had the last lines to shore cut, and was quoted as saying, "We'll float tonight, or we'll go to Hell!" Thirteen years earlier, he and *Circassian* survived her Sable Island grounding and he intended to repeat that experience.

Those ashore were convinced that nothing could save the vessel. Men on horseback traveled east and west along the beach to summon lifesaving crews for the impending rescue. The storm soon turned into an icy hurricane, driving tremendous seas over *Circassian*. She was in desperate trouble, and all aboard knew it. Rescue was out of the question in the turbulent sea. Lifeboats could not be launched, and efforts to reach the ship with a breeches buoy fell short against the violence of the storm.

By 8:00 p.m., a leak developed and the ship rapidly flooded, dousing the galley fires and driving everyone above deck. The men sought shelter from the tumult in the rigging to avoid being washed overboard. More than 100 people kept vigil from shore, lifesavers, salvagers, and concerned local residents. The full moon that Captain Lewis had been waiting for lit the sky, and those on shore listened while the men who had lashed themselves to the rigging sang hymns that could be heard above the raging wind. The men in the frozen rigging were visible through glasses from on shore, but nothing could be done to save them—only 400 yards away.

THE SINKIING

Early in the morning of December 30, 1876, after a night of relentless pounding, *Circassian*'s hull broke in two and the stern portion, carrying her mizzen mast, slid into deep water and disappeared from sight. With it went all but four of the 28 aboard. Credit for the rescue of those four goes to Superintendent Huntting, who felt duty-bound to make an almost futile effort to find survivors. He organized a lantern patrol to search the beach at forty-foot intervals.

The leading patrol spotted a small cluster of figures on the ocean, drifting rapidly eastward. Luther Burnett and Gordon Ludlow pulled four survivors out of the freezing surf onto the beach: First Mate Henry Morle of Taunton, England, Second Mate John Rowland of Cardiff, Wales, Wrecking Company Engineer Charles Campbell of Newark, New Jersey, and Ship's Carpenter Alexander Wilson of Birkenhead, England.

In their story of survival, the men said there were only a few life preservers and a couple of cork fenders from the ship's remaining boats to help them. Morle gave a life preserver to John Walker, a Shinnecock, and cut loose one of the canvas covered cork fenders for himself. Morle had been shipwrecked before and knew he could remain alive only if he remained calm and developed a survival plan. He took the fender below and rigged it with wooden cleats and ropes.

Morle jumped overboard and shared his buoy with Rowland, Campbell, and Wilson with two men on each side of the float. They put their arms through the ropes and around the cylinder, clutching the lines and locking legs with each other under water. Morle instructed the others to breathe before each icy wave struck, and ordered them to rest whenever possible. Within minutes, they almost drowned, numbed by cold and weakened by their struggle. In a desperate effort, they plunged through the breakers and headed for shore. Everyone else aboard perished. The names of victims from the original crew, Coast Wrecking Company employees, Shinnecock Indians, and a local resident, 28 in total, are listed at the end of this chapter.

In 1934, Charles Bennett, one of the lifesavers, when asked

about Captain Lewis' last words to the lifesavers, expressed his fury with, "That man went to Hell and I'm glad of it."

AFTERMATH

At least 40 children were left fatherless and 16 women were widowed by the needless disaster. The entire Indian reservation went into mourning. Every home on the Shinnecock reservation felt the effects; many of the lost men were related. Three, the Bunns, were cousins; three Cuffees were of the same family. One woman lost her husband and her brother. In another household, a husband and a brother-in-law were lost, leaving a widow, a widowed daughter and several fatherless children. No shipwreck in Long Island history was responsible for so much devastation to so many closely related families.

The disaster is immortalized in the following selected stanzas of a poem by Harriett Brown, a Shinnecock:

> *Slowly the ship seemed to settle,*
> *Higher the waves lashed and beat,*
> *Eyes closed that no longer wanted to watch*
> *Men going to their Maker to meet.*
>
> *It was the message of Henry Herrick,*
> *Who brought the news to town,*
> *That a storm of great violence had come up,*
> *And our twenty-eight* [sic] *braves had drowned.*

In 1998, Reverend Michael Smith, pastor of the reservation's Shinnecock Church, stated:

"It was never determined what caused *Circassian* to sink, but three factors contributed:

1. All the freight removed from her hold was from midship, leaving the rest of the cargo in the bow and stern. With so much weight concentrated at either end, and her midships hull resting on the sandbar, the ship sagged and snapped in two.

2. Captain Lewis was over-confident because he had been able to free the vessel once before.

3. Captain Lewis under-estimated the violence of the storm and its effect on the stranded ship."

The *Annual Report of the Operations of the United States Life Saving-Service for 1877* states: "The undue reliance of the persons in charge of the ship upon her power to withstand the force of the seas which broke her spine, and which led them, in the face of warnings of a storm of more than ordinary violence, to refuse to maintain connection with the shore, was undoubtedly the cause of the loss of life which followed. A line drawn between the vessel and the beach would have enabled the Life-Saving crews to have effected a rescue at any time prior to the breaking of the hull, which forced the hapless wreckers and mariners to mount to the rigging. It is evident that from that moment no earthly power could save them."

At the time of the disaster, ship owners had no liability for loss of life on a vessel, and wreckers worked entirely at their own risk. There were no settlements, no lawsuits, nothing in the way of monetary compensation. The fates of women and children deprived of husbands and fathers was left to the generosity of friends and neighbors. The *Circassian* tragedy made life difficult for bereaved families in England, Finland, Italy, and the United States, but none felt their loss more than those left behind on Long Island's Shinnecock Indian Reservation. They were the living victims of the sinking of the ship with its Indian-sounding name.

CASUALTIES OF THE *CIRCASSIAN* SINKING
Original Crew:

Richard Williams, Captain	*Welshman from Liverpool, 35 years old, married, two children*
Evan Johnson, Third Mate	*Liverpool, 20 years old, unmarried; just completed apprenticeship*
Thomas Orr, Carpenters Mate	*Liverpool, 25 years old, married, no children*
William Keefe, Boatswain	*Finland, unmarried*
Henry Freeman, Sailmaker	*Philadelphia, 30 years old, married, two children*
John Grant, Cook	*About 45 years old*
Frank Wright, Apprentice	*Liverpool, 18 years old*
Andrew Nodder, Apprentice	*Wavertree, England, 17 years old*

Walter Colburn, Apprentice   *Liverpool, 18 years old*
James Scott, Seaman   *England, 23 years old,*
    Royal Navy Reserve
Andrew Ladago, Seaman   *Italy, 30 years old*
Horatio Johnson, Steward   *Liverpool, 45 years old, married,*
    several children
John Mc Dermott (stowaway)   *Liverpool, 19 years old*

Local Men:
Lewis Walker, Shinnecock   *26 years old, married, three children*
John Walker, Shinnecock   *51 years old, former whaler, married,*
    nine children
David W. Bunn, Shinnecock   *47 years old, former whaler,*
    married, five children
J. Franklin Bunn, Shinnecock   *39 years old, former whaler,*
    married, no children
Russell Bunn, Shinnecock   *49 years old, former whaler,*
    married, four children
William Cuffee, Shinnecock   *23 years old, unmarried*
Warren N. Cuffee, Shinnecock   *33 years old, Civil War Veteran,*
    married, three children
George W. Cuffee, Shinnecock   *25 years old, married, one child*
James R. Lee, Shinnecock   *33 years old, former whaler,*
    married, no children
Oliver J. Kellis, Shinnecock   *39 years old, former whaler,*
    married, no children
James Thurston, Southampton   *24 years old, unmarried*

Coast Wrecking Company Employees:
John Lewis,   *45 years old, married, no*
Wreckers Foreman   *living children*
Luke Stillman, Engineer   *Brooklyn, 30's age, eight children*
Philip Dearns, Engineer   *Staten Island, 30's age*
Patrick Donohue, Engineer   *30's age, married, several children*

CLAN GALBRAITH—QUITE A SIGHT

Type of vessel: four-masted bark
Where built: Russell and Company, Glasgow, Scotland
Launched: 1894
Length/beam: 282'9" / 40'4"
Gross tons: 2,168
Stranded: July 22, 1916
Cause of incident: fog
Location: Flying Point, south of Water Mill
Approximate depth of water: refloated

IT WAS EARLY Saturday morning July 22, 1916, and Captain A.E. Olsen turned the air blue with seafaring profanity. His graceful Norwegian bark *Clan Galbraith* had just rammed into an offshore sandbar, leaving her stranded near Flying Point (south of Water Mill). The tall masts of the beautiful ship drew huge crowds of sightseers. The masts stood like probing fingers above the flat southern Long Island landscape. By late afternoon, everyone for miles around had come to view the unusual sight. Republican presidential nominee Charles E. Hughes, with his wife and daughters, was prominent in the throngs of spectators. Drivers parked their cars on every dry spot within half a mile, after struggling through mud holes and a road saturated by the heavy surf.

The four-masted, square-rigged bark ran into dense fog off the south shore of Long Island while she was enroute from Bristol, England to New York. She was almost at the end of her transatlantic voyage when she ran into the fog that blinded Captain Olsen and his helmsman. By dead reckoning, Olsen calculated that he was 40 miles off the shore of Long Island. He was totally unaware of danger until the moment of grounding. Although the bark was sailing under little canvas, she struck hard. Captain Olsen and his crew refused requests for details of the disaster. Twenty-eight years later, the *Bridgehampton News* reported that the ship "was probably the largest sailing vessel ever grounded along this coast."

Surfmen of the Mecox Life-Saving Station were first to see the ship's distress signals. They alerted the Southampton station crew, but the fog was still so thick that the men from the two stations passed each other on the beach several times before they located the stranded ship.

The fog lifted by noon, revealing the bark grounded on the sandbar. When she struck, the tide was low, leading to the hope that the rising tide would float her off the bar. Instead, it edged the ship higher on shore; by night she was within 50 feet of the beach, firmly embedded in the sand, with not more than three feet of water around her.

PRECAUTION

During the afternoon the lifesavers carried lines to the ship and rigged a breeches buoy as a precaution against a storm overnight. The vessel seemed to be in no danger, so Captain Olsen and his crew of 30 remained on board.

The New York Times reported: "Mrs. Hughes and her daughters were among the first to reach the scene of Bridgehampton's wreck. They were notified while out for an early morning automobile ride, and joined the crowd of 500 which had collected to cheer the lifesavers. Mr. Hughes was hard at work on his speech of acceptance, and was not bothered until luncheon time. Then for an hour he put work aside and went to the beach with his family.

"No resident of Bridgehampton could remember anything to match the shipwreck of today for picturesque features. Some recalled a wreck of 50 years ago, when a Spanish ship was tossed ashore and spilled a cargo of fine wines along the same beach, but none in recent years."

The 2,168-ton *Clan Galbraith* was built in Glasgow, Scotland in 1894 to carry cargo between Great Britain and India. However, by the time she grounded on Long Island she had been converted into an oil tanker and was in ballast on her way to pick up another load of oil for England.

REFLOATED

The beautiful, steel-hulled ship showed little damage as she lay on the beach for about two weeks, continuing to attract sightseers. The Long Island Rail Road even featured a special train for the occasion. The multitude of spectators watching the salvage operation attracted an influx of food vendors. Many said it reminded them of the Riverhead Fair in the old days. The carnival atmosphere ended on August 4, when Merritt-Chapman Company salvage tugs pulled *Clan Galbraith* into deep water.

The only casualty of the grounding was the election bid of spectator Charles E. Hughes. He lost the 1916 presidential election, with 48% to Wilson's 52% of the electoral vote. More time spent electioneering instead of admiring the stranded *Clan Galbraith* from the beach might have made a difference.

Clan Galbraith returned to service, still carrying Norwegian flags painted on her sides to indicate her neutral status during World War I. That precaution did little to save her from the torpedoes of a German U-boat that sank her later in the war.

H.M. sloop *SYLPH*—DISASTER OFF SOUTHAMPTON

Type of vessel: sloop-of-war
Where built: Bermuda
Launched: 1812
Length/beam: about 100' / 30'
Gross tons: about 325
Sunk: January 17, 1815
Cause of sinking: blizzard / ran aground
Location: off Southampton
Approximate depth of water: wreckage has not been located

EASTERN LONG ISLAND'S worst maritime disaster occurred near the end of the War of 1812. The United States declared war on Great Britain June 18, 1812, following more than a decade of the impressment of American merchant seamen by the Royal Navy. In March 1813, eight British warships sailed into Eastern Long Island waters to blockade Long Island Sound, one of the two entrances to New York Harbor.

On a snow-swept January night of 1815, the 22-gun British sloop *Sylph* went ashore on Shinnecock Bar, west of the village of Southampton. The location was about opposite Sugar Loaf, the highest Shinnecock hill. Most of the 121-man crew aboard the five-year-old sloop-of-war perished despite the heroic efforts of local residents who rescued one officer and five seamen. Captain George Dickens and 11 of his officers were casualties. The local residents salvaged part of the ship's stores, copper, iron, cordage, and other materials.

The district wreck master auctioned the materials recovered from the ship, and paid the salvors for their efforts. The money remaining from the auction was divided among the religious societies of Southampton Town.

During the War of 1812, British warships blockaded some of the important American ports to shut down the import of war materials. Joel and Esther Steele covered that critical phase of the war in their *A Brief History of the United States*: "The British blockade extended this year [1814] to the north. Commerce was so completely destroyed that the lamps in the light-houses were extinguished as being of use only to the English."

A peace treaty was signed at Ghent, Belgium on December 24, 1814, but before the news reached America, an unnecessary bloody battle was fought on January 8, 1815, at New Orleans. In the confrontation that would have been avoided with modern communication, the British lost more than 2,000 men. By contrast, there were only 13 American casualties, seven killed and six wounded.

The 22-gun sloop-of-war *Sylph* wrecked
off Southampton with the loss of 115 men.

One night, a week after that battle, *Sylph* cruised off Long Island's south shore into blinding snow and gale force winds. Captain Dickens knew the coast well from many months of patrolling, but with limited visibility he could not see the shore. Soundings were difficult in the mountainous swells produced by winds that gusted up to 40 knots. He ordered several crewmen to the bow when visibility dropped to 100 yards. The snow thickened until he could not see the bow of his vessel. He did know approximately where he was and he hoped to clear Montauk Point before daybreak.

Suddenly a lookout on the bow shouted "Breakers ahead!" The captain heard the crash of waves as his ship hit the sandbar and threw him and his men to the deck. The storm ran *Sylph* hard aground off Shinnecock Point. The following morning Nathan White of Wickapogue (east of the village of Southampton) sighted the stranded ship and sounded an alarm. Local residents gathered at the shore recognized the stranded ship as a blockading vessel but, their only concern was to save the men clinging to her shrouds. However, snow, gale-force winds, high surf, and freezing temperature discouraged any rescue attempt. By afternoon the sloop-of-war began to break up. Each wave breaking over the warship plucked one or two of the crew into the boiling surf. Under the impact of a tremendous breaker, the ship capsized, sparking action from the beach. Despite the pounding surf, two local men, Sylvanus Raynor and Ephrain White, and others manned a fishing boat and managed to reach *Sylph*. They recovered only six men who were found clinging to the wreck. Some had to have the frozen rigging cut away from their arms and legs. Although the British blockading warships had caused many hardships for the Americans, Southampton residents took the British seamen to a tavern at the end of Jobs Lane and plied them with brandy. A newspaper reported that one of the rescuers asked the British officer "Why were you so near the shore on such a bad night?" "Damn you! There would have been a number of you Americans laid low if we had come ashore under other circumstances," was the reply. The local residents resented the response and the British survivors were treated "coarsely until they left town."

A letter in the East Hampton Library from an American soldier, J.M. Williamson of Sag Harbor, to his father in Stony Brook tells the story of the disaster. The letter's last paragraph reads: "The loss of this vessel may be considered as a national benefit to us, but the loss of so many lives in this manner can not give a pleasing sensation to any but a savage. They were ... our enemies, but in the same time were our fellow creatures. The human treatment showed the survivors denote that they fell among

among people possessing human feelings and not among savages."

Many bodies drifted into Shinnecock Bay and 21 corpses washed ashore opposite Sugar Loaf. One of those who witnessed the rescue from the beach could not believe his eyes, "Seeing a spar with men lashed to it coming ashore through the breakers with 12 pairs of frozen legs sticking up in the air."

One story relates that the warship's angry helmsman, upset over bad treatment from the ship's officers, swore, "I'll send some of them to Hell tonight, if putting her ashore will do it."

A memorial plaque is displayed inside Southampton's St. Andrews Dune Church. The border and the wheel above the plaque are made of red cedar from the sloop-of-war.

Many items from the wreck ended up in the homes of Southampton residents, including a book with Captain Dickens' name in it and his leather trunk with a brass plate inscribed with his name on top.

Stephen Sayre, of Bridgehampton, recovered one of *Sylph*'s cannons. It was displayed on the village common for many years and then on the lawn of a private residence. The cannon was often fired in celebration of the Fourth of July and other important events such as weddings. An article in the October 14, 1910 *Bridgehampton News* reported: "The most hilarious times were when the old gun was borrowed to congratulate the newly married. The wonder is, that nobody ever got killed or hurt. Twice that I know of, the old cannon came to Wainscott, when James Topping was married and when Charles W. Strong brought his wife home. The Sagg boys brought the gun and the Wainscott boys had a lot of tar balls made up so that they had pretty noisy times.... But the biggest time of all was when Captain Charles A. Pierson was married. He had always set the boys on and furnished them with powder, so they thought he was deserving to be paid up. They got the old gun so near the house that some 40 panes of glass were broken and other damage was done."

In 1916, James Tuslow Adams wrote in *Memorials of Old Bridgehampton* that the cannon was beginning its second century as the village's plaything. The remains of the old cannon, damaged at the Pierson wedding, were in the Bridgehampton Library for many years, but the current director of the library has not seen them in the nine years of her tenure.

Many years after *Sylph* ran aground, a large steam dredge cut a new inlet from the bay to the ocean over the wreck site. Two weapons that survived the War of 1812 were recovered, a musket and a sword inscribed with the sloop-of-war's name.

The bodies of British seamen that washed ashore were buried in the hills overlooking Shinnecock sandbar where one of Long Island's worst maritime disasters occurred in a war that ended more than three weeks earlier.

The Wreck of the Sylph

'Tis nigh on seventy years ago
Since the "Sylph" came ashore
Twas the war of eighteen hundred and twelve,
And she was a British sloop of war.
Lord, I can see it all again,—
The gale, and the spray, and the wild surf's roar,
And the wave-lashed corpses of drownded men;
Though I was but a lad of ten
When the "Sylph" came ashore.
And the old sea-captain's silver hair
Fluttered and tossed in the summer air,
As he leaned at ease oer his garden gate,
And told me the tale of the "Sylph's" hard fate.
Did we know the craft? Ay, we knew her well,
From Montauk Point to Fire Island light.
Many a time from her decks had a shell
Screamed through the air in the quiet night,
Waking the silent village street
With its roar and tramp of flying feet!
Many a night had a ruddy glare
Lighted the landscape far and near,
As some old homestead and barns were burned,
And the labor of years unto ashes turned.
And so, when one cold December morn,
Ere the moon's pale light had faded out,

The Bell Tolls

A hurrying sound of feet was heard,
And on the chill night air rang forth the shout, —
"The Sylph's ashore on Southampton beach!"
We wasted no time in idle speech;
But each man sped to the beach away
To meet the foe that was now at bay.
This was the sight that met our eyes
In that cold dawning dim and gray, —
A white-capped mass of swirling foam,
Filling the air with its icy spray;
Out of its midst there rose a mast
Black with the bodies of men lashed fast;
And each wild wave, as it came ashore,
With its icy fingers some poor wretch tore
From his frail hold, and with wrathful hand
Beat out his life on the hollow sand.
What could we do in a strait like this?
What ship could live in so mad a sea?
Women wailed as they watched it all;
Strong men looked on helplessly.
Crash! all at once the mast went down,
Hurling them sheer in the surf to drown.
One mad struggle, then all was still;
Only the wind whistling shrill.
Out of a hundred and twenty men
Only six walked the earth again
We buried the dead that came ashore;
You may see their graves at the inlet still.
But the wreck turned out a prize indeed,
And we picked her bones with a right good will
From her guns and timbers of cedar-wood
We built us a meeting house strong and good,
And I've often heard the parson tell
That he heard these words in her swinging bell,
"To pruning hook ye shall beat the sword;
praise the Lord."

—Richard Markham

• 158 •

"MONEY SHIP"—MYSTERY SHIP

Type of vessel: brig
Where built: unknown
Launched: unknown
Length/beam: unknown
Gross tons: between 150 and 350
Sunk: November 1816
Cause of sink: drifted ashore
Location: about two miles west of the village of Southampton
Approximate depth of water: wreckage has not been located

RESIDENTS OF SOUTHAMPTON gathered on the beach two miles west of the village in November 1816 during a severe autumn storm. Such storms were not uncommon on the south shore of Long Island, but the observers peered intently at the horizon. It was not the storm that held their attention but the indistinct outline of a ship in trouble. They shielded their eyes from the driving rain and squinted to watch it first drift out of control as the gale slackened, then surge like a released cheetah as it intensified. Obviously, no one was at the helm of what one observer identified as a brig (a two-masted, square-rigged sailing vessel with the mast carrying a large fore and aft sail in addition to the square rig). An abandoned ship would make a great prize, but there was no one willing to risk his life in a boat through the heavy surf. Instead, watchers waited for the sea to drive the lost ship to them.

The wind and tide cooperated to keep the helpless brig from drifting away. Then, with a flourish, the wind carried her through the surf and dropped her hard aground. There were no signs of life aboard, but there were ample indications that a crew was aboard when her voyage started. The sails were half-furled, lifeboats were missing, and food, furnishings, and clothing were scattered about below decks. Everything indicated that the ship had been deserted in haste.

AUCTION

The hopes of would-be salvagers to strip the stranded ship were foiled by the district wreck master. Before that could happen, he took possession of the wreck in the name of the State of New York. The sails, rigging, and other materials were auctioned on Southampton's Main Street. During the auction, one man showed interest in a deadeye (a rounded wood block pierced with holes to receive fastening lines). He examined it and found a Spanish piece of eight (silver coin) wedged tightly in one of the openings. That launched a frantic search of the auction goods, but no more coins were found. Jokes circulated through the village about the unknown sailor who chose such a strange hiding place for his wealth.

The next day, the wreck master held his auction on the beach to sell the wooden hull. The successful bidder was a salvage company that planned to profit from the sale of its planks, timbers, and copper fastenings. During the auction, another silver coin was found in the sand near the wreck. That night, the "Money Ship" dominated conversation at the Ship and Whale Tavern in Southampton.

TREASURE

Several weeks later, two young residents, Henry Green and Franklin Jagger, were duck hunting on the beach where the mystery ship washed ashore. The wreck remained where it grounded because the new owners wanted to wait until later in the year to begin working on it. The two hunters, intrigued by the hull's unusual design, agreed that it seemed to be Spanish. They climbed aboard the listing ship, up its sloping deck and down into the cabin. The wood hull was holed in the stern from the grounding. Although the cabin was dry, shells and sand in the corners indicated that water entered the cabin at high tide. Green continued his examination, then fell on his knees to claim a shiny, silver coin that glinted merrily in the center of the cabin. It might have been a random piece that washed in with the tide, but to be sure, he and Jagger searched the cabin carefully. They found no more.

In 1816, the popular Ship and Whale Tavern was Southampton's reference library for fact and rumor. It was there that Green and Jagger learned that other coins had been found, one from the deadeye, the other from the site of the grounding. Green realized that his find was more than coincidence; it must have come from the ship.

The two youths returned to the wreck with a small candle lantern (a small metal cylinder with perforations). They waited until they were inside the cabin to light the lantern to avoid detection from shore. Although it was not high tide, an occasional wave brought water rushing into the cabin. That and the sound of waves striking the hull made Jagger uneasy. Green calmed his partner and the two carefully searched the cabin while seawater washed around their ankles. Their search was unrewarded and they were about to leave when the flickering candlelight revealed a glint of silver from a split board in the low wooden overhang.

Green carried a knife that he used to pry the board loose while Jagger held the lantern. When the board pulled free, a shower of silver coins followed. In his excitement, Jagger dropped the lantern. It went out and followed the silver coins as they rolled down the slanted floor into a pool of water at the bottom. Coins continued to spill out of the hiding place while the two men floundered through the swirling water feeling for treasure in the dark.

BEACH DOLLARS

Green and Jagger made frequent trips to the wreck—always at night. Continued search produced other caches of Spanish pieces of eight. Henry Green's share was reported to be 500 coins. Green had some of the silver coins melted down and made into tableware for his mother and himself. Green and Jagger kept their secret well, but several weeks after the discovery, a violent winter storm split the hull and spilled more silver coins into the surf. Local residents who flocked to the beach to find Spanish coins referred to their pieces of eight as "beach dollars." Farmers plowed the beach with teams of horses in search of beach dollars; one uncovered 60 of the coins. Beachcombers came across them in the sand for years afterward.

The salvage company that purchased the hull at the auction knew nothing of the clandestine treasure hunts by Green and

Jagger, but the recovery of beach dollars spurred them to action. They dismembered the hull, and in the process found 486 pieces of eight. Their auction bid turned out to be one of the firm's best investments.

WHALING

Twenty-two-year-old Henry Green went on to become a whaler. A private journal tells of his first voyage: "On the 7th day of June 1817, I sailed as a foremast hand in the ship *Fair Helen*, Oliver Fordham, Master. [The remains of *Fair Helen* are embedded in the sand off Conklin's Point, Sag Harbor.] We were 12 months and 12 days at sea." For the next three years he sailed aboard *Abigail*, progressing from boat steerer to second mate, first mate to master. *Abigail*'s ship log carries the following May 24, 1821, entry: "Captain Henry Green, Master. I got the ship away with a fine pleasant breeze from the southwestward." A few lines later he added: "This is the first voyage I ever took charge of. I am very young at the business and my ship very old. I am 26 ½ years old and the ship is 29."

For 22 years Captain Green commanded whaling ships, the first of his family to do so, but three younger brothers and a brother-in-law followed him as whaling ship captains. After *Abigail*, he commanded *Octavia, Hannibal, Phoenix, Hudson,* and *Huron.* Eight years after retirement from the sea, he started to farm 40 acres in Peconic on the North Fork of Long Island. That home, still standing on Route 25 opposite Skunk Lane, is known as "one of the North Fork's most important architectural landmarks." He died at the age of 79, leaving a wealth of seafaring memorabilia, including his 1840 portrait and several spoons made from silver coins from Southampton's mystery ship, for display in the Nautical Museum in Southold's Horton Point Lighthouse.

RUMORS

Stories circulated about what became known as the "Money Ship." Some believed she was a pirate ship that may have been blown away in a storm while her crew was ashore burying other plunder. The Sag Harbor *Suffolk County Recorder* reported on

November 2, 1816, that papers found on board indicated that the brig was "a Spanish vessel captured by a Carthaginian privateer." Two weeks later the same newspaper reported: "The brig that came ashore near Southampton on the 31 of October is the *Mary Manuel* from St. Cruz, Teneriffe to Amelia Island in ballast. The

brig was abandoned off Moriches, on account of her being waterlogged. In crossing the outer bar the boat capsized, and the master and all hands, except two, perished. John Sloan, seaman, a native of Ireland, and an English boy are the two persons saved.... A chest drifted ashore containing specie to the amount of $400, which the Irishman claimed as his property. The brig was ... sold for $18."

Years later, a man named Sloane, who lived in Moriches, said the ship was captured from the Spanish by rebelling Mexicans. Sloane claimed he had been sailing the ship to New York to be converted into a privateer for use by Mexicans against the

Spanish. Some of the silver on board was to pay for outfitting the ship and obtaining guns. During a "screaming gale," some of the crew discovered the silver and mutinied. They grabbed all the available money and abandoned ship in two boats, which were soon swamped. Sloane claimed that he and the cabin boy made it ashore in a third boat.

Sloane's story, like the other rumors has never been verified. Most are fanciful, but they do add to the mystery of the unmanned "Money Ship" that showered silver coins with a bountiful hand.

COIMBRA—U-BOAT VICTIM
Type of vessel: tanker
Where built: Howaldtswerke A.G., Kiel, Germany
Launched: 1937
Length/beam: 422' / 60'
Gross tons: 6,768
Sunk: January 15, 1942
Cause of sinking: torpedo of German submarine
Location: about 28 miles south of Shinnecock Inlet
Approximate depth of water: 180'

LIKE WORLD WAR I, World War II opened as a European conflict, with Great Britain and Germany as the major adversaries. As in the first war, American neutrality was heavily biased in favor of the British. Within days after Pearl Harbor, Germany's declaration of war made the United States an active belligerent. That provided Nazi Germany with the opportunity to stem the flow of United States war materials that had so far deprived the Nazi war machine of total victory. The German Kriegsmarine (Navy) followed the declaration of war with a concerted attack on American shipping at the source. Admiral Doenitz dispatched all the long-range U-boats (submarines) he had available to attack large merchant ships along the eastern seaboard of the United States.

Fortunately for the Allied cause, only five Type IX U-boats were initially available in early 1942 for the first of the three waves of the two-month-long attack code-named Paukenschlag (Drumbeat). Those five, and the others (including short-range Type VII boats) that followed through March 20, 1942, sank 84 merchant ships and the U.S. destroyer *Jacob Jones*, for a total of 486,761 tons.

The first Paukenschlag U-boat was *U-123* with Kapitänleutnant Reinhard Hardegen in command. En route to the U.S. coast he sighted the British passenger liner *Cyclops*, 300 miles east of Cape Cod. At 6:49 p.m. on January 11, 1942, Hardegen fired a torpedo at the British ship. It struck just aft of the forward smokestack, blowing the funnel into the sea. The liner's crew scrambled into lifeboats and abandoned ship. At 7:18 p.m., Hardegen fired a second torpedo, the coup de grace. *U-123* headed eastward for her assigned patrol area, the approaches to New York Harbor.

In the early morning of January 14, 60 miles southeast of Montauk Point, *U-123* sank the 9,577-ton Panamanian tanker *Norness* with torpedoes. The first torpedo missed, but the second struck the tanker midship sending a column of flame 500 feet into the air. After the tanker's crew abandoned ship, Hardegen fired another torpedo that struck beneath the bridge. The violent explosion caused incredible damage, but *Norness* would not sink. Reluctantly, Hardegen decided to expend another of his precious torpedoes. Another miss. Bewildered that he could miss a stationary target only 2,000 meters away. Hardegen sacrificed another torpedo. This one was a success, striking the engine room, blowing off the tanker's deck, and she began to sink by the stern. As soon as Hardegen was certain that the tanker would transport no more fuel to support the Allied war effort, he resumed course for New York Harbor.

Thirty-eight of the 40-man tanker crew survived.

The next day, at 1:40 a.m., traveling on the surface off Long Island, the U-boat's lookouts sighted a large vessel steaming at 10 or 11 knots. The ship was another tanker, fully loaded and like *Norness,* lighted as though there was no war.

The opportunity to attack shipping in American waters provided an inviting prospect for U-boat commanders. United States coastal defenses were inexperienced in antisubmarine warfare. Months would be required to organize defenses and group merchant ships into protective convoys under naval and air escort.

Events proved that the optimism of U-boat commanders was well-founded. American merchant ships sailed the eastern seaboard with normal peacetime lighting, and brightly illuminated coastal cities offered a silhouette of passing ships to prowling U-boats. Lighthouses and buoys continued to display invaluable navigational information. U-boat commanders intercepted uncoded communications between merchant ships and shore concerning speed, course, and position as well as radio details of destroyer sailings and aircraft patrols.

What a successful mission this was proving to be for *U-123*—the second tanker in only two days, and sinking the British passenger ship *Cyclops* while en route, as a bonus.

SINKING

Hardegen waited for the heavily-loaded oil tanker to come into close range (800 meters), then fired a single torpedo that struck it starboard, aft of the bridge. The violent explosion that blew sections of the ship high into the sky was followed by red and yellow flames that revealed the severely damaged vessel listing to port with her bridge ablaze, but still afloat. A second torpedo struck about 150 yards forward of the stern breaking the tanker in two. She went down by the stern and, like *Norness* the day before, her bow remained above water, at an angle of about 30 degrees.

The sinking tanker was the British 6,768-ton *Coimbra*, built in 1937 for Socony-Vacuum, Ltd.; like *Norness*, she was built by a German shipyard. Her 422-foot-long hull, with a 60-foot beam carried more than 80,000 barrels of oil for delivery to England when she went down. The triple disaster that cost the Allied cause critical war materials, a sound ship, and 36 lives might have been avoided if the tanker had observed the normal wartime precaution of traveling darkened. Only six aboard survived, although the sinking occurred close enough to the south shore of Long Island for residents of Quogue and Hampton Bays to watch the flames of the wreck from on shore.

At 9:00 a.m. on January 15, seven hours after the attack, a patrol plane radioed the position of *Coimbra* survivors to the destroyer *Rowan*. It took another six hours for *Rowan* to rescue two survivors from a small boat that originally held 12. Four others were picked up from a raft by the destroyer *Mayrant* and three men were rescued by another vessel. The harsh winter conditions had taken a heavy toll, *Coimbra* had a crew of 42, including four Navy and two Army gunners for her stern deck gun. By that time, *U-123* was well under way, looking for new victims in the approaches to New York Harbor.

Between January and June 1942, 100 ships were sunk along the eastern seaboard, many of them tankers. The oil spills from those wrecks totaled 145 million gallons, a formidable amount that created temporary problems of shore pollution. Fortunately, it seems to have had no lasting effect on sea life, birds, or beach recreation. But the rusting hulks of the tankers that make up a large portion of those wrecks is a potential threat to environmentalists; they fear the effects of a sudden rupture of their cargo tanks. *Coimbra* is one such deteriorating example. One estimate claimed the equivalent of 28,500 barrels of lubricating oil remaining on the wreck in the 1970s. Environmentalists were concerned that if a severe storm ruptured the oil tanks, Long Island's sandy beaches would be severely contaminated. In response, the U.S. Coast Guard, during 1975, dropped 20 sealed drift cards per month over the sunken tanker. The drift cards were questionnaires to be filled out and returned to the Coast Guard when found by beachcombers. The result of the test was inconclusive. Even today droplets of oil float to the surface over the sunken tanker. Environmentalists continue to be concerned, even though U.S. government inspection of the wreck has found· that the oil left on *Coimbra* poses no pollution threat.

PRESENT CONDITION

The wreck is in 180 feet of water about 28 miles south of Shinnecock Inlet. It lies on its starboard side, with the hull broken at each of the torpedo impact points. The stern is the shortest of the three sections, but the most intact. It rises about 30 feet above the bottom. There, the deck is canted about 80 degrees to starboard, with the stern deck gun still in place, and the large bronze screw-propeller exposed. The midship section has an even more severe list of 100 degrees. The crumpled and twisted bow is heeled over so far that it is almost upside down.

PANTHER & LYKENS VALLEY—TUG & TOW

Type of vessel: Panther, tug; *Valley,* schooner-barge
Where built: Panther, Chester, Pennsylvania; *Valley,* unknown
Launched: Panther, 1870; *Valley,* unknown
Length/beam: Panther, 191' / 36'; *Valley,* 186'
Gross tons: Panther, 712; *Valley,* unknown
Sunk: August 24, 1893
Cause of sinking: storm
Location: 1 ½ miles south of Southampton; close to shore
Approximate depth of Water: 55'; unknown

THE TRANSATLANTIC CROSSING of the American steamship *Savannah* in 1819 did not end the "Great Age of Sail," but it did spell the beginning of the end. Shippers learned that they could save time and money with steam-powered freighters, and fear of mechanical failure was dispelled by improvements. Before the 19th century ended, sail-powered transports were so outmoded that their ample hulls were filled with cargo and they were towed behind steam-powered transports or tugs that also carried cargo. The cost saving was obvious, but the risk of loss in foul weather was a constant concern for shippers, ship owners, and the men who manned the tethered ships.

Philadelphia is one of the major shipping ports of the United States although the "City of Brotherly Love" is 100 miles inland. Only her fine deep water harbor and 40-foot channel through the Delaware River elevate her to the status of Atlantic coast seaport. In the late 1800s, coal ranked high on the list of cargo carried from Philadelphia in the holds of ships to foreign ports and eastern seaboard cities.

On Monday morning, August 21, 1893, Captain George W. Pierson stood by the wheel of his steam-driven, but still sail-rigged ocean tug *Panther* as she eased her way down the Delaware River to the sea. The iron-hulled tug, one of the largest of her kind afloat, was one of 20 such ships owned by the Philadelphia and Reading Railroad Company. She carried a crew of 16 and a cargo of 739 tons of coal from Pennsylvania mines. Cape May lay ahead and Philadelphia was behind the steaming tug. Trailing, but not that far behind, *Lykens Valley*, a 186-foot, three-masted schooner-barge followed obediently at the end of the hawser that coupled her to the tug's stern.

STORM

The schooner-barge carried a crew of only four—even under sail, there was little to keep them busy, with the tugboat doing all the work. Her cargo was 2,350 tons of coal for delivery to Newburyport, Massachusetts.

Captain Pierson checked the barometer and shook his head. He knew that the bad weather they'd had since leaving Philadelphia would thicken before it improved. It did, all day Monday through Wednesday morning. Gale force winds and heavy seas rocked both vessels, but *Panther* stood up better than *Lykens Valley* under what proved to be the edge of an offshore hurricane.

Both ships were in trouble by 6:00 a.m. Thursday. The tug used both steam and her sails to maintain headway against the gale that threatened to swamp both ships.

The captain estimated that the ships were off the south shore of Eastern Long Island. There was still a long way to go to reach Newburyport, high up the northeast coast of Massachusetts. The wind lulled, then it struck with an angry blast that tore away the tug's mainsail. All hands struggled to rig another aft of the smokestack, but that too was torn away. At 7:00 a.m., the tug and tow were about six miles off the shore of Southampton, Long Island when Fireman Edwin Cummings was half drowned by a tremendous wave that engulfed the deck and drove into the tug's engine room. The cold seawater striking the hot furnace and pipes generated clouds of vapor that blinded him as he struggled topside.

DECISION

Words tumbled out as Cummings described the flooded engine room to Captain Pierson. "This is the end if you can't do something to give us an even break against this blasted storm. We can't last another hour." Pierson nodded, "Aye, I've got to get you and the ship home safe. Its been a rough night for all of us. My problem is the tow. She's my responsibility too, ship, crew, and cargo. Without her, I think we can make it. We could drop the line, but God knows where she'll end up. There must be another way. I've been beating my brains out all night trying to find that other way."

Cummings had never taken issue with his captain before, but this time the stakes were life or death. "Your pardon, Captain, but I think you know the only answer is to cut loose and let the chips fall where they may. I feel sorry for the men on the barge, but we're 16 and there's only four of them. If we've got a chance, I respectfully suggest we take it."

Captain Pierson recognized his own reasoning, that the men were his first responsibility. "If there was any way I could pick up those four, the barge could fend for itself."

"But there's no way, Captain."

"I know. If we pulled the barge close enough, this blasted gale would batter both of us to splinters. I swear, Cummings, I'll never haul another tow without a breeches buoy on the towline. They'd probably drown on the way across, but at least they'd have a chance."

The fireman watched Captain Pierson decide the fate of two ships and 20 men. When tears welled in the captain's eyes, Cummings turned away, embarrassed. It was unnerving to see into the bared soul of another, especially when it belonged to a gruff, demanding tugboat captain. When he turned back, the captain's eyes were clear. Any tears were carried away by the rain streaming down his face.

Pierson breathed, "God, forgive me," then he bawled to the mate at the stern, "Signal we're dropping the line, then cut the hawser!" He dismissed Cummings with a scowl, "Fireman, be sure the mate got that order."

Relieved of her burden, *Panther* surged ahead while *Lykens Valley* floundered helplessly as the storm carried her off. She twisted and turned at the whim of the waves until breakers drove her onto a sandbar one-half-mile east of Southampton's St. Andrews Dune Church. Two of the four-man crew disappeared into the sea when

20-foot waves washed them overboard. The other two drowned while occupants of a house near the beach watched helplessly. Within an hour, the coal-laden barge broke up. One observer noted, "There was nothing to see but wreckage chopped up by the force of the sea as to be hardly recognizable as that of a ship."

Captain Pierson headed *Panther* into the storm and moved offshore, but there was no hope. Towering waves pounded the tug's deckhouse to pieces, seawater poured into her engine room and drowned the boilers. The tugboat was as helpless as the abandoned barge. The crew donned life preservers and many climbed into the rigging, then were swept into the sea by relentless waves. Fireman Cummings survived by climbing into the rigging. His description was: "The waves took the men off the rigging like flies. The mate and myself were way up in the mainmast rigging ... We saw every other man aboard go over [including the captain].... A huge roller broke over us and took him off.... The waves fell on me again and again as if there were a hundred ropes pulling at every limb in my body. My wrist, as I hung with one hand only, was terribly strained."

The next wave carried him off: "The next thing I knew ... the mate was close by me, swimming.... then he was carried out of sight.... I saw Billy Dailey [steward] and the little mess boy. They were swimming with planks across their chests."

Cummings sighted the top of the pilothouse floating nearby. He climbed aboard and drifted until a wave turned it over. That was all he recalled until he came to on shore.

Another crew member estimated that he had been in the water for about three hours before he felt land under his feet. He clawed his way in the sand bottom to grasp the hand of one of the members of the Southampton Life-Saving Station rescue team that formed a human chain off the beach. Two more survivors were rescued by volunteers from neighboring cottages.

Local physicians tended the survivors who lapsed into periods of unconsciousness. Their close brush with death at sea left them exhausted—physically and mentally. Their black and blue bodies were evidence of the severe pounding they had suffered from the mass of floating wreckage.

For several weeks, bodies in various stages of decomposition washed onto southeastern Long Island beaches. The corpses of all but one of the 16 victims from the two ships were recovered. Most are buried in the northwest section of the North Road Cemetery, with a memorial stone marking the modest 10- by 20-foot plot.

Souvenir hunters had a field day collecting the wreckage that washed ashore. It included a small boat, an oar, a life preserver marked *"Panther,"* a crushed small boat bearing *"Lykens Valley, Philadelphia"* painted on it, and a brass plate with the inscription "P. and R.," undoubtedly for Philadelphia and Reading.

Panther remained upright when she sank, and pretty much intact except for her deckhouse. Her heavy coal cargo kept her in a fixed position. At low tide on a clear day, several feet of her mast was visible from shore. Lying in only 55 feet of water, she was a menace to navigation. On October 11, 1893, a nine-pound dynamite cartridge was detonated on her deck by surfmen of the local lifesaving station. A six-pound cartridge completed the task of dismasting the tugboat. Many timbers surfaced and three days later, a headless body washed ashore near Bridgehampton, accounting for all the victims. The latest was probably dislodged from the wreck by the explosions. It was buried with the other victims.

Lykens Valley's 1,200-pound anchor was discovered on September 28, between the offshore sandbar and the beach. Two boats brought it ashore with rope and tackle, then it was sold to the congregation of St. Andrews Dune Church. It now graces the front lawn of the church as a memorial to the 16 victims. The church, originally built as a lifesaving station in 1851, almost 20 years before the U.S. Life-Saving Service came into being, was ideally suited for such a memorial. Inside, one brass wall tablet records the wreck of *Panther* and *Lykens Valley*. Another memorializes the destruction of the British sloop-of-war *Sylph* on the night of January 16, 1815, with 115 of her 121-man crew lost. A cannon from the French ship *Alexander*, wrecked in 1874, shares the front lawn of the truly maritime church with *Lykens Valley*'s anchor.

The old lifesaving station became the nucleus of the new St. Andrews-by-the-Sea church in 1879. The name was changed to the present name in 1884. The church was expanded and remodeled several times. It was badly damaged in the 1938 hurricane.

The unique church's bells, appointments, and windows are memorial gifts, including a marble table base from Netley Abbey, founded in the 13th century near Southampton, England by Henry III. An Irish silver paten (plate) made in 1684, a Florentine chalice of 1550, two early English chancel chairs, an English Bible printed in 1639, carved stones of the 12th century, and oak corbels (used to support a cornice or an arch) from England's Blytheburg church, built in 1442, are among other gifts.

PRESENT CONDITION

Panther's remains have been a favorite spot for fishermen for a century. The site has been visited by scuba divers since the late 1950s. Only a small amount of wreckage remains, scattered over the bottom. The engine, with 30 feet of shaft and an iron screw-propeller, extends about 14 feet off the bottom. With part of a boiler and a few flattened iron plates, that is all that is left of the iron-hulled ocean tug.

To our knowledge, *Lykens Valley*'s remains have never been found.

NAHUM CHAPIN—SWIFT DESTRUCTION

Type of vessel: three-masted schooner
Where built: Cobb, Wight & Co., Rockland, Maine
Launched: 1882
Length/beam: 145' / 35'
Gross tons: 597
Sunk: January 21, 1897
Cause of sinking: fog / ran aground
Location: Quogue
Approximate depth of water: wreckage has not been located

AT 4:00 A.M. on January 21, 1897, surfman Harry Carter left the Quogue Life-Saving Station and headed east on his beach patrol. The night was pitch black and the gale force wind, heavily laden with sharp sleet and stinging rain, was from the southeast and in his face. A tremendous sea pounding on the shore sent the surf rolling close to the sand dunes. A local newspaper reported it "one of the worst nights ever seen" with southeast winds of 60 miles per hour blowing almost directly on shore, producing breakers which came "booming over the bar with a deafening roar ... men could not hear each others' shouts mouth to ear."

SHIP IN DISTRESS

The surf was unusually high, forcing Carter to walk in the dunes rather than on the beach. He was no more than 50 feet from the station, at the top of a sand dune, when he spotted two or three lights flickering downshore and to seaward. He knew it could only be a vessel in distress on the sandbar that preyed on careless navigators. He went back to the station to arouse the lifesavers, then returned to the dune and fired three red Costen flares in rapid succession to signal that help was on the way. Each flare burned for 90 seconds.

The ship ran aground about one-mile southeast of the village of Quogue and between one-half to three-quarters of a mile east of the Quogue Life-Saving Station. The station was 200 yards east of the foot of Beach Lane.

The lifesaving crew assembled their surfboat and beach rescue equipment from the boathouse while Captain Herman telephoned for assistance from adjacent Tiana and Potunk (Westhampton) stations. The Tiana station was four miles to the east and Potunk three and one-half miles to the west. Herman's own men set out for the beach abreast of the flickering lights. Less than 30 minutes after Carter's discovery of the lights the Quogue lifesaving crew stood on the beach with rescue gear ready for action. By then, only one light could be seen. There was no way to tell if the vessel lay broadside to the shoreline. However, the Lyle gun was positioned and fired. Its projectile either fell short or went clear of the vessel. A second shot drew no response from the stranded ship.

Captain John E. Carter and the Tiana station crew arrived at about 5:00 a.m. The gun was fired again, but still without success. Up to then, not even the faintest outline of the vessel could be seen. There was no way to tell her size and rig, number aboard, or if any were still alive. Whatever she was, rapidly accumulating wreckage on the shore revealed that the mountainous seas were beginning to batter her into fragments. At 5:20 a.m., the gun was fired again. The line was reeled back without strain because it missed the ship.

A few minutes before 6:00 a.m., Captain Franklin C. Jessup and the Potunk station crew joined the other two crews. At about 6:20 a.m., there was sufficient daylight to see the ship and her condition. She was a three-masted schooner, about 500 yards offshore. Her three headsails, foresail, and reefed spanker were still standing, evidence that her mishap was due to an error in heading. The schooner struck the sandbar while she was under nearly full sail. Her captain must have been unaware of the ship's position, and did not realize the danger until the schooner plunged bow first onto the bar. He most likely believed his position was east of Montauk Point. It is possible that, like *John Milton*'s captain 39 years before, the stranded schooner's captain mistook the beacon from Shinnecock Lighthouse for the Montauk light at the end of Long Island.

The schooner rolled violently, and was so completely deluged by huge waves that her hull was practically submerged. With dawn, the lifesavers could make out nine survivors on the ship, six high in the fore rigging and three on the end of the jib-boom.

Even though the ship was stranded far offshore, the lifesavers were confident that all could be rescued by breeches buoy if the ship held together for another hour and the survivors could handle the life lines.

The Lyle gun was fired again. The surfmen followed the flight of the shot as it soared over the schooner, laying its line safely between the fore and main masts. However, with mountainous waves sweeping the deck, none of the men in the rigging left their precarious perches to secure the line. Another shot carried its line across the head stays, but still no one moved to get it. Although they wouldn't have to descend to the deck, the half-frozen men were afraid to release their holds in the rigging to climb even higher for the line.

HELPLESS ON SHORE

Shortly after the shot line settled over the rigging, a huge wave struck the schooner with such violence that the masts whipped back and forth, catapulting two of the six survivors in the rigging from their sanctuary into the sea. The other four shared the same fate when the next wave struck. Will S. Terrell, a surfman of the Tiana station said he saw one man projected "like an arrow 50 feet out to sea and saw him drop with a splash in the boiling breakers."

Another tremendous wave snapped off the three spars like matchsticks. They fell with a crash, carrying with them the jib-boom and the three remaining survivors. In hardly more than ten minutes, the schooner was stripped of its nine survivors. Not even the most powerful swimmer could survive in such a heavy sea, with spars, timbers, and a mass of tangled rigging swirling around the ship's hull. The tragedy ended at 7:00 a.m., only 40 minutes after dawn.

The disaster was as quick as it was overwhelming for those on shore. The schooner's masts were still standing, but the lifesavers could hardly see her shattered hull above the hollows of the great green waves. Less than an hour after daylight, much of the wreck lay in fragments at the feet of the helpless lifesavers.

The ship's masts collapsed from the repeated onslaught of waves. Her hull continued to break up as lifesavers scattered along the shore in a search for survivors. A newspaper reported: "... the wreckage was in slivers (scattered over four miles) ... the sea had ripped the large schooner as though she had been a plaything."

Another newspaper stated: "There are parts of sides, parts of bottoms, parts of the bow and parts of the stern, but not a whole piece of the ship is left. Even the schooner's name is not complete. One piece, cap of the hatch, carries the name and the register carved with a chisel, as the law commands."

About 8:30 a.m., one surfman discovered a body in the rolling waves about a half-mile to the west. He removed the body from the surf and tried resuscitation, aided by three others. Their efforts were fruitless, and the body was carried to the lifesaving station. The *Riverhead News* reported: "During the day, a large crowd of sightseers visited the beach, and the terrible tragedy brought into Quogue's quiet life by this fatal January storm was the sole topic of conversation."

At a coroner's inquest the following morning, the man's brother identified the corpse as the schooner's captain, Ernest L. Arey. The captain's body was interred at Malden, Massachusetts. The body of the mate, Alfred E. Davis, was recovered from the surf at 8:00 a.m. the following day. Three more bodies were recovered, but they were so mutilated by pounding from wreckage, that they could not be identified.

Five men from the schooner were buried in the Patchogue cemetery in a plot adjoining one where the men from the schooner *Louis V. Place* are interred. Six men were lost on *Louis V. Place* when she ran aground in 1895 at Moriches. The two burial sites are called the Sailors' Plot.

The stranded vessel was the 596-ton American schooner *Nahum Chapin*, with a captain, mate, and seven sailors. Her home port was Rockland, Maine, but she was en route from Baltimore, Maryland to Boston, Massachusetts with a cargo of coal consigned to the West End Railway Company. Unconfirmed reports suggested that the captain's wife and child were aboard when the storm drove the schooner aground. Terrell, the surfman of the Tiana station, reported he saw: "six [men] in the forward rigging, and three on the gibbon's rope. What struck me most forcibly was the figure of a man of great stature low down in the forward rigging. Lashed to him and to the rigging was a smaller figure in white, which I took to be a woman in her nightclothes. It might have been a smaller man, but as the others were not lashed together, and this was the only figure in white, I had no doubt that it was a woman. I saw a girl pick up on the beach a hairbrush, delicate of pattern and evidently the pride of a woman. I saw this girl take out of it long silken hairs, dark brown in color. These hairs must have come from a woman's head. There is no getting away from the evidence, and the girl put the brush under her shawl to treasure it as a keepsake."

The presumption that a child perished with the schooner was based upon debris that washed ashore; a tangled clump of water-soaked doll's clothing, a broken, little red chair, and a box of Mother's Milk, which must have contained a baby food of some sort. These articles attracted the interest of the women and girls who thronged the beach all day.

Lieutenant Failing, of the Revenue Cutter Service, conducted an inquiry. His official report of the disaster included the following statement: "There never was a time from the discovery of the vessel until she went to pieces when any type of surfboat could have put off through the breakers. This surely was an occasion when human agency was powerless to save life."

The largest piece of wreckage from *Nahum Chapin* washed ashore near Post's Pavilion (now the Quogue Surf Club). The schooner's insurance underwriters disposed of what little salvage there was from the wreckage in lots, one of which included a kedge anchor (a small anchor used for changing location while at anchor).

Selden H. Hallock, proprietor of the Quogue House Hotel on Beach Lane, bought the lot with the anchor and in 1919 presented the anchor to the Quogue Library where it is prominently displayed on the front lawn.

AUGUSTUS HUNT—HEROIC LIFESAVERS

Type of vessel: four-masted schooner
Where built: Bath, Maine
Launched: 1883
Length/beam: 208' / 40.7'
Gross tons: 1,141
Sunk: January 22, 1904
Cause of sinking: fog / ran aground
Location: between Westhampton Beach & Quogue
Approximate depth of water: wreckage has not been located

"ANOTHER NIGHT OF fog, and this one's a beaut," complained surfman Levi Crasper as he left the Quogue Life-Saving Station. It was midnight and he was on patrol to the west of the station, along Long Island's south shore. In good weather he enjoyed the half-hour tour to the halfway house, where he would meet his counterpart from the Potunk (Westhampton) station. There, they would exchange brass tags and return to their home stations with proof of a completed patrol.

Clear skies, moonlight, and the constant surf were soothing on a warm summer night, but this was winter, January 22, 1904. It was bitter cold, the night was damp, and the fog was a gray wall that blotted out everything more than ten feet ahead. He looked to the left toward the unseen turbulent sea and wondered what good he might serve if someone was in distress out there, someone he could neither see nor hear.

STRANDED

Crasper was on time arriving at the halfway house at 12:30 a.m., but surfman Bishop was late arriving from the Potunk station. With nothing better to do, Crasper walked to the edge of the water and peered out to sea through the fog. For a moment the fog thinned, revealing a dark object almost directly off shore. For the next 15 minutes Crasper tried to determine if the unlighted, indistinct image was a ship. If it was, it was surely in trouble because it was directly over a shallow sandbar. When Bishop arrived, the two concluded that it was a ship, and it was stranded on a sandbar that was well known locally, but apparently not to the captain of the stranded vessel.

Lifesavers were furnished with Coston signal flares. Crasper lit his for the benefit of any survivors and to mark the location. The Coston signal emitted a brilliant red flame for 90 seconds. Survivors aboard the stranded ship saw it as an occasional flash of red light and cried out for rescue, but by that time both surfmen were headed back to their stations for help.

The lifesavers returned with reinforcements, but there was little they could do but listen to the cries of the stranded sailors. Tremendous waves produced by the storm surge prevented the lifesavers from reaching them with a surfboat. An attempt was made to launch one, but the craft was tossed back onto the beach by an enormous wave. One lifesaver later testified, "there was white water clear to the bar," where the ship was stranded. Five efforts to fire a Lyle gun projectile with a line attached for breeches buoy rescue failed, partly because of limited visibility through the fog. It was later learned that one or two shots struck within 15 or 20 yards of the ship that, even after daylight, was invisible behind the dense fog that cleared only intermittently.

A drowned member of the ship's crew washed ashore, but there were no papers on the body to aid in identification of the victim or the ship. Cries for help became fainter as the morning wore on, indicating that the crewmen were exhausted and probably succumbing to the frigid conditions.

At 9:10 a.m. another Lyle gun projectile was fired. At first it was thought that the line reached the stranded vessel. It was taut, as though it was tied it off on the ship, but instead it was entangled in a piece of drifting wreckage.

Captain Carter of the Tiana Life-Saving Station arrived with men to assist those from Quogue and Potunk. That made a total of 17 lifesavers and several local residents who were on hand to rescue survivors. By afternoon, however, there were no more cries from offshore. The lifesavers could only patrol the beach searching for bodies. Two more were recovered.

RESCUE

A little after 1:00 p.m., one of the lifesavers spotted two men floating on the remains of their ship's jib boom. He called for the Lyle gun and a line was fired to them. The shot fell within four feet of one man, but he was unwilling to relinquish his hold on the wreckage that kept him afloat. A second shot was more successful; the line fell almost on top of one survivor. He deftly slipped down the boom, and pulled the line to him with one foot. He regained his hold and tied the line to the piece of wreckage that so far had saved both men. Then he attempted to pull himself ashore, hand over hand, through the mass of wreckage that packed the water. He lost his hold once, but regained the line and worked his way about ten more yards. By then he was so cold and exhausted that the next wave that struck him loosened his grasp and he fell into the sea. William Halsey of the Quogue Life-Saving Station, tied a line to a life preserver and went into the frigid surf to his rescue. Although Halsey was a strong swimmer (he had won a silver cup and a gold medal in surf competitions), it was a desperate struggle for him to reach the drowning sailor. He pulled the half-drowned and almost frozen survivor onto a piece of wreckage. Several other lifesavers followed close behind Halsey. Their combined efforts managed to get the man ashore.

The survivor was too weak to say more than the name of his ship, *Augustus Hunt*. The lifesavers took him to the Quogue Life-Saving Station where massage restored his circulation and rest restored his strength. Those who witnessed the rescue proclaimed Halsey a hero, an opinion that was obviously shared by the United States Government. The Secretary of Treasury later awarded him a gold lifesaving medal for the act.

The lifesavers turned their attention to the second sailor, still holding onto the broken boom. They watched as, with almost frozen fingers, he tried to climb higher out of the frigid water. A moment later he lost his grip and dropped into the mass of wreckage. He scrambled to make his way to the beach across floating masts, spars, rigging, and sails but fell into the turbulence. Halsey was too exhausted to go out again. Surfman Frank D. Warner, also of the Quogue Life-Saving Station, and several lifesavers with Winfield Jessup of Westhampton Beach and other local men dashed into the surf to save him.

Warner fought the towering surf to reach the sailor and pull him onto a piece of wreckage as Halsey had with the first survivor. Both were pulled ashore by the others. The rescued man was beginning to turn blue from the cold. He was covered with bruises and small cuts, completely exhausted, and unable to speak. He too was taken to the lifesaving station, where massage and rest restored him to an almost normal state. Warner's action was also rewarded with a gold medal of honor.

On June 30, 1874, Congress had passed the Life-Saving Act, authorizing awards of gold and silver medals to individuals who save, or attempt to save, persons from drowning. The gold medal is awarded to those who risk their own lives in the attempt. Since its inception about 600 gold medals have been awarded to civilians and military personnel.

Surfmen Halsey and Warner were awarded their medals by the Life-Saving Service's Assistant General Superintendent Horace S. Piper at the annual dinner of the Long Island Lifesaving District. The following letter from the Secretary of the Treasury L. M. Shaw, dated June 11, 1904, accompanied the gold medal awarded to surfman Frank Warner: "Transmitted herewith is a gold lifesaving medal of honor awarded you under the provisions of Acts of Congress ... in recognition of your heroic conduct in saving life at the wreck of the schooner *Augustus Hunt* ... without any line about you and with apparently no thought on your own safety, you boldly jumped in and made all possible haste to the perishing sailor ...

"How great the danger was that you might be killed by the wreckage is shown by the fact that the bodies of the drowned sailors afterward recovered showed by pitiful wounds that death was due to this cause, one of them having one leg torn off at the hip so that it was held only by a single ligament.

"Your conduct was most highly courageous and commendable. You voluntarily jeopardized your life by assuming an undertaking of extreme peril where no keeper [lifesaving station captain] would have ordered you to go, and in so doing

The submarine chaser *Eagle 17* was lost near Amagansett in 1922. *Courtesy of Brian Campbell.*

The 283-foot long *Clan Galbraith* was the largest ship to come ashore on the south fork of Long Island when she grounded at Flying Point, Water Mill. *Courtesy of the Suffolk County Historical Society.*

The U.S. destroyer *Baldwin* ran aground at Montauk Point in 1961. During salvage operations a cable snapped, killing one man. *Courtesy of Albert R. Holden.*

Above: *Augustus Hunt* ran aground at Quogue in 1904. Wreckage scattered on the beach. *Courtesy of the Quogue Historical Society.* Bottom Left: Susanne and Carol Small sitting on the remains of *Hunt.* The girls enjoyed playing on and swimming off the wreckage as a precious summer time tradition of their childhood. *Courtesy of Pat Shuttleworth.* Bottom Right: William Halsey (shown here) and another surfman of the Quogue Life-Saving Station plunged into the ocean to save *Hunt* crew members at great risk of injury from heavy surf and floating wreckage. Both men received USLSS gold medals for their heroism. *Courtesy of Van Field.*

William Halsey (X on his back) inspecting the frozen corpse of Hunt's captain. *Courtesy of the Quogue Historical Society.*

performed an act that could have been dictated only by an extraordinary sense of duty and humanity. The danger of losing your own life would seem to have been as great if not greater than the probability of saving the imperiled sailor.

"I am glad to have the privilege ... of awarding the accompanying medal to so brave a man."

Their low pay led to frequent resignations of many of the best surfmen of the U.S. Life-Saving Service. Its 1893 annual report acknowledged that a recent increase from $50 to $60 a month (but only for stormy winter months) slowed the rate of loss. Eleven years later, the actions of Halsey and Warren inspired Congress to grant the low-paid surfmen of the service a further increase.

Twenty-five-year-old Halsey, of East Quogue, entered the service at the Blue Point station on Long Island four years before his heroic rescue. During compulsory unpaid summer vacations he was the Quogue beach lifeguard. By saving the lives of many swimmers, he gained the gratitude of Quogue residents, who presented him with a gold watch. Warner, also in his 20s, had two years of service, the first at the Long Island Bellport station.

SURVIVORS

The two survivors were Second Mate George Ebbets of Cleveland, Ohio and Carl Sommers of Finland. When they recovered they identified their ship as the four-masted schooner *Augustus Hunt*, carrying 1,718 tons of coal from Norfolk Virginia to A. Gove & Son in East Boston, Massachusetts. The schooner was considered one of the most seaworthy four masters of the coastal trade. She was known as "jumbo," because of her unusually large (1,141 tons) size.

Sommers, a survivor of the schooner *Joseph Paro* that wrecked near Cape Charles, Virginia on January 2, returned to the sea immediately. He shipped out of nearby Norfolk on *Augustus Hunt*, then endured his second shipwreck in less than three weeks.

Ebbets said the large schooner left Norfolk on January 13. She put into Hampton Roads and left that port on January 17, under the command of Captain William H. Connary, of Bath, Maine. Captain Connary was actually the mate of the schooner, her regular commander, Captain Blair was ill in Boston.

Augustus Hunt enjoyed fair weather until she encountered dense fog and high seas off the south shore of Long Island. Captain Connary believed they were "many miles off the Long Island coast," and no depth soundings were taken. He had no idea that the schooner was in shallow water until, under full headway, she ran aground between Westhampton and Quogue on January 22, just before midnight, about where *Nahum Chapin* was wrecked seven years earlier.

Ebbets said that only five or ten minutes before the schooner struck, the forward lookout reported a light ahead that the first mate thought was the light of a steamer. Instead, it was the Shinnecock (Ponquogue) Lighthouse on Ponquogue Point, west of Southampton village. Ebbets described the disaster that followed: "Only a moderate gale was blowing, but the sea was very heavy, and all hands had been called earlier in the night to furl some of the sails, which had been done, leaving the foresail, mainsail, and four headsails standing. All of these were drawing and drove her so far and deep into the bar that she held fast, whereupon the sea instantly swept her from stern to stem, breaking halfway up the spars."

It was apparent to everyone on board that the position of the ship was hopeless. Seven men took to the rigging, but Ebbets and Sommers lashed themselves to the jib boom. They were convinced that the swaying masts would not stand for long. The stranded crew could hear voices from shore answering their cries for help, but neither group could understand the other.

After the crew endured a night of frozen terror, Ebbets' and Sommers' fears were realized when all four masts crashed to the deck and the pounding waves washed them into the sea. The crash when the masts went down was heard by those on the beach. Captain Connary and six members of the crew who were perched in the rigging went with the masts, and none survived. Neither Ebbets nor Sommers, were able to help their drowning shipmates from the jib boom they floated on. They couldn't even hear each other over the thunder of the waves and the tearing apart of the schooner, and they were only a few feet apart.

Most of the bodies recovered were bruised and battered by the floating wreckage. Four that washed ashore were First Mate Matt Torrey and Steward Charles Sherman, both of Boston, Seaman Charles Hudson of Malden, Massachusetts, and John Miller. Captain Connary's frozen corpse was found on the shore, entangled in wire cables and a mast.

In 1948, George E. Winters described the recovery of Connary's body in a letter to Harry Squires: "The body was under a piece of wreckage and low water, about all that was showing was the body. I stood on the wreckage with Dr. John Nugent the Coroner, (I many times took testimony for him at inquests) and he turned to me [and said], 'We can't get the body out unless we chop off the leg' which was fast under the wreckage and he told Halsey to take the ax and chop it off, which he did. I do not believe there was a bone left unbroken in the body and it was carried off in a piece of canvas no larger than a bath towel. Connary, Torrey, and Hudson, with one child, were married."

There is a memorial stone to crew member John Miller by the east fence in Westhampton Cemetery.

The mass of debris that used to be *Augustus Hunt* was strewn for several miles along the beach. The remains were sold where they lay to Silas Tuttle for $15, probably a fair price. But for a four-masted schooner?

The hulk was in the surf off the Quogue Bathing Pavilion (now the Quogue Surf Club) for four years before a storm-aided high tide moved it westward one-quarter of a mile to Dr. Robert L. Dickinson's summer cottage, between the Westhampton Beach and Quogue bridges. In 1955, his daughter, Mrs. T.S. Potter of Amherst, Massachusetts, wrote: "A side of the ship was in our beach for years—occasionally showing when the beach was deeply gouged. The prow and a section of keel and ribbing protruded in front of Mr. Small's [Charles Small, grandfather of Ted Shuttleworth] house [east of Quantuck Beach Club]. We used to run between waves, climb up on the high prow and watch the water swirl around us, sometimes getting punished for getting wet if the waves were too high and splashed on the planking. As this wreck was at normal water level it gathered sand and a sort of point was built around it. Then a terrible winter storm from the east swirled out around that point and turned inland an equal amount just at our house, and again an in-sweep at Dr. Dudley Roberts' home."

The Small and Roberts homes were almost lost to beach erosion caused by the point that was built up by the wreck. Mrs. Potter continued: "Because the wreck was dangerous to our house, Father acquired rights to it and tried to burn it up, but the tar or whatever was used simply burned off the old saturated timbers. Dynamite did not seem to do any good; the beams sprung apart and together again. Finally, the following winter, the ocean delivered the goods' right UP on our beach, a great joy to all youngsters.... 'Our wreck' was a precious tradition of our childhood."

As young girls, Mrs. Potter and Ted Shuttleworth's (his wife Pat is Chairman of the Quogue Historical Society) mother Carol Small, with her sister Susanne, enjoyed playing on and swimming off the wreckage of *Augustus Hunt*.

In 1915, the Life-Saving Service became part of the Coast Guard Service and the Quogue Life-Saving Station was sold and moved back from the beach. A new Quogue Coast Guard station was built on the old site, but the tradition of heroism displayed by two surfmen the night the four-masted schooner *Augustus Hunt* was lost remains. The Coast Guard station is still there, but has been privately owned since 1948.

MILES M. MERRY & WILLIAM C. CARNEGIE

Type of vessels: schooners
Where built: Percy & Small, Bath, Maine
Launched: *Merry* 1901, *Carnegie* 1900
Length/beam: *Merry* 215.2/43.2, *Carnegie* 289.2/46.3
Gross tons: *Merry* 1,589; *Carnegie* 2,664
Sunk: *Merry* February 17, 1909; *Carnegie* May 1, 1909
Cause of sinking: ran aground
Location: Eastport, New York
Approximate depth of water: wreckage has not been located

THE FOUR-MASTED schooner *Miles M. Merry* ran aground twice in her career, both times at the same location on Long Island. The first grounding occurred September 10, 1907, in fair weather on the barrier island off Long Island's south shore. The location was near the Moriches Life-Saving Station (Eastport). The next day the salvage tug *Ira J. Merritt* refloated the ship without removing her cargo of coal. The second time, only 17 months later on February 17, 1909, she came ashore at the same spot, but with a more severe result.

The 1,589-ton schooner was en route from Boston to Newport News, Virginia to take on another load of coal when she grounded at 4:15 a.m. in bitter cold weather. A copy of a July 2, 1977, handwritten document titled "Ships and the Sea" was given to Harry Huson, teacher, principal, then chief administrator at East Moriches School for 37 years. The author, son of the surfman who discovered the ship in distress, described the grounding: "... surfman Earl W. Suydam had the last west beach patrol from Moriches Life-Saving Station. The weather was foggy and suddenly he was dumfounded to see a four-masted schooner 'beating' its way eastward between the bar and the beach. [The schooner must have struck so hard she was driven over the offshore sandbar.] He fired a Coston signal [hand held flare] to alert those on board that she had been sighted and after observing her make several tacks between bar and beach, first nudging one and then the other, he ran back to the station and alerted the crew to this strange and practically unheard of circumstance. Shortly thereafter she grounded fast almost opposite the station [700 feet to the east]. She had made her way eastward for about a mile from where first sighted by surfman Suydam."

THE SCHOONER "MILES M.MERRY" WRECKED OFF EAST MORICHES, FEBRUARY 17, 1909.

The wind was moderate with little sea and thus the ship's crew were not endangered nor was the vessel in danger of further immediate damage.

The lifesavers must have rubbed their eyes in disbelief at the schooner's nameboard. It was same ship that had grounded in front of their station less than a year and a half earlier. They shrugged off their surprise and tackled the job of getting *Merry*'s captain and his ten-man crew ashore by breeches buoy. The lifesaving station provided the men with shelter.

The handwritten document continued: "Again the tug *Ira J. Merritt*, with Capt. Edward G. Denisen and a crew of 20, began refloating efforts. After three weeks of fruitless endeavors a terrific easterly gale came up driving high seas over the vessel. She broke in two and both the on board salvage and ship's crews were rescued [with breeches buoy] by crews of the Moriches, Potunk [Westhampton], and Forge River [west of the Moriches station] lifesaving stations operating jointly under the command of Captain Charles T. ("Rose") Gordon of the Moriches station.

The wreck was abandoned and in appreciation for services rendered Captain Farrow [J.O. Farrow, master of *Merry*] advised the lifesavers to salvage whatever they could for their personal use. "

Subsequently on March 15, 1909, the hulk caught fire and burned to the water's edge. The remains were visible for many years alternately covered and uncovered by sand as shifted by storms and wind driven tides. The author of the document, Commander Elmer J.J. (Jim) Suydam, U.S. Coast Guard (Retired), added the following anecdote: "After entering the service [Life-Saving Service] on his 21st birthday in 1905, Earl married Viola E. Brown of Eastport and in 1909 they resided in a small house 'on the beach' close by the station. On March 12th he was on *Merry*'s fore top helping to strip the vessel's rigging. Viola had gone to the mainland a few days previously expectant with their first born to be. On this day a message had come by boat—another surfman came over the dunes and called 'Hey, Early! Hey, Early! You've got a boy!' Dad, in his exuberance, took the quickest way down. He slid down the forestay from the topmast to the outer end of the bowsprit and dropped from there to the sand, landing running. That to my Dad was when I entered the world on his 25th birthday, March 12, 1909."

In July 1977 Elmer Suydam donated a leather-upholstered, wooden chair from *Merry*'s captain's cabin to the Moriches Bay Historical Society in the name of his mother.

WILLIAM C. CARNEGIE

During the investigation of the stranding and loss of *Merry*, the captain of the five-masted schooner *William C. Carnegie*, owned by the same company, Clark Brothers of Portland, Maine, testified, "that only a fool would run a ship ashore on the south shore of Long Island." He proved his point less than three months after *Merry*'s loss when he ran his own ship *Carnegie* aground at almost the same spot, within a mile of the wreck site. His scathing indictment of his fellow captain had returned to haunt him, although his excuse would be that gale force winds forced him ashore. The 2,664-ton *Carnegie* was en route from Newport News to Boston with a cargo of 4,400 tons of coal when she went aground.

When 20-foot seas prevented the lifesavers from launching a surfboat, the schooner's captain and her 14-man crew launched the ship's longboat and rowed offshore to be rescued by the revenue cutter *Mohawk*.

In 1966, Samuel B. Cross of Westhampton Beach reported two large anchors buried in the sand to the Suffolk County Department of Public Works. The anchors were dug up and removed to Yaphank, Long Island. Although they were believed to be *Merry*'s, that seems unlikely. Joseph Tuttle of Eastport and Hubert Tuttle of Speonk, members of the Moriches Life-Saving Station's 1909 crew attested that the anchor from *Merry* was taken off and sent by freight to the owners, Clark Brothers, in Portland, Maine. They added that after *Carnegie* stranded, Clark Brothers gave her gear and anchors to the lifesaving crew at Moriches. Winfield S. Jessup, a house-mover [from Westhampton], sold the anchors to a Mr. Rodgers of Bay Shore, who never took them from the beach.

On February 2, 1967, *The Hampton Chronicle* (Westhampton Beach) published a photograph borrowed from Winfield Jessup's daughter Margery. It depicted an anchor, presumably from *Merry*, being moved by her father across Moriches Bay on a scow (a large flat-bottomed boat with square ends). One cart on the scow holds the anchor chain and a second holds the anchor itself. The anchors dug up by the Suffolk County Department of Public Works remain unidentified.

Many of the old lifesaving stations, including the Moriches and Potunk stations were destroyed by the hurricane of 1938 and were never rebuilt. Like manned lighthouses, they had served their purpose and were no longer needed.

> *"To every thing there is a season, and a time for every purpose under the heaven ..."*
>
> Old Testament — Ecclesiastics, III, 1-8.

Above: *Miles M. Merry* went aground twice in her career, both times at the same location near the Moriches Life-Saving Station. The schooner was a total loss when she stranded in 1909. *Courtesy of Harry Huson.* Below: this piece of wreckage that washed ashore in the early 1990s could be from the schooner *Merry*. *Photo by H. Keatts.*

The loss of the transatlantic liner *Oregon* off Long Island was Cunard's first major disaster. *Courtesy of Frank Braynard.*

In 1909, less than three months after *Merry* stranded, a northeast gale drove the five-masted schooner *William C. Carnegie* ashore at almost the same site. *Top photo courtesy of Van Field*; bottom, *courtesy of William P. Quinn.*

GATE CITY—COTTON CARGO

Type of vessel: coastal passenger liner
Where built: John Roach & Son, Chester, Pennsylvania
Launched: 1878
Length/beam: 275′ / 38.5′
Gross tons: 1,997
Sunk: February 8, 1900
Cause of sinking: fog / ran aground
Location: about ½ mile east of Moriches Inlet, approximately 50 yards offshore
Approximate depth of water: 15′

INSHORE WATERS ARE constantly in motion. They respond to currents and changing tides with a restless action that carries sand from one place to another. That process results in a continuing cycle of beach erosion and buildup. As a consequence, many inshore shipwrecks are periodically exposed more at one time than another. The coastal passenger steamer *Gate City* is an outstanding example of such a wreck, and is at the mercy of the shifting sands of Long Island's south shore.

Gate City was built for the Ocean Steamship Company of New York by John Roach at Chester, Pennsylvania in 1878. Her cost was approximately $375,000. The 1,997-ton vessel was 275 feet long, 38.5 feet beam and 15 feet draft. She was equipped with compound engines of 1,500 horsepower, steam steering gear, four hoisting engines and one engine to run a 5,000-candlepower light in the bow. Stateroom accommodations accommodated 114 cabin passengers, and less luxurious accommodations served 30 steerage passengers.

The steamer carried six metal lifeboats, two rafts, and 200 life preservers. *Gate City* could carry a cargo of 3,700 bales of cotton and miscellaneous freight in addition to passengers. Her main saloon was 80 feet long and 30 feet wide, finished in French walnut, birdseye maple, rosewood and mahogany, all accented by elegant red plush upholstery.

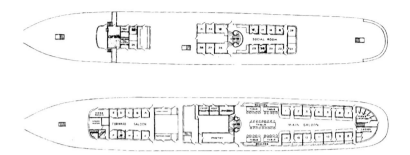

GROUNDING

The Boston and Savannah Steamship Company bought the vessel in September 1882 and placed her under the command of Captain Hedge. She was run between the two ports that made up the company's name, and she served in that role for almost four years. On July 16, 1886, *Gate City* left Savannah en route to Boston with 52 passengers and a full cargo that included a shipment of 53,000 watermelons. Three days later, dense fog drove in from the east as the vessel entered Vineyard Sound. The engines were stopped while the ship waited for the fog to lift. After four hours, Captain Hedge felt that he could wait no longer and ordered slow speed ahead, with one of the seamen taking soundings to ensure against grounding. The seaman heaving the lead raised the alarm, "We have no water," at the instant the vessel ran aground off Naushon Island.

Passengers who recalled that only 30 months earlier *Gate City's* sister ship, *City of Columbus*, was lost only 11 miles away were shaken by the prospect of a repeat performance. Ninety-seven passengers and crew were lost in that sinking at Devil's Bridge on January 18, 1884, the worst marine disaster to occur off Martha's Vineyard.

The first mate was sent off in a small boat to summon assistance. The small tugboat *W.O. Brown* of New Bedford provided that aid by coming alongside to pick up 37 passengers for the balance of their trip to Boston. Fifteen other passengers who were headed for Wood's Hole preferred to wait until they could be taken directly to their destination. The next morning, the steamer *Monohansett*, of the Vineyard Line, removed them for the completion of their journey.

Gate City was moving cautiously through the heavy fog at the time of the accident and seemed to ground so lightly that it was felt she could be refloated without much of a problem. To lighten the steamer, the 53,000 watermelons were thrown overboard, transforming Vineyard Sound into a bobbing sea of green capsules. Many small craft harvested the unexpected crop; 10,000 of the melons that floated ashore on Naushon Island were forwarded to Boston, their original destination.

A salvage vessel carrying hard-hat divers arrived at the scene on July 20th. When they determined the extent of the damage and the probable expense of raising and repairing the ship, the owners decided to abandon it. Insurance coverage was $200,000, of which $150,000 was placed with foreign companies. The cost estimate for refloating the vessel was $100,000, and the domestic underwriters were reluctant to proceed until the foreign companies would agree to bear their proportion of the expense.

Agreement was reached by the owners, underwriters, and the Boston Towboat Company to retrieve the steamer. A Boston steamship builder estimated her value before the accident at $300,000. The towboat company was to receive a salvage fee based upon the value of the wreck. Although many experts believed that it would be almost impossible to get *Gate City* afloat, the salvage company had little difficulty. They found the principal damage directly under the fire room, where a large boulder had forced through the plates. The opening was closed by sewing a dozen blankets together and wedging them into the hole. A huge canvas boot was placed under the bow to cover another large hole on the starboard side. On July 26, the vessel was pumped out and she was refloated. She steamed into Boston Harbor under her own power, accompanied by two tugs. The boot and blanket plugs had served their purpose.

Gate City resumed transporting cargo between southeastern cities and New England as soon as repairs were completed. She did so for the next 14 years, except for a brief enlistment as a troop transport in 1898. She carried 556 Spanish-American War soldiers from Cuba to Camp Wikoff, Montauk, New York, then returned to her familiar run.

SECOND GROUNDING

On February 8, 1900, *Gate City* was en route from Savannah to Boston with Captain Goggins in command when she ran into a dense fog bank off Long Island. The shoreline was invisible and he was unaware of his exact position. Perhaps because of faulty instruments or his own error in thinking his ship was clear of the Montauk Point tip of Long Island, he headed directly into shore. The vessel was under almost full steam when she drove hard onto the outer sandbar, east of the Moriches Life-Saving Station.

With her whistle blowing for almost an hour, the steamer had been driving through the fog at a speed that was probably too high for the limited visibility. The station's beach patrol had monitored *Gate City*'s whistle, but the fog was too dense for their responding Coston flare signals to be seen aboard the ship.

The sea was calm and the lifesaving crew launched a surfboat at once, guided to the stranded ship by her bell and steam whistle. Their offer to take off as many of the 49 passengers (including three women) and crew as their boat could carry was accepted only by the women. The others elected to stay because the steamship did not seem to be in immediate danger.

The following day, the remaining passengers and 18 of the crew whose services were not required were taken off. It appeared that *Gate City* could be refloated without much problem; her hull was in good condition and she was facing toward the beach. A salvage steamer stood by and removed 2,713 bales of cotton and some barrels of turpentine. Then, a storm arose and worsened as the day progressed. That night the stranded steamer was driven over the sandbar that had supported her, into a section of shoaling beach, which is almost always fatal to a stricken ship.

Salvage of the cargo continued after the storm subsided. All of the cotton and much of the turpentine was recovered, but the ship was creeping closer to the beach with each tide. Several powerful tugs strained to pull the vessel back over the sandbar into open water at each high tide for more than a week before the effort was abandoned. Instead of trying to save the ship, valued at $100,000, efforts were redirected to dismantling and removing everything of value. Even huge iron hull plates were removed for sale as scrap.

A salvage tent camp, appropriately named "Sand Hill City," was set up on the beach, with one large tent serving as a hotel. The operation was so massive that a rail line was constructed over Moriches Bay to the wreck site for transfer of the salvaged material. The magnitude of the large wreck and the massive recovery effort attracted hordes of spectators to the scene. The large ship was almost close enough to walk aboard from the beach at low tide. There were no roads on the barrier island, but hundreds arrived by boat to view the spectacle. The railway was dismantled when salvage ceased, and *Gate City* was soon forgotten.

In March 1931 a gale struck Long Island with such fury that it opened a new inlet at Moriches, affecting tide and current action. Boatmen using the inlet began to report a wreck exposed on the west side of the inlet, where none had been observed earlier. It was *Gate City*, rediscovered after 38 years of oblivion. It soon became a favorite fishing spot for large blackfish, attracted by the mussels that cover the wreck by late summer. Most of those who were interested in the wreck were unaware of its identity, only that it provided good fishing and was a potential menace to navigation.

PRESENT CONDITION

Over time, the inlet migrated westerly along the beach until it stabilized after jetties were installed by the U.S. Corps of Engineers. The wreck is now about one-half-mile east of Moriches Inlet and approximately 50 yards offshore in about 15 feet of water. Scuba divers have explored the remains since the early 1960s. They never know from year to year how much of the wreck will be exposed above the shifting sands. Wooden barrels of solidified turpentine in a cargo hold were in view in 1978; the next year they were deep in sand.

A savage winter storm ripped a new inlet through the barrier island in January 1980, exposing *Gate City* more than any time since divers first visited her. During the diving season it was hard to believe it was the same wreck, with steel plates containing portholes exposed and dead eyes, block and tackles, and other artifacts strewn about.

The U.S. Corp of Engineers filled in the new inlet with sand and the longshore current covered the newly exposed areas of wreckage with sand. The coastal passenger steamer *Gate City* continues to present an ever-changing image to those who are interested in her history and the adventure of underwater exploration.

In February 1900, after the ship was lost, *Gate City*'s cabin boy, H.J. Elmore of East Boston, wrote a poem. The following are selected stanzas.

The Wreck of the Gate City

The Steamer Gate City *for Boston sailed,*
With the weather bright and clear,
None thought of danger on that trip.
As the ship her course did steer;

The weather changed, the fog shut down,
There was trouble then in store,
With Shinnecock Light almost in sight,
The ship she went ashore

It was a welcome sound to the shipwrecked crew,
The brave Life Savers' cheer,
They knew that help was close at hand,
They had no cause for fear.

A man is rescued from *Gate City* by breeches buoy.

Center: the stranded steamer quickly became a tourist attraction.

Below: steam powered equipment was used to salvage the wreck and even iron hull plates on the land side were removed. *Courtesy of Harry Huson.*

Bottom: An aerial photo of *Gate City* taken by Ed Pinto in 1994

Above: Some of the trees and shrubs that grace the Hamptons owe their lineage to trees and shrubs from *Louis Philippe* that ran aground at Mecox in 1842. *Courtesy of the Enoch Pratt Free Library, Baltimore.*
Bottom: *Elmiranda* stranded in 1894 off Wainscott; crew member coming ashore in breeches buoy. *Courtesy of the Suffolk County Historical Society.*

Benjamin B. Church aground at Mecox in 1894. *Courtesy of Southampton Historical Museum.*

R.M.S. OREGON—
CUNARD'S FIRST DISASTER

Type of vessel: transatlantic passenger liner
Where built: John Elder & Company, Fairfield, Scotland
Launched: 1883
Length/beam: 520' / 54'
Gross tons: 7,375
Sunk: March 14, 1886
Cause of sinking: collision
Location: about 15 miles south southwest of Moriches Inlet
Approximate depth of water: 130 feet

THE TRAVELING PUBLIC has always been in a hurry to get from one place to another, whether in cars, trains, planes — even on luxury ships. That fascination for speed was responsible for the steamship *Oregon*'s existence. The course of the maritime race was the breadth of the Atlantic Ocean. The contestants were the steamship lines and the prize was the Atlantic Blue Riband (ribbon), a British maritime term for outstanding achievement. It was awarded for the fastest transatlantic passage, and served to inspire designers, builders, and owners to new levels of ocean liner speed.

Cunard took the record from America's Collins Line in 1862 and held it till the British Inman Line took it in 1867 with *City of Paris*. The other British steamship company vying for the honor, White Star Line, established a new record with *Britanic* in 1876. Stephen Guion, president of the Guion Line, vowed to break the British monopoly and bring the Atlantic Blue Riband back to the United States. His earlier attempts with *Dakota*, *Montana*, and *Nevada* were unsuccessful. He had experimented with a new water-tube boiler design. The money wasted on the project eventually contributed to the financial collapse of the Guion Line.

In 1879, Guion launched *Arizona*, built by John Elder & Company of Fairfield, Scotland. Elder later became Fairfield Shipbuilding and Engineering Company. To Guion's delight, *Arizona*'s was the fastest maiden voyage on record, but it did not win the Blue Riband. That was to come later the same year. He followed with the larger and more powerful *Alaska*, which won the award with a crossing in under seven days.

Cunard reacted by ordering two new superliners, *Eturia* and *Umbria*, from the builders of *Arizona* and *Alaska*. Guion struck back in 1881 with an order for the builders to lay the keel of *Oregon*. She was the leading edge of ocean transportation, swift, immense, and beautiful. Three years later, she won the Blue Riband with a speed of 17.48 knots.

The new empress of the sea was constructed of iron, 501 feet 5 inches in length at the waterline and 520 feet overall. She had a beam of 54 feet 2 inches and displaced 7,375 gross tons and a displacement of 12,966 tons at a draft of 28 feet.

Oregon. Sketch by Frank Braynard.

Oregon was fitted with four complete decks, a turtle back deck forward and aft, and a long promenade deck. The hull had nine bulkheads, seven of which extended to the upper deck. Her three-cylinder compound engine operated at 64 r.p.m., to produce 3,000 n.h.p. and 12,000 i.h.p.—the most powerful machinery afloat. Nine steel boilers, including one auxiliary, were 16 ¾ feet long and 16 ½ feet in diameter. Each was fired by eight furnaces operating at 110 pounds per square inch. The engine room required a crew of 87 engineers, a chief, ten assistants, and 76 firemen and stokers, and consumed 268 to 280 tons of coal daily at full speed. Her single iron screw-propeller measured 24 feet in diameter.

Shipbuilders of the day shied away from total reliance on steam power. Guion also included four full-rigged masts and sails, two forward square rig and two fore-and-aft rigs. There is no record that the cumbersome reserve power was ever used, even at the end of her career when *Oregon* drifted helplessly while she was sinking.

The new liner was a "traveling palace," with 153 large, ventilated, and well-lighted staterooms, mostly on the main deck. Accommodations were provided for 360 first-class and 92 second-class passengers. The majority of the first-class cabins were designed for two passengers only. That was an improvement in comfort over the more crowded contemporary facilities. An elegant ladies room graced the Promenade Deck. Its extravagant furnishings contrasted sharply with the less commodious accommodations in the stern that handled 1,100 steerage passengers. The 'tween decks were fitted so they could be cleared of cargo to accommodate 1,000 more steerage passengers.

The grand saloon was on the main deck, forward of the engines. Its dimensions were 65 feet long by 54 feet wide, so lofty that the lowest ceiling was nine feet high. Parquet flooring underfoot and a white-and-gold ceiling overhead were separated by walls adorned with satinwood panels and gilded walnut pilasters. A massive cupola extended 20 feet above the center of the ceiling to a skylight of multi-colored glass that remained open for ventilation, even in inclement weather.

Like Guion's *Arizona* and *Alaska* before her, *Oregon* was lighted by the new Edison electric lamp. They were the first to adopt that scientific marvel to illuminate luxury liners.

Oregon flew the American flag for only 12 months. By June of 1884, Guion was in desperate financial condition. Boiler design problems in *Dakota* and *Montana* and the too rapid expansion of his fleet, three large liners in four years, had depleted his resources. The shipbuilder, still waiting to be paid, repossessed *Oregon* and sold her to the Cunard Line for 616,000 pounds sterling ($3,080,000). It was a bitter blow for Guion, particularly two months later, when the new Cunard liner re-captured the Blue Riband for the British with a crossing in six days, nine hours and 42 minutes at an average speed of 18.14 knots. A year later another Cunard liner, the giant *Etruria* captured the coveted award at an average of 18.93 knots.

An ornate award was created in 1935 by Britisher Harold Hales to embody the mythical Blue Riband.

Oregon was the last American ship to hold the transatlantic record until 1952, when *United States*, which had a maximum speed of 38.32 knots, made the crossing in three days, ten hours and 40 minutes. None of today's liners can come close to that record passage. The British, however, won back the coveted award by using a small passenger ferry to break *United States'* record in 1990.

Oregon had contributed only briefly to Cunard's long reign as the steamship line with the fastest transportation between Europe and America. But she would be long remembered as the victim of the shipping line's first major disaster in 43 years.

COLLISION

In the dim predawn of Sunday, March 14, 1886, *Oregon*, steaming at full speed toward New York, was five miles off the shore of Fire Island. There were 673 passengers (186 first-class, 66 second-class, and 421 steerage) and a crew of 205 aboard. Although those numbers may seem impressive, they were less than half the vessel's capacity.

At about 4:20 a.m., most passengers were still asleep, but the decks were being stacked high with their baggage in preparation for entry into port. First Officer William George Matthews was on the bridge. The few passengers who were awake and on deck observed the lights of a vessel approaching on a northeast tack. No one aboard the liner granted the approaching vessel more than passing attention until she suddenly loomed up on the port rail, a deeply laden three-masted schooner that seemed oblivious to the luxury liner in her path. The schooner drove hard into the iron plates of *Oregon's* port hull, amidships. The liner shuddered, and the wooden schooner rebounded and drifted off, seemingly out of control.

The collision opened gaping holes in the Cunard steamer's hull. One, as large as a 9- by 12-foot room, was below the grand dining saloon, fortunately above the water line. Two others were smaller, about a quarter the size, but one was below the water line. The sea gushed in and flooded the liner's boiler room, stopping the engine. *Oregon* drifted without power, with more than 30 square feet of her hull open to the sea.

Captain Cottier was asleep when the schooner struck. He rushed to the bridge and concluded that the luxurious liner was in no immediate danger of sinking, but passengers were awakened and ordered to the decks as a precaution.

ABANDON SHIP

One cabin passenger, Mrs. W.H. Hurst of Brooklyn, described the scene as "something awful." Confused passengers milled aimlessly on the open decks, half-dressed or in pajamas and nightgowns. Steerage passengers were crying, screaming, and praying. She could hear the horrible profanity of begrimed and half-dressed firemen and stokers above the uproar. They seemed to have mutinied; officers had little or no control over them. She added, "Myself and other ladies and some children were so roughly pushed about that several of us were thrown violently to the deck." The officers, assisted by some of the male cabin passengers, had to use belaying pins to subdue the mutinous men and prevent them from taking all the lifeboats. However, according to Mrs. Hurst, "The first away was filled with them."

Another passenger complained, "... a more cowardly set of rascals than some of the crew of the *Oregon* were never got together outside of a jail ..." He accused one group of firemen of taking possession of a lifeboat and preparing to leave without any passengers. An officer interceded, but although he beat them with a heavy piece of wood, they would not give up their places. However, he did manage to get some passengers into the boat.

One of the passengers, a Mr. Sturges, commented that he had not used a profane word since the first night of the Chicago fire. But he "cursed frightfully" when he saw a lifeboat half filled with firemen leave the ship. He called them to return but was ignored. Then he drew his revolver, aimed at a crew member who seemed to be in charge and threatened, "... if you don't come back I will kill you ..." They returned and loaded 16 passengers into the boat. Mr. Sturges observed that he felt he would have been "... justified in killing some of the rascals ..."

The lifeboats that were not commandeered by the firemen and stokers were filled with passengers in an orderly manner. But there were too few boats. Mrs. Hurst said that her heart sank when she saw from her lifeboat that half the passengers, all male, and crew were left behind with only life preservers, and would not survive for long in the cold water. It seemed that there was no hope for them. She said "... the suspense was simply horrible, while minutes seemed to grow into hours and hours into years ..."

RESCUE

Oregon was to have been guided through Ambrose Channel into New York Harbor by a pilot who was aboard the pilot boat *Phantom*, waiting to be placed aboard the liner when *Oregon*'s distress signals were sighted. The pilot boat arrived at the scene at about 7:00 a.m., followed two hours later by the schooner *Fanny A. Gorham*, bound for Boston out of Jacksonville, Florida. Her skipper, Captain Mahoney, reportedly was reluctant to take passengers aboard because he lacked provisions until *Oregon*'s Captain Cottier convinced him that the need was not for food, but to keep the survivors afloat.

By 11:00 a.m. all the passengers and crew were temporarily aboard the two small vessels. An hour later, the German steamship *Fulda* appeared and transferred the survivors aboard for transportation to New York. Her Captain Ringk extended every consideration to make the short stay aboard his vessel as comfortable as possible.

SINKING

At 12:45 p.m., approximately eight hours after the collision, *Oregon* went to the bottom.

The Cunard Line had lost a magnificent ship, but had been spared its first loss of a passenger. Some passengers ascribed the accident to "gross carelessness" by the ship's officers, who had miscalculated their distance from the schooner. That does not seem to have been the case, based on the testimony of First Officer Matthews at the Board of Trade inquiry that followed. He testified that he took charge of the ship at 4:00 a.m. on the starboard side of the bridge, with the Fourth Officer on the port side. The night was clear and three men were on lookout duty.

The first sign of another vessel in the vicinity was a single bright light off the port bow. Matthews described it as a light just held up for a time because it disappeared instantly. He thought it might be a pilot boat with her mast headlight out, because pilot boats do not carry side lights. When asked about the height of the light, Matthews responded that it seemed to be in the hands of a man standing on deck. There were no colored port or starboard lights, nor were there any other lights at all.

Matthew's first impression was that someone on the deck of a vessel without regulation lights had been startled by the approach of the liner, and had reached for the most accessible light and held it up. Officers and lookouts saw the light at the same time. Matthews immediately ordered the helm put hard aport, but too late to change course before contact was made. At full speed, the ship might run a quarter of a mile after the wheel was spun before changing course.

Matthews had seen neither sails nor the outline of a schooner until it was on the point of striking the steamer. He described it as a large schooner, but could tell little else because everything happened so quickly. Two of the three lookouts said that they saw the schooner 30 or 40 yards away, off the port bow of the steamer, bearing down on her under full sail. That was too late for evasive action. Any object would have to be sighted at least a mile away to ensure safety of the steamer.

The schooner struck a few feet forward of the bridge with shuddering impact, and Matthews signaled the engineer to stop the engines. He turned to look for the schooner, but there was nothing. He testified that he heard no noise or conversation from the schooner's crew. No words were exchanged between the two vessels at any time. Matthews had not ordered a boat lowered for the schooner after the accident because it was still dark and he had no idea where the unknown vessel was.

Captain Cottier wanted everyone assembled on deck. However, once they were on deck, little was done for them. Most of the passengers and crew lost all their personal effects, except for the clothes they wore and an occasional purse. If the ship's officers had issued clear, uniform instructions to stewards during the crisis, valuable papers, money and costly personal effects might have been saved.

Oregon veered off immediately after the impact. Crew members confirmed that the schooner's foremast went by the board; they saw the mast topple. Captain Cottier, First Officer Matthews and the Fourth Officer agreed that the schooner probably sank at once because the tremendous force of the collision must have split the colliding vessel from stem to stern.

The New York Times offered an explanation of why the schooner's lights might not have been seen. The steamer was heading west and was struck on the port side. The wind was blowing from the west and the schooner was on a port tack, her sails bellying out to starboard as she approached the liner. The schooner's head sails would have concealed her starboard light and her port light would have been out of view on the opposite side of the ship. The momentary white light was probably the binnacle light, seen momentarily between her sails when she was close upon the steamer.

On Thursday, March 18, a fishing vessel retrieved a schooner's yawl, 25 miles southeast of the *Oregon* wreck. The capsized boat showed no ship's name, but obviously had been cut loose in a hurry. The connecting lines had been clumsily hacked with a knife or ax and the drain was open; the drain plug was still in its storage compartment. A link was established between the yawl and the colliding schooner when one of *Oregon*'s mail bags and several broken wooden cases were found near the yawl.

Wreckage identified as the cutwater of a medium-size vessel washed ashore at Asbury Park, New Jersey on Saturday, March 20th. It was undoubtedly part of the bow of a schooner, but was without identification. The most likely prospect was the schooner *Charles H. Morse*, which left Baltimore for Boston on March 6, with a cargo of coal. An accompanying schooner, *Florence J. Allen*, was separated from her the night of the disaster, near the collision site. Two days later, *Allen* arrived at Boston, but *Morse*, with her captain, Alonzo Wilder, and eight others were never seen again.

A Captain Manson, who had sailed aboard *Morse*, identified the yawl that had been found as one of hers.

Oregon was valued at $1,250,000 and her cargo of china, earthenware, fruit, fabrics, and sundries at $700,000. Other losses included $216,000 in personal effects and $1,000,000 in negotiable coupons and currency.

Several private boats cruised the area of the sinking for days, recovering cases, barrels, mail bags, and steamer trunks. Trunks, valises, and other personal effects were sent to Brooklyn for identification and claiming. Floating mail bags were picked up by passing vessels many miles from the accident. The R.M.S. before the name *Oregon* denotes Royal Mail Steamer. There had been 620 sacks of mail on board; 75 were taken off before the ship went down, and 237 others were eventually recovered. Much that was recovered from the sea was so water-soaked that names and addresses were indecipherable.

INVESTIGATION

The extent of the Cunard Company's liability developed into a major issue. The line's chief agent in New York protested the claim of one female passenger for $15,000 worth of diamonds. It was his opinion that she had enough time to recover her gems before the ship was abandoned. Another claimant explained that securely barred iron doors blocked his effort to return to his stateroom for his currency.

Cunard could be held legally responsible for personal losses only if there was evidence that the sinking resulted from the negligence or incompetence of the ship's crew. The Liverpool Board of Trade was to conduct a full investigation of the disaster, and the company would be bound by its findings. However, passenger tickets included a $50 limitation on individual liability.

The Cunard agent authorized feeding and caring for immigrant passengers at company expense. A few, who were headed west for Minnesota, Dakota and Nebraska, had lost their railway tickets with their luggage. About 80 steerage passengers continued their journeys at Cunard expense. Many also hoped for compensation for their lost luggage, but were turned down.

A Court of Inquiry was held in England by the Liverpool Board of Trade, with a finding for the owners and officers of the steamer, relieving them of liability. However, it did find First Officer Matthews remiss in his calculation of distance between *Oregon* and the schooner, but not sufficiently remiss to warrant punishment. Cunard, however, held Captain Cottier responsible for the loss of *Oregon*, and released him, even though he was not on the bridge at the time of the collision. He was 45 years of age, the youngest captain in the fleet, and had held his Master's papers for 20 years in the employ of Cunard. His dismissal was justified by Cunard by failure to check bulkhead doors daily, as specified by company policy. He had testified that with her large engine compartment bulkhead doors jammed open by coal dust he could not save the ship. He was also criticized for not recognizing the vessel's plight sooner, and beaching her or reaching shallow water, where she might have been raised.

Oregon had been heralded as one of the few large steamers that could remain afloat, even with her large engine compartment flooded. It was feared that her sinking might destroy confidence in the watertight compartment system. There were stories that the bulkheads at either end of the engine compartment might have been closed, but did not remain water-tight. But those doors were not closed. They were jammed open, and water could flow freely into adjoining compartments. If they had been closed, the collision probably would not have cost Cunard their beautiful liner. In a similar collision in June 1880, the steamship *Anchoria*, of the Anchor Line, had been struck in the side by *Queen*, of the National Line, and reached port safely because of her watertight compartments.

No lives were lost in the *Oregon* disaster, but if there had been only two instead of eight hours between collision and sinking, many would have gone down with the ship. Fewer than half the 878 passengers and crew could have been crowded onto the lifeboats and life rafts. The lifeboats would hold only 365, but that was more than was required by the current regulations. The timely arrival of the rescuing pilot boat and schooner allowed each of the ten lifeboats and three life rafts to make four to five trips back to the sinking steamer.

A year later, the House of Commons appointed a Select Committee to investigate lifeboat requirements. Despite the evidence of need in *Oregon*'s sinking, the committee found that regulations should not be changed. It concluded that passenger ships could not, without great inconvenience, carry enough lifeboats for all passengers and crew. Twenty-six years later, on April 14, 1912, *Titanic*, the largest passenger ship in the world, sank on her maiden voyage. More than 1,500 of 2,206 passengers and crew aboard perished because the Board of Trade had ignored the warning provided by *Oregon*. A maximum of 1,178 could have been accommodated by *Titanic*'s lifeboats, even if they had been filled to capacity.

SALVAGE

The day after *Oregon*'s sinking, the Merrit Wrecking Company dispatched the tug *Rescue* and the schooner *Post* to the scene with hard-hat divers aboard. Three of *Oregon*'s masts were still above water. The foremast had disappeared, but her mainmast stood 30 feet out of the water. Her mizzenmast was 25 feet high and the jiggermast 11 feet.

The wreck was considered a navigational hazard, so the Lighthouse Board placed a lightship at the site (for one year, the shortest official time for a U.S. lightship station) to alert shipping to the potential danger.

Inclement weather limited divers to only one half of a day of work out of the first ten days. They and the salvage crew spent that time recovering floating baggage and freight from the sea.

The only personal property that bore identification was a leather stateroom trunk with the initials "E.D.M." marked on one end. It probably belonged to a Mr. E.D. Morgan, who was listed as a first-class passenger. Ninety-three years later, co-author Henry Keatts, less encumbered than the earlier, hard-hat divers, recovered a brush bearing the same "E.D.M." initials—too late to return it to Mr. Morgan.

When the weather cleared, diver examination of the port side of the wreck revealed that the vessel had broken in two between hatches #2 and #3, and there was a 3 ½- by 9-foot hole about 25 feet aft of the break.

The divers concluded that *Oregon* could not be raised. Tackle so large that it didn't even exist would be needed to lift her through 132 feet of seawater, even in calm conditions, and heavy seas prevail in the area of the wreck. No vessel of her size had ever been raised from such a depth.

A Merritt Wrecking Company diver with *Oregon*'s masts and salvage vessels in view. *Frank Leslie's Illustrated Newspaper.*

Six Merrit Company divers under the supervision of Captain Edward S. Dennison worked through that spring and summer, removing mail and cargo while the ship gradually broke up. Steam pumps supplied them with air through a five-ply rubber hose that was resistant to breaking or cutting. Their copper helmets, with three glass viewing ports, were connected to brass and rubber suits. Lead weights attached to their chest and back, and heavy lead-weighted boots allowed them to walk on the wreck. A lifeline (rope) attached to their waist allowed them to be pulled to the surface in an emergency. Also, it was their only means of communication with the tenders. One or more tugs on the rope could signal hoist the crate of cargo or pull me up. The deep-sea-diving gear, weighing more than 150 pounds, was cumbersome and dangerous. The air-hose could be cut by a sharp piece of wreckage or the lifeline could become entangled in the wreck. Also, divers had to contend with caisson disease, named for the affliction that paralyzed or killed men working in pressurized chambers (caissons) while laying the foundation for the Brooklyn Bridge, today commonly known as "the bends." At the time, divers did not know the problem involved compressed gases saturating body tissues, but they knew their "bottom time" was limited, or they would contract the debilitating, often fatal, disease. Today's divers use dive tables that list bottom times at different depths. The Merritt salvage divers worked under water in their hard-hat equipment from 30 minutes to an hour at a time. Today's dive tables limit dives at *Oregon*'s depth to only 20 minutes unless the diver plans to decompress (off-gas) before surfacing.

Bill Dwyer's, one of Merritt's hard-hat divers, job was to recover cargo. After he attached a rope to a wooden crate of cargo he would move out of the way and signal the salvage vessel to use its steam-powered winch to hoist the heavy crate. During one dive, after signaling for the crate to be lifted, Dwyer watched in horror as his air-hose started rising with the rope. He quickly looked up and saw that the air-hose and rope were fouled, but more frightening his lifeline was entangled in an iron beam.

As Dwyer was pulled off the bottom his air-hose snapped and air began to gush out of the separated hose. With his heavy dive gear he could not swim or jump to retrieve the air supply. He could not signal to the men above, because the lifeline was wrapped around the beam.

The tenders on the salvage vessel noticed an increase in air bubbles streaming to the surface, but were not alarmed. Dwyer could have been adjusting the air in his suit by venting air out of the valve in the helmet. However, when the crate reached the surface they saw the ruptured air-hose and immediately started pulling on the lifeline. Fortunately, the line did not break, and after a hard struggle it pulled loose from the wreckage allowing them to pull Dwyer to the surface.

Dwyer survived the incident and continued the salvage work on other, uneventful by comparison, dives.

By late August, the divers reported that the wreck was rapidly disintegrating and the bow had fallen over into the sand. They ended their salvage efforts after recovering most of the cargo, and *Oregon* was left undisturbed until World War II. The Navy knew it only as an unidentified wreck that was occasionally depth-charged during training exercises.

PRESENT CONDITION

Beginning in 1958, scuba divers (an acronym for self-contained underwater breathing apparatus) heard reports of large codfish being caught on a wreck referred to as *Oregon*. The location about 15 miles south southwest of Moriches Inlet, corresponded to what was known of the Cunard liner's sinking. In 1960, divers recovered plates, cups and chamber pots bearing the Cunard Steamship Company emblem from the wreck. Other plates bore the Guion Line insignia. No more positive proof of *Oregon*'s identity could be desired.

More than 100 years after the steamship brought transatlantic speed honors to the United States, she has become recognized as one of the most interesting and exciting dives on the northeast coast. Her depth varies from about 130 feet in the sand to approximately 120 feet on top of the rubble. A giant steam engine extends 60 feet from the bottom, and divers can cruise around the huge boilers. Two large blades of the iron screw-propeller thrust boldly out of the sand.

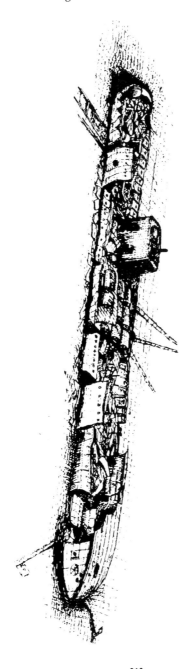

The wreck's condition in 1980. *Courtesy of Captain Steve Bielenda.*

The 130-foot depth is at the limit of safe diving according to scuba certification agencies. Although no lives were lost when she sank, since her rediscovery, *Oregon* has claimed the lives of at least two scuba divers.

MISCELLANEOUS SHIPWRECKS

JOHN & LUCY—1668

On March 22, 1668, *John & Lucy* was en route from Rhode Island to New York when she struck a rock off Fishers Island. The East Hampton Town records of Justice of the Peace John Mulford state that on board were "15 men and 2 sheepe, 2 goats, 3 mares and the ship's Dogg called Lion, and several Catts. The ship remained stranded on the rock and there was nothing but a terrible distraction and confusion all the night long, one erging this the other that, doing one thing and then undoing it, doing all things and yet nothing ... at break of day the ship beating so extremely that all courage was taken way, and suddenly the boats were full of men."

In the confusion and haste three men were left behind when the others abandoned ship. The ship floated off the rock at high tide and drifted ashore near Montauk Point.

CAPTIAIN BELL—1700s

In the early 1700s, tea was introduced to the East End, but few people knew how to brew it. One family boiled it and ate it like porridge and a man spread the leaves on his bread and butter. An old copper teakettle at the East Hampton Historical Society museum in Clinton Academy, Amagansett was recovered from the beach after the ship *Captain Bell* wrecked at Montauk in the 1700s. It was the first teakettle seen on the East End and no one could imagine its use. Finally the farmer who found it carried the object to East Hampton and showed it to Samuel Hedges, who was considered to be the wisest person in the village. He decided it was the ship's lamp, and all agreed.

Clinton Academy, founded in 1786, was the first private school chartered by New York State.

MARY—1701

During the early Colonial Period, the British Government forbade commerce "with foreign plantations." Smuggling between French Canada and the British Colonies flourished. *The Journal of the voyage of the sloop Mary,* written by E.B. O'Callaghan and published in 1866, describes the cargo the sloop transported to Canada and the contraband she was carrying back when she ran aground at Montauk Point in 1701. The sloop transported cheese, flour, tobacco, and shot to the French in Quebec and loaded brandy, claret, wine, furs, cotton cloth, and beads in Canada. On the return trip she anchored off Cape Ann, stopped at Misery Island off Salem Harbor, rounded Cape Cod, and reached Martha's Vineyard 25 days after leaving Quebec. The *Journal* states that the sloop encountered "thick weather," and her crew was navigating by taking "Latt'd by Judgment." The *Journal* stops at Martha's Vineyard, but records in Albany, New York, state that seven days later *Mary* "drove on shore as a Wrecke, not having any p'rson on Board her the 23 day of November, 1701."

The sloop's captain and owner, Samuel Vetch, mysteriously turned up later, but the vessel was seized by the East Hampton Justice of the Peace, who condemned the sloop and her cargo for smuggling. Prominent citizens, including John Gardiner, Lord of the Manor of Gardiners Island, and Sheriff John Wick were responsible for supervising recovery of the sloop's cargo. However some cotton cloth and barrels of brandy disappeared while en route from the wreck site to the warehouse where they were to be stored. The goods were transported by wagons to the warehouse and later in an affidavit it was reported that some unknown person "did bair away to the woods." Captain Vetch was arrested and fined for trading with the French.

One hundred copies of the *Journal* were printed by J. Munsell in Albany, New York in 1866. One copy is in the New York City Public Library, a copy is in the Suffolk County Historical Society, and another is in the East Hampton Public Library.

OCEAN—1800

The brig *Ocean* was en route from Bremen, Germany to Philadelphia with a cargo of wine and brandy on January 17, 1800, when a violent storm drove her ashore near Sag Harbor. The stern filled with water and the captain drowned in his cabin. Waves destroyed the lifeboats before they could be launched. John Hulbert, a Sag Harbor notary public, was told by a member of the crew that the ship's mate, "at the risk of his Life cast himself into the Surf and got on Shore and Assisted in getting the Passengers and Crew on Shore, and in half an hour after the people were Landed the Quarter Deck burst off and the main deck went to Pieces and the Brig became a Wreck."

VERONI—1806

The brig *Veroni* was en route from the West Indies to New London, Connecticut under the command of Captain A. Clark on January 6, 1806, when she ran aground off Westhampton Beach. The cargo was salvaged, but the brig was a total loss.

MARIA LOUISA—1811

The great Christmas blizzard of 1811 sank many ships around Long Island. In *History of Long Island* (1839) Benjamin F. Thompson wrote: "On the night of the 23rd of December ... commenced one of the most remarkable snowstorms and gales of wind ever experienced together, upon Long Island. It came from the northeast, and swept over Long Island with dreadful violence."

In his version of *History of Long Island* (1845), Nathaniel S. Prime wrote: "The change took place suddenly in the night, the mercury falling almost to zero. Between 50 and 60 vessels foundered in the Sound, or were driven on the northern shore of the Island in that terrible night. In some cases the entire crews perished, while in others, those who found their way ashore were objects of greater commiseration than the dead, being horribly frozen. The writer can speak with entire confidence on this subject, as he was an eyewitness to some of the ravages of that awful tempest."

About 20 people perished within ten miles of Prime's home; he helped bury four, all from the same vessel, on Christmas Day. Prime wrote, "That storm will never be forgotten by the last survivor of that generation."

In *Memories of Gardiners Island*, Sarah Diodati Gardiner wrote that the 230-ton French ship *Maria Louisa* wrecked at Gardiners Island on Christmas Day, but in 1812, not 1811. That story of the disaster, handed down by word of mouth, was almost certainly the Christmas blizzard of 1811.

Some of the ship's crew perished, but those who survived were cared for at the manor house on Gardiners Island.

Jeannette Rattray wrote in *Ship Ashore* that John Lyon Gardiner, great-grandfather of Miss Gardiner, "was supervising the work of salvage on horseback from the shore, when he noticed a Maltese cat clinging to a floating piece of wood. He told his men to rescue the cat and brought it home tied up in a big silk bandanna handkerchief. The cat's descendants were numerous. As a little girl, Miss Gardiner was given a descendant of the celebrated Gardiners Island cat, and named it Maria Louisa, for the ill-fated French ship."

Rattray also wrote of a ship, *Maria L. Stowell*, that wrecked on Gardiners Island on December 25, 1811, with three lost and 18 saved. The full name of Miss Gardiner's ship was most likely *Maria Louisa Stowell*.

LIVE OAK—1814

The American ship *Live Oak* became known as the "Gunpowder Ship" after a fire erupted while at sea and she was run ashore at Shinnecock Point in July 1814. The burning ship's cargo was 900 kegs of gunpowder and the fire was beyond control. The captain and crew abandoned ship a few hours before the fire reached the gunpowder. A tremendous explosion tore the ship apart and broke hundreds of windows in Southampton Village. One scrap of iron from the ship was found a half-mile away.

HELEN—1820

On January 17, 1820, *Helen*, en route from France to New York, ran aground off Southampton. Six crewmen in the bow survived, but Captain Huguet, his officers, and eight passengers were lost. A memorial stone in Southampton's North End Burying Ground is inscribed, "Sacred to the Memory of Major Robert Sterry, who was shipwrecked and lost with the ship *Helen*, Jan. 17, 1820, aged 37 years."

VINEYARD—1830

The remains of the brig *Vineyard* lie about 15 miles south of the village of Southampton. The ship left New Orleans on November 9, 1830 with a cargo of cotton, molasses, sugar, and $54,000 in Mexican gold consigned to Stephen Girard of Philadelphia.

Off Cape Hatteras, sailor Charles Gibbs and cook Thomas Wansley, killed the captain and mate and threw their bodies overboard. Gibbs took command of the brig and sailed to Long Island's south shore. He scuttled the ship off Southampton. Gibbs and Wansley took the brig's longboat (the longest boat carried by a sailing ship) and $21,000 in gold, and sailed to Coney Island. The rest of the crew put off in the brig's jollyboat (a medium sized ship's boat) with $33,000 in gold, but a storm capsized the smaller boat and the gold and men were lost.

Gibbs and Wansley were apprehended, but not before burying their gold in the sand. After a lengthy trial, they were convicted of the murders, and on April 22, 1831, they were hanged on Ellis Island before a huge crowd of spectators.

During the trial it was discovered that over 14 years, Gibbs had taken part in the pirating of 40 ships. For some disaffected sailors, the rewards of piracy outweighed the risks. The infamous Captain Bartholomew Roberts (Black Bart) most succinctly summed up the pirates' view: "In an honest service there is thin rations, low wages and hard labor; in this, plenty and satiety, pleasure and ease, liberty and power; and who would not balance credit on this side, when all the hazard that is run for it, at worst, is only a sour look or two at choking. No, a merry life and a short one shall be my motto."

In 1722, at the age of 3?, Black Bart was killed during a battle with the British warship *Swallow*. His crew was captured and taken to Cape Coast Castle on the coast of Africa, where they were tried for piracy. Seventeen were sentenced to prison in London, but 13 died during the voyage home. Fifty-two were hanged and the bodies of the 18 men considered to be the worst offenders were dipped in tar, bound with metal straps and hung in chains from gibbets (T-shaped, wooden structures from which executed criminals were hung for public viewing) on three prominent hills as a reminder of the consequences of piracy to those passing on the road below. Their bodies rotted rapidly in the tropical climate, then dried in the sun and swayed back and forth in the offshore breeze—macabre sentries looking out across the sea where they had plundered so many helpless merchant ships.

EDWARD QUESNEL—1839

In May 1839, the sailing vessel *Edward Quesnel* ran aground near the Napeague Life-Saving Station. Heavy breakers tore the wooden-hulled ship apart, and scattered her cargo of 2,300 barrels of whale oil and the bodies of the second mate and six other men along the beach. Fifty-eight years later, H.P. Hedges in the *History of East Hampton* wrote: "The bodies were drawn up on the beach near the banks. A ghastly array of corpses, pitiful to behold.... That vision of lifeless bodies lying in a row on Napeague beach, pale, motionless, ghastly, has followed and haunted me in the darkness of night from that day to this."

POCAHONTAS—1839

The brig *Pocahontas* was en route from Cadiz, Spain to Newburyport, Massachusetts under the command of Captain James G. Cook. During the night of December 22, 1839, the brig struck a rock reef off Plum Island. By morning she was dismasted and breaking up by the waves sweeping over her. Spectators on the beach could see one man, apparently dead, lashed to the taffrail (the rail around the stern) and two others clinging to the bowsprit. One was washed off and disappeared from sight. Shortly after the other man was swept off, but he managed to grab a dangling rope and climbed back up. Again a wave pulled him off and this time he did not reappear. None of the 12-man crew survived and the brig was a total loss.

LOUIS PHILIPPE—1842

Some of the trees and shrubs that grace the Hamptons owe their lineage to trees and shrubs from the landscape of France. The Union Line's 794-ton, square-rigged ship *Louis Philippe* was en route from Havre, France to New York when she ran aground on April 14, 1842, at Mecox, between Bridgehampton and Southampton. The 92 officers, crew, and passengers were safely landed.

Eighteen days later the ship was refloated by tugboats and taken in tow by the steamer *Mutual Safety*. However, in order to pull her off the beach she was lightened by removing part of her cargo of dry goods, trees, shrubs, and champagne. The trees and shrubs she carried were thrown overboard and floated ashore where they were recovered by the locals and planted in their yards. The most beautiful were the lindens. Other types recovered were larches, beeches, chestnuts, elms, and fruit trees. It was reported in the *Long Island Forum* that some of the elms that lined East Hampton's main street until the 1938 hurricane blew them down came from *Louis Phillippe*.

The shrubs included laburnum with their drooping clusters of yellow flowers and rose bushes. The hardy rose bushes produced flowers known as "Shipwreck Roses." They were fragrant and deep pink in color. Some descendants of the original plants are still around.

MAJESTIC—1845

When the brig *Majestic* ran aground in 1845 near today's west jetty of Moriches Inlet, her cargo calmed the heavy breakers. Oil of peppermint and anise poured out of the broken wooden hull, smoothing the seas, allowing the crew to lower lifeboats and row ashore.

HENRY—1851

A surfman, Samuel A. Cook, at the Mecox Life-Saving Station

recorded the following in his diary: "June 27th, 1851. Came on shore, Barque *Henry*, of London, loaded with Chalk and Linseed Oil, and 104 passengers, who were all saved. Oil saved also, Ship and Chalk lost."

PERSIAN—1853

The first Moriches station was built by the Life-Saving Benevolent Association of New York with money furnished by the U.S. Treasury Department. The Association built 14 stations on Long Island during 1849-50. The importance of the Moriches station and its equipment was demonstrated by the grounding of the passenger ship *Persian* in April 1853.

The station keeper, E.D. Topping, wrote the following letter concerning the rescue of the 218 passengers and crew and the ship's cargo to the president of the Atlantic Mutual Insurance Company: "... The unfortunate passengers have expressed their thanks for what your Benevolent Association has done erecting houses for the shipwrecked on our shores. The storm ... was very severe. Many of the passengers are sick (smallpox); and one of them, who was unable to walk, had to be lifted on a litter. The women and children, and the sick, would have perished but for the life-boat building, as it was nearly impossible to get them off the beach.... We have not been able to get at the cargo today; but hope to do so tomorrow. The ship is badly broken up, and I presume she will be a total wreck...."

ROBERT—1855

In 1855 *Robert*, out of London with a cargo of 1,000 casks of Madeira wine, came ashore off Wickapogue. The cargo was saved and transported to Sag Harbor for reshipment. However, during the overland shipment 400 casks of wine disappeared. During the trip from Sag Harbor up Long Island Sound to New York City another 100 casks mysteriously disappeared from the transporting vessels.

DANIEL WEBSTER—1856

The brig *Daniel Webster* was en route from the Canary Islands with a cargo of fruit, nuts, rice, and salt when she ran aground at

Amagansett on March 25, 1856. John Lawrence a member of the crew, married a 17-year-old Amagansett girl and settled in East Hampton.

FLYING CLOUD—1856

Lighthouse keepers were often involved in the rescue of wrecked mariners. On December 14, 1856, the brig *Flying Cloud* ran aground near Montauk Lighthouse. Keeper Patrick T. Gould rescued six sailors and was awarded the Gold Life-Saving Medal by the Life-Saving Benevolent Association for his actions.

SOLICITOR—1859

On December 4, 1859, *Solicitor* was en route from the Island of Cephalonia to New York City when a storm blew her ashore off Old Town. Her cargo of 1,605 barrels of Zante currants was strewn along the beach and in subsequent puddings of Long Islanders. All aboard were saved by volunteers from shore. One crewman grumbled because he and his shipmates got their clothes wet during the rescue. The caustic reaction of one lifesaver was the hope that, "the next time they were wrecked it would be in a dry time."

AMSTERDAM—1867

Many ships have grounded on the treacherous reefs and shoals of Montauk Point, even in clear weather. When that projection of land is shrouded in fog, the navigational hazard is immeasurably worse. That was particularly true before the invention of radar and loran (lo[ng] ra[nge] n[avigation]).

   In 1867, the 639-ton, iron-hulled British steamer *Amsterdam*, loaded with a cargo of fruit, wine, and lead, left Malaga, Spain, en route to New York. On October 21, while in a dense fog, she struck rocks about three miles west of Montauk Point, on the south shore. The freighter's hull was badly damaged and she was partially filled with water. Cargo, strewn along the beach for miles, was quickly gathered up by the locals. The cargo was insured for 6,000 pounds sterling by the Great Western Insurance Company. An agent of the company traveled to Montauk to oversee salvage of what remained of the cargo. The 211-foot-long freighter, less than a year old, and valued at 30,000 pounds, was declared a total loss. Only half of the cargo could be salvaged. None of *Amsterdam*'s crew survived. They were buried one-and-a-half miles east of the lifesaving station.

The wreck is only about 50 yards offshore in about 15 feet of water, but lies off property that is privately owned, so access is by boat only.

The freighter's engine extends above water at low tide. The steam engine, covered with seaweed, is often mistaken for a rock, but closer inspection reveals the cylinder openings. Sections of iron hull are scattered about the bottom. From year to year the shifting sand exposes or covers much of the wreckage.

In 1970, a snorkeler found the ship's brass builder's plaque, inscribed with:

AMSTERDAM
Andrew Leslie & Co.
Iron Ship Builders
New Castle on Tyne
1866

In 1978, while scuba diving, a marine biology student found a complete porthole lying in the sand about 50 yards south of the engine. The following year several deadeyes were recovered from a large piece of wreckage west of the engine.

MARY MILNESS—1869

Strong winds, described by the Sag Harbor *Corrector* as a tornado, drove the schooner *Mary Milness* ashore at Montauk on September 8, 1869. The wreck was sold at auction to M.H. Gregory for $670.

The September 18, 1869, *Corrector* stated: "The bodies of the 2nd mate [the captain's brother] and a seaman, lost in the time of the wreck, washed ashore.... The remains of the seaman was interred on Montauk. Those of the mate were taken by Captain F. Parker for interment."

MASSACHUSETTS—1870

At 12:20 a.m. on October 5, 1870, the side-wheel steamer

Massachusetts ran aground off Rocky Point (Southold Town) en route from New York City to New England. The steamer's pilot missed the Horton Point Lighthouse when the side-wheeler passed it five miles to the west.

At the time there was no lifesaving station along the Eastern Long Island shore. The Rocky Point Life-Saving Station was not built until 16 years later. That building is still there, but today it is a two-family residence. The steamer's crew managed to lower a lifeboat on the lee side, but could not handle it in the breakers. They were freight handlers, not seamen.

Using a team of horses and a farm wagon, local residents hauled two rowboats from Orient Harbor to the Sound. They rowed out and rigged lines from the ship to shore and rescued the passengers by pulling the boats back and forth. As the boats neared shore other residents picked up the passengers and carried them over the surf to the beach. They were landed without even getting wet.

Rumors spread that the two men who first boarded the steamer were later rewarded with two barrels of Pillsbury's Best flour because Mr. Pillsbury was among the rescued passengers.

Massachusetts was refloated and continued to transport passengers through Long Island Sound until she was scrapped 11 years later.

ROSINA—1871

The grounding of the bark *Rosina* on February 1, 1871, near the Moriches Life-Saving Station was a boon to local residents. The pounding breakers broke apart the wooden hull and the cargo of brandy was strewn for miles along the shore. Twenty-nine years later the *Brooklyn Daily Eagle* reported that there were still bottles of brandy from the wreck to be found in East Moriches homes. The same newspaper reported on September 1, 1934 that an 80-year-old man said that he was at the wreck site and "walked miles on the cases of brandy that were strewn on the beach." He carried 17 cases home, but when his father found out he "ran a high temperature and made me give them up."

A three-foot long swivel cannon was recovered from wreckage

that washed ashore. Many years later it was donated to the Long Island Maritime museum in West Sayville.

PACIFIC—1871

For generations, beachcombers at East Hampton and Wainscott have occasionally found clay pipes from the sailing ship *Pacific*, that went ashore on June 3, 1871 under full sail. The ship was en route from Glasgow, Scotland to New York when she ran aground. The crew was rescued, but her cargo of clay pipes was thrown overboard to lighten the ship. Almost all the local residents picked up a "beach pipe." Beach pipes are occasionally found today. *Pacific* was refloated.

ROBERT FLETCHER—1872

A year after *Rosina* ran aground off East Moriches, the British bark *Robert Fletcher* stranded about 100 yards from the same spot. Captain Brown ordered his crew to cut away the masts and rigging to prevent the strong wind from tearing the bark to pieces. The ship was en route from China to New York with a valuable cargo of silks and tea when she ran aground. An agent for the Coast Wrecking Company organized removal of the cargo.

A cannon recovered from the ship was often fired to celebrate holidays. Twenty-six years later the cannon exploded when it was fired in East Moriches on Washington's birthday, but no one was hurt.

ALEXANDER LA VALLE—1874

The French steamer *Alexander La Valle* ran aground about one-half-mile east of the village of Southampton, off Wickapogue on January 23, 1874. The 1,500-ton, iron-hulled ship was 243 feet long and was built in 1870 at Nantes, France. The steamer was en route from London to New York with a cargo of 400 tons of ale, port, and other wines, dried fruit, potash, zinc ingots, and rags.

Due to a dense fog, the stranded steamer was not discovered until after daylight. Though there was a heavy surf at the time, the men from the lifesaving station safely removed all 33 on board with a surfboat. The *Sag Harbor Express* reported on January 29, 1874:

"With a pilot on board and no storm prevailing at the time, it seems that there must have been unpardonable carelessness somewhere."

Hundreds of people from Southampton and neighboring villages gathered to see the stranded steamer and watch the salvage operation. On January 29, the Coast Wrecking Company, under the watchful eye of *La Valle*'s captain, E. Courtoir, placed two anchors offshore with hawsers fastened to the steamer. Several days later, with the help of the tug *Relief*, the ship was hauled off the sandbar. However, the steamer was taking in water faster than her pumps could remove it. The following day the hawsers were released and she was allowed to drift ashore, more than a quarter of a mile farther east. The steamer stranded so close to shore that at low tide people could go aboard dry shod.

Some of her cargo was removed while a schooner from New York City brought heavier anchors and a steam pump. Mrs. E.P. White in a paper read before the Colonial Society of Southampton in 1914 said: "Some of her cargo found its way to the cellars of our villagers and even now, on rare occasions, an inquiry as to the origin of some choice brand of 'good cheer' meets with the response of '*La Valle*.'"

After the equipment arrived, the salvors worked for three months but could not refloat the ship. By May, constant pounding of the surf gradually weakened the ship, so bulkheads were installed and a large quantity of cement was used to make them tight. Still the salvors could not budge the steamer.

In August the steamer's French owners decided to sell the ship by auction where she lay. The *Sag Harbor Express* reported on August 27: "... a large crowd of ladies and gentlemen gathered on board to take a look at this vessel and to be present at the auction. Every part of the craft underwent scrutiny and was the subject of inquiry. There were, however, but few persons on board who meant business.... M.H. Gregory of Sag Harbor promptly made the first bid, $500 and in a few minutes the last, $3375."

Captain George G. White, of the lifesaving station at Southampton, was presented a spy glass by A. Pommeray, *La Valle*'s second officer. The testimonial accompanying the gift thanked him for his "great courage" in commanding the surfboat that rescued them "from a death that appeared imminent."

For about 60 years the iron hull was visible at low tide. A cannon from *Alexander La Valle* is on display in front of St. Andrew's Dune Church in Southampton.

EXPERIMENT—1874

A storm and fog combined to bring the British schooner *Experiment* ashore near the Shinnecock Life-Saving Station in February 1874. After grounding, a tremendous wave struck the schooner, flooding the cabin where Captain McFadzen's wife and seven-year-old son were. The captain rushed below and pulled them to the deck. As waves continued to pound the stranded ship, he lashed his wife to the rigging while the mate did the same for the small boy.

A surfman on patrol spotted the schooner and returned to the Shinnecock station to raise the alarm. Men from that station and the Southampton station to the east rescued all on board the stranded schooner. The captain's wife and son were suffering from severe frostbite. One of the surfmen almost drowned when a tremendous wave struck the surfboat, tossing him into the water.

HILL BAXTER—1875

The coastal schooner *Hill Baxter* was en route from Turks Island to Boston when she ran aground on December 26, 1875. The schooner stranded on the beach opposite Shinnecock Hills. The six-man crew was rescued by the lifesavers. The schooner's home port was Canning, Nova Scotia.

JACOB C. THOMPSON—1876

The coastal schooner *Jacob C. Thompson* was en route from Baltimore to Groton, Connecticut on March 26, 1876 when she was driven ashore by strong wind at Shinnecock. Lifesavers fought through the heavy surf to rescue the captain and five-man crew. The schooner's home port was Philadelphia.

ANNIE C. COOK—1876

The 223-ton schooner *Annie C. Cook* was en route from Bonaire, West Indies to Providence, Rhode Island with a cargo of salt when she ran aground off Shinnecock Point, Southampton on November 19, 1876. There was no loss of life, but the schooner was a total loss. One of her masts was used from 1876 to 1930 as the Liberty Pole for the village of Southampton.

JAMES A. POTTER—1878

When the three-masted schooner *James A. Potter* ran aground near the Mecox Life-Saving Station on December 22, 1878, huge breakers swept a sailor to his death. The waves were breaking so far up the dunes that the lifesaving crew could not set up their mortar directly opposite the wreck. Finally, with the beach rescue apparatus set up at an angle, they fired a line over the topmast and removed the seven survivors by breeches buoy.

Later, the unmanned schooner drifted free and came ashore at Amagansett, near the spot where a German submarine landed saboteurs during World War II.

The schooner was en route from Pensacola, Florida to Boston with a cargo of yellow-pine lumber. The lumber was put to various uses by East End residents. A counter at the country store at The Springs, a carriage house (now a cottage), and numerous fences and small buildings were constructed from the salvaged lumber.

NARRAGANSETT—1880

The steamer *Narragansett*, owned by Joseph Church & Company, was fishing off the south shore of Long Island near Bridgehampton, when she struck the wreck of *Circassian* (see index) on April 29, 1880. The 97-ton fishing vessel began to leak badly and headed toward Montauk Point in an attempt to make it back to Newport, Rhode Island, her home port.

The steamer made it only as far as East Hampton. Captain Church ran her aground between the Georgica and Amagansett lifesaving stations to keep her from sinking. The lifesaving crews rescued the captain and his 14-man crew, then housed them overnight at the two stations. All the crew's personal and fishing gear were recovered, but the steamer broke up in a storm before she could be refloated. Seven years later, her boiler and engine were recovered by Hopping and Topping Salvage Company.

JOHN D. BUCKALEW—1882

Few ships have run aground on the north shore at Montauk. One that did, the collier *John D. Buckalew*, was driven ashore about five miles west of Montauk Point by a strong northerly gale on February 18, 1882.

The schooner was old and in danger of being pounded to pieces by the heavy breakers. The captain and his two-man crew lowered a lifeboat, but the crewmen refused to leave the ship. The captain made it to shore, wet and with his clothes frozen stiff, but he wandered around until he found a house. He was taken to the Ditch Plain Life-Saving Station to summon help. Lifesavers hurried to the wreck site, but by then the schooner was broken up, with wreckage strewn along the beach for miles. The bodies of the two crewmen were found among the wreckage.

DAYLIGHT—1882

En route from the West Indies to New Haven, Connecticut with a cargo of sugar, the brig *Daylight* ran aground at Georgica Inlet, East Hampton, about 100 feet from shore on June 1, 1882. The lifesaving crew at the Georgica Life-Saving Station, a half-mile to the east, had been released from duties for the summer season. A local man drove his team of horses to the station and, with help from others, hitched them to the lifesaving equipment cart. When they reached the wreck site, Keeper Barnes of the Georgica station and Keeper Filer of the Hither Plain station had arrived. They set up the Lyle gun and fired a line to the stranded ship. Captain Thomas Gibson and his crew were rescued by breeches buoy.

Life-Saving District Superintendent Huntting, who lived nearby, arrived and heard that the captain's wife and daughter were still on board the brig. He went aboard and persuaded the daughter to leave but the wife refused. That evening she became ill and a doctor had to be put aboard by breeches buoy. He insisted she go ashore, she finally agreed and the lifesavers took her off.

The brig was refloated and the local newspaper reported that the ship's owner said that Gibson "... must have been looking for a short cut to New Haven...."

EUROPA—1886

The 1,003-ton steamer *Europa* was en route from Hamburg, Germany to New York City with a 27-man crew when she ran aground at Quogue on March 30, 1886. All aboard were rescued, but the cargo valued at $140,000 was thrown overboard to lighten the ship. Thirteen days later, *Europa*, although badly damaged, was refloated.

George E. Winters, in a letter dated May 13, 1948, wrote: "I do remember seeing the *Europa* as a small boy. I remember she was painted white and her cargo, at least in part, was Swiss music boxes, Swedish matches, and briar pipes. I am smoking one of the pipes now. The cases of matches were wet but the inside of the cases were dry and everyone had matches a plenty. Pipes in cases were taken in charge by the wrecking master, but cases were broken in the surf and picked up. They were good briar pipes [with] short amber bits. Very few are around now and of course none of the matches, but at the time I thought no one would ever have to buy another match."

JAMES T. ABBOTT—1886

The 200-ton brig *James T. Abbott* was en route from Turks Island to Vineyard Haven, Martha's Vineyard, when she ran aground at Wainscott on June 24, 1886. The brig's manifest stated there was a cargo of salt on board. She struck in daylight, in fair weather, and her rotted and shipworm-eaten wooden hull was demolished.

A local newspaper reported the opinion of the East End residents: "She was run ashore for the insurance. She was rotten all right, rotten as punk; an old vessel. There was little surf when she came ashore. The crew jumped off the bowsprit onto the sand. The owner was on board; he was one of only three white men, the other six crewmen from the West Indies. They brought off some gin and bay rum. There was no salt on board."

If the locals were right, the cargo of salt could not have been verified by insurers. It would have dissolved in the sea. The owner would have collected on an old ship and a nonexistent cargo.

CARRIE A. LANE—1886

The 703-ton, four-masted schooner *Carrie A. Lane* stranded off

Shinnecock on September 18, 1886. She was 178 feet long and 35 feet wide, with a crew of eight under the command of Captain John B. Phillips of Sag Harbor. The schooner was refloated and resumed operation until she was lost off the west coast of Africa about 1919.

CITY OF CHICAGO—1887

The 5,202-ton passenger ship *City of Chicago* was en route from Liverpool to New York when the steamer ran aground off Westhampton on March 6, 1887. All 639 passengers and crew were rescued.

LEWIS A. KING—1887

The 142-ton, two-masted schooner *Lewis A. King* was en route from Boston to New York with a cargo of dates and pipe-clay when she ran aground at 12:30 a.m. on December 18, 1887. She came ashore a mile and a half west of Montauk Lighthouse at an area known as Stony Brook. The schooner's captain, H.C. Farnham, had mistaken Montauk Lighthouse for Watch Hill Lighthouse on Rhode Island.

The closest lifesaving station, Ditch Plain, was three miles to the west. The stranded ship was not within their patrol area, but that afternoon the schooner's crew of five and the captain's sister came ashore in a lifeboat and walked to the lighthouse seeking assistance. Captain Farnham believed the lifesaving station was near the lighthouse. The schooner had run aground bow first and distress signals were fired from the starboard side toward the lighthouse, so the men at the lifesaving station, to the west, did not see them.

The 300-pound sacks of dates were salvaged and date pudding was served as dessert in East Hampton Town households for many months.

Scott Wrecking Company salvage vessels came from New London to refloat the ship, but Captain Farnham was unwilling or unable to pay the salvage fee, so the wreckers left. The schooner could not be refloated and three years later, in November 1890, she broke up in a storm.

GEORGE APPOLD—1889

The grounded two-masted schooner *Lewis A. King* was still in sight in the breakers when the passenger/freighter *George Appold*, later designated the "Shoe Wreck," ran aground at high tide at the same spot on January 9, 1889. The ship was en route from Providence, Rhode Island to Newport News, Virginia with a cargo of shoes, clothes, 100 barrels of New England rum, and calico cloth. The men at the Ditch Plain Life-Saving Station attributed the stranding to "extraordinary steering" by the ship's second officer. They said that two years before, with the same officer at the helm, the schooner was about to run aground at the same spot and they warned the ship off with a Coston signal (a hand-held flare).

The 1,456-ton, wooden-hulled, schooner-rigged steamer was broken up in a storm on January 26 and the part of her cargo not recovered by salvors washed ashore.

A newspaper reported: "Several parties obtained a whole wagon-load of shoes, boots, stockings, hats and underwear, enough to last them their natural lifetime. Small boys stowed bundles of stockings, etc., under their coats. Isaac Conklin's house on Montauk was broken into, and goods stored there by the wrecking company were stolen. The Coast Wrecking Company's agent, Mr. Pierson, will try to compel people to return the goods."

Edna Howell Yeager, in the *Long Island Forum* wrote: "Days were spent trying to pair up those ugly, copper-toed, high laced shoes, mainly children's shoes. Oh! the sore feet that resulted from these poorly fitted and often times not even paired correctly shoes ... I know for I have one of these 'wreck shoes' ..."

Paul Bailey, in *Treading Clams*, included his poem *Shoes From the Sea*:

> There were shoes galore along the shore
> In assorted styles of leather,
> But the undertow had scattered them so
> There wasn't a pair together.

In *Around the Forks* Yeager wrote that the shoes from *George Appold*: "... were a hurtful reminder for many a year. Parties were held where people brought all their mis-mated shoes in the hopes of finding a mate. If a pair was found that half way fit, how the kids hated to wear them, because their copper toes marked them as 'wreck shoes.'"

A newspaper reported that on February 2, the local wreck master held an auction of wreckage and recovered cargo. He attempted to induce those who had carted off plunder to return it and receive half the sale price. The newspaper did not say how effective the inducement was.

The "wreck calico," as the cloth was called, was a dismal brown with circles of white or red and yellow. Many dresses and other apparel were made from that salvaged material. In *Ship Ashore* (1955), Jeannette Rattray wrote that bedquilts lined with the material "are still in use around the Hamptons."

ELSIE FAY—1893

A section of beach between the Ditch Plain Life-Saving Station and Montauk Point became known as coconuts in commemoration of the wreck of the schooner *Elsie Fay* on February 17, 1893. The 172-ton schooner was en route from Grand Cayman Island, West Indies to Boston with a cargo of coconuts when she encountered a blizzard south of Long Island. After she grounded, the lifesavers rescued the captain and his six-man crew by breeches buoy, but the ship's mascot, a parrot, froze to death in the rigging. Jeannette Rattray in *Ship Ashore* wrote that the pessimistic parrot called out, "We'll all go to Hell together, boys!"

The schooner broke up in the heavy surf and scattered her cargo of coconuts along the beach. The local residents harvested the coconuts and Rattray, in her book written in 1955, stated that the senior citizens of East Hampton Town recalled: "Montauk people had coconuts in every style for about a year, and were sure to be given coconut cake whenever they were invited to a ... meal in Amagansett or East Hampton."

Van Field wrote in *Wrecks and Rescues On Long Island* (1997) that the coconut cake was "probably ... a break from the *Lewis King* date pudding."

The schooner's nameboard is on display at the East Hampton Town Marine Museum at Amagansett.

FANNY J. BARTLETT—1894

A Long Island Rail Road station between the Amagansett and
Montauk stations was known as Fanny Bartlett's Station. Actually
it was a flag-station with a platform used by fishermen to ship fish
and for the men of the Napeague Life-Saving Station.

In 1954, Captain Samuel S. Edwards of Amagansett told
Jeannette Rattray of East Hampton: "The Long Island Rail Road
really used to run accommodation trains. There were two other
flag-stops between Amagansett and Montauk. One of them had a
regular platform like Fannie Bartlett's, fish were also shipped
from there. That was where the automobile road crosses the tracks
today, east of George's Inn; and another stop was where the track
went into a branch at Promised Land. The Bartlett stop was at the
east end of what we call The Pines."

The stop was used for about 30 years, but few railroad
passengers knew that the station was named for a shipwreck. The
ship the station was named after was the three-masted schooner
Fannie J. Bartlett. The schooner was en route from Philadelphia to
Boston with 1,250 tons of coal when she ran aground at Napeague
on January 16, 1894. Her ten-man crew was saved, but the ship
was a total loss.

In 1894, the Long Island Rail Road was extended from
Bridgehampton to Montauk, and the first train ran to the Fort
Pond Bay Station the following year. Someone christened the flag-
station between Amagansett and Montauk by nailing the
schooner's nameboard to it.

JOSEPH F. LOUBAT—1894

Pilot boats from New York Harbor were in fierce competition with
each other and would sail hundreds of miles to reach New York
bound ships before their competitors. They would put a harbor
pilot aboard to guide the ship through the treacherous Ambrose
Channel into New York Harbor.

The pilot boat *Joseph F. Loubat*, in search of a customer, was
driven ashore on the same day, January 16, 1894, as *Fannie J.
Bartlett* and just a little east of where she struck.

The pilot boat had driven over the sandbar and close to the

beach. The crew was rescued by the Amagansett and Napeague lifesavers. Later the crew returned and made several efforts to kedge the pilot boat off, but their anchor was too light. During one attempt a sailor fell from the rigging and broke a leg. A Chapman Wrecking Company salvage tug arrived and set a two-ton anchor offshore outside the bar and ran a hawser from the anchor to the pilot boat. The end of the hawser was tied off to the tug's stern. The tug pulled the pilot boat back over the bar and into deep water.

BENJAMIN B. CHURCH—1894

During a blinding snowstorm on April 7, 1894, *Benjamin B. Church* grounded on the sandbar opposite the Mecox Life-Saving Station at 11:00 p.m. The eight-man Portuguese crew and a fox terrier were rescued by lifesavers in less than an hour. The next day the sailors rowed out to the wreck for a Maltese cat. The ship was a total loss.

ELMIRANDA—1894

The 622-ton, three-masted bark *Elmiranda*, named for two sisters, Elmira and Miranda, was en route to Portland, Maine when she left New York on April 9, 1894, with a cargo of 1,100 tons of coal. Two days later and 50 miles south east of Sandy Hook she ran into gale force winds. Her cargo shifted and the schooner almost capsized.

On the third day the captain hailed a passing schooner, but his request for assistance was refused. A seaman from Liverpool, England died of exposure and was buried at sea. On the fourth day, after having been continuously blown south, the bark put in at Hampton Roads, Virginia and two of her crew, who were suffering from exhaustion and exposure, were left there hospitalized.

After *Elmiranda* left port she encountered another storm which drove her ashore at East Hampton, about a mile-and-a-half west of the Georgica Life-Saving Station on April 21. The nine-man crew, the captain and the captain's 19-year-old son were rescued by breeches buoy by the men from the Georgica and Mecox stations. Heavy seas rocked the stranded ship back and forth.

Each time the vessel rolled toward shore the breeches buoy line slackened and several of the ship's crew dropped into the waves; one was almost lost. Another came ashore with a bottle of whiskey tied around his neck and a parrot inside his coat. A third brought ashore a monkey that had been shipwrecked with him in China eight months earlier. The parrot, whose vocabulary was said to be mostly profanity was sold to Condit Miller, one of the lifesavers from the Georgica station, for two dollars. Fifty tons of coal were thrown overboard to lighten the bark and she was pulled off by a tugboat.

ORIOLE—1894

The year 1894 recorded another shipwreck for Long Island's East End when the schooner *Oriole*, en route from Providence, Rhode Island to New York City, ran aground late in the year at Fort Pond Bay. Her captain and four-man crew were saved, but the schooner could not be refloated and was sold at auction for $26. Her cargo of 1,000 barrels (full or empty we do not know) were sold for $110. One of the schooner's spars was bought by Peter Koppleman and given to the village of Springs to be used as a flag pole.

GEM—1895

The brig *Gem* was en route from St. Martin, West Indies to New York City with a cargo of salt. On February 6, 1895 she came ashore near the Potunk (Westhampton) Life-Saving Station. After the captain and eight-man crew abandoned ship, the brig drifted eastward and stranded again at Quogue. The locals recovered some of the salt cargo before the ship broke up, earning her the name "Salt Ship."

The wreck's wooden-hull slowly decomposed and was covered by sand. In 1950, beach erosion exposed the shipworm eaten ribs and timbers of a wreck that former lifesavers Joe Tuttle and Andy Jacobs identified as the "Salt Ship."

Again sand covered the remains of the wreck, but severe beach erosion in 1973 and 1996 exposed them in front of the Quogue Surf Club, once known as Hallock's Beach, and later, Cooley's Beach.

PURITAN—1895

In a dense fog, on November 9, 1895, the Fall River Line steamer *Puritan* ran aground at 3:00 a.m. on Great Gull Island. The 418-foot long steamer was carrying 176 passengers when she grounded at high tide.

The following day two tugs from the Scott Wrecking Company, one from the Chapman Wrecking Company, and two Fall River Line steamers tried unsuccessfully to pull the stranded steamer off the rocks. After her cargo was removed to lighten her, the steel-hulled steamer was refloated on November 12, and steamed to New York for repairs.

CENTRAL RAILROAD OF NEW JERSEY NO. 6— 1896

On July 4, 1896, the tug *Nottingham* was towing three coal laden barges in a dense fog. All four vessels ran aground at Southampton Beach near Shinnecock Inlet. The tug worked free and managed to pull one barge off. A second barge broke in half during the salvage effort and was abandoned. *Central Railroad Of New Jersey No. 6*, the third barge, was refloated by the Chapman Wrecking Company about a week after the grounding, and was towed to Providence for repairs.

PRAIRIE—1898

During the Spanish-American War the U.S. troopship *Prairie* was used to ferry soldiers between Montauk's Camp Wykoff and Cuba. On August 26, 1898, the troopship was en route to the Army camp with 400 sick and wounded soldiers when she stranded on a sandbar near the Napeague Life-Saving Station. The lifesavers and others from neighboring stations rescued the men. One man died from his illness, not injury, soon after reaching shore. The following day the ship was refloated.

McCAULEY, NEVERSINK, AND ESCORT—1898

The Inlet Mill at Peconic (Goldsmith) Inlet was a prominent landmark near Horton Point Lighthouse on Southold Town's north shore from 1839 until 1900. For more than 30 years the grist mill

Severe erosion at the Quogue Surf Club in the winter of 1973 exposed the skeletal remains of the brig *Gem* that wrecked in 1895. The wreck has always been called "The Old Salt Ship" because of the cargo she carried. Top: Pat Shuttleworth is standing on the wreck. The wreck was exposed again in 1993 (center) and 1996 (bottom). *Courtesy of Pat Shuttleworth.*

In 1898, gale force winds drove three coal barges ashore. One, *McCauley* grounded in front of the old mill at Peconic (Goldsmith) Inlet (top). The Inlet Mill suffered severe damage (including complete destruction of its wind wheel). The barge *Escort* stranded near Duck Pond Point to the west (center and bottom). The following summer two young artists from New York City decided on *Escort* as a low cost summer residence. *Courtesy of Southold Historical Society.*

power was generated by a wheel moved by the waters of the inlet. However, the tide wheel would only turn during part of the rise and fall of the tide, so a wind wheel was added in 1870 to assist the water wheel and increase the mill's efficiency. The old mill has been immortalized in verse by Reverend Daniel H. Overton, of Brooklyn, in an illustrated booklet titled *The Old Tide Mill on the Sound*.

The old mill saw numerous shipwrecks, including one at the mouth of the inlet during the great November blizzard of 1898.

On November 22, 1898, three large coal barges, *McCauley, Neversink,* and *Escort,* were being towed in Long Island Sound by a steam tug when gale force winds parted the towline. *Neversink* and *Escort* drifted ashore near Duck Pond Point just to the west of Peconic Inlet. The third barge, *McCauley,* stranded in front of the old mill.

The three barges, converted schooners, were owned by the Boston Towboat Company. *McCauley,* which was high and dry at low tide, was the most valuable of the three, being a former White Star Line transatlantic sailing vessel. *McCauley,* after five months of hard work that cost more than she was worth, was hauled off the beach by the Merritt Wrecking Company.

Neversink and *Escort* were not considered valuable enough to pay for salvage tugs to pull them off. The following summer two young artists from New York City decided *Escort* would make a cheap summer residence. A newspaper reported: "They set up housekeeping aboard and almost developed one short leg as she was somewhat canted over. Their little dog definitely ran crookedly while ashore. The young men rigged up a hoisting arrangement like a breeches buoy and kept a rope ladder on the high side. Callers had to be daring souls to get aboard."

The old mill also suffered great damage from the blizzard, the wind wheel being completely destroyed. It was never repaired, and all grinding was done by the water wheel for her last two years. In 1900, the mill was dismantled.

E.W. STETSON—1898

E.W. Stetson, built as a schooner in Maine in 1862, was later converted into a barge. During a gale, on November 27, 1898, she was driven ashore near Jamesport.

INDEPENDENT—1898

The same storm that grounded *Stetson* drove the coal barge *Independent* ashore near Riverhead. The barge was refloated, but was lost with all hands on November 14, 1908 off Hog Island, Virginia.

JANE N. AYERS—1898

The schooner *Jane N. Ayers* foundered in a storm in Peconic Bay off the village of North Sea on November 27, 1898. The bodies of Captain Ross, of Sag Harbor, and seaman Nathan Hand were recovered immediately, but it was two weeks before the body of seaman Winfield Rockwell was found on the beach at North Sea where the schooner's small boat had been found a few days earlier. It was believed that he reached shore alive but exhausted, then froze to death and a snowstorm covered his body.

The schooner, in 20 feet of water, was a total loss.

ARGUS—1899

In 1899, the tug *Argus* was en route from Perth Amboy, New Jersey to New London, Connecticut towing two coal barges, when a storm drove her ashore near Montauk Point Lighthouse. The tug was a total loss but her captain and 11-man crew were saved. Eleven years later the fishing vessel *Betsy Ross* struck the tug's engine and sank.

BRAZIL—1899

The barkentine *Brazil* was en route from Jamaica, West Indies to New York when she ran aground a mile and a quarter west of the Moriches Life-Saving Station (west of Westhampton) on February 10, 1899. The lifesavers rescued her captain and seven-man crew, but the ship was a total loss. *Brazil* stranded almost a year to the day before *Gate City* (see index), at almost the same spot. The wrecks are within 170 feet of each other.

ELLEN—1899

In September 1899, during a severe thunderstorm, Captain Judas Paine of the sloop *Ellen*, out of Shelter Island, sought shelter in

Napeague Harbor. After anchoring, he and his crew rowed ashore. Standing on the beach they saw lightning strike the sloop and sink her.

After the storm passed, Captain Paine and his crew rowed out to the sloop which was sitting on the bottom in shallow water. The lightning bolt had hit the top of the mast, followed it down and exited out both sides of the hull, leaving large holes. The men from the Napeague Life-Saving Station and the crews of several vessels in the harbor helped patch the hull and pump out the water. Then the sloop was towed to a shipyard for permanent repairs.

RABBANO—1900

A gale struck Long Island during the first week of 1900. The two-masted schooner *Rabbano* was caught in the storm near Horton's Point on Long Island's north shore. Men at the Rocky Point Life-Saving Station (East Marion, Southold Town) saw that the ship was in distress. Captain Brown and his crew of lifesavers fought through the breakers to launch their surfboat.

They took the schooner's crew aboard the small surfboat. Spectators on shore watched anxiously as the overcrowded boat almost foundered several times. When it neared shore, spectators became participants by wading into the water and helping the rescued and rescuers make their way through the heavy surf to the beach. When the schooner drifted ashore she was quickly broken up by the pounding surf.

Captain Brown and his men received special mention from the Treasury Department and praise from the local press for their heroic action. The lifesaving station is now a private residence at the end of Rocky Point Road.

S.P. HITCHCOCK—1900

About the same time that *Rabbano*'s crew were being rescued on Long Island's north shore, lifesavers on the south shore were busy rescuing the crew of a three-masted schooner.

S.P. Hitchcock was en route from Brunswick, Georgia to Bath, Maine with a cargo of lumber and large, heavy timbers. The schooner had fought bad weather all the way up the coast and had lost some of her sails and rigging. Her captain decided to seek shelter inside one of Long Island's south shore inlets.

Leaking from the pounding of the heavy seas and from the constantly shifting cargo of lumber and timbers, the schooner was unable to maintain her heading in the teeth of the frigid gale. Before dawn on January 3, she ran aground between the Potunk (Westhampton) and Moriches lifesaving stations.

The schooner's crew fired distress signals that were spotted by surfmen Henry Griffin and Fred Tuttle who were patrolling the beach between the two stations. They ignited their brilliant red Coston signal flares to alert the ship's crew that they had been discovered and help was on the way. The surfmen then ran to alert the stations.

Within 30 minutes the lifesavers were at the site with rescue gear, but several attempts to launch a surfboat through the mountainous breakers proved futile. At dawn the Lyle gun was used in an attempt to fire a line over the ship.

The first projectile fell short but a second try was successful and the schooner's crew used it to haul a cable from shore to ship. However, the high seas and the swaying ship kept the cables so low that survivors riding the breeches buoy were submerged most of the trip ashore. Nevertheless, everyone was brought safely to the beach. As each man was lifted from the breeches buoy he was wrapped in blankets and rushed to the Moriches station, the closer of the two stations. There the stove, roaring from a driftwood fire, together with a round or two of steaming grog, soon lifted his spirits.

Although badly battered, the schooner was hauled off the sandbar by salvage tugs and towed to New York. She was repaired, recaulked, and returned to service a few months later.

WILLIAM T. SEWARD—1900

In the early morning of May 16, 1900, the fishing sloop *William T. Seward* was destroyed in an explosion off Gardiner's Island. A fire started in the sloop's cabin and spread to a tank containing naphtha (a highly volatile, inflammable liquid), which exploded. Captain Frank J. Tuthill, of East Marion, and his crew escaped before the explosion, but the sloop was a total loss.

ROSINA—1900

The schooner-yacht *Rosina* was launched on December 1, 1900, at Lynn, Massachusetts. The same month, her owner, Harry T. Malpass of Philadelphia, wanted to take her on her maiden voyage. The yacht's captain, A.L. Matthews, a crew of three, Malpass and his guest Miss Florence Jones sailed for Florida. After rounding Cape Cod, *Rosina* encountered strong winds and rough seas that carried her lifeboats away. Captain Matthews headed into Long Island Sound looking for protected waters, but his vessel was in such distress that he was forced to run her aground in Southold Town.

The men from the Rocky Point Life-Saving Station (East Marion), seven miles to the east, managed to launch their surfboat and reach the stranded vessel to rescue those on board.

Captain Matthews telegraphed the Thomas A. Scott Wrecking Company of New London for salvage tugs, but high seas kept them in port. By the time the tugs arrived, the following day, *Rosina* was high and dry on the beach. That night the new, powerful tug *Chapman* of the Merritt-Chapman Wrecking Company of New York City arrived at the scene. The big tug's efforts to pull the yacht off the beach were unsuccessful because the yacht's keel was imbedded in two feet of sand. The salvors shoveled the sand away from the keel and a six-inch hawser was run from *Rosina*'s bow to the big tug a quarter of a mile out in the Sound. At high tide four unsuccessful attempts were made to haul the yacht off the beach. The fifth time, however, succeeded.

Rosina proved seaworthy and the tug towed her to New York City for repairs. Malpass, Matthews, and her crew went on board for the trip. Miss Jones, who was one of the many spectators of the salvage operation, insisted on being taken aboard the yacht. A yawl from the tug came in after her and on its first attempt to reach the yacht was overturned by a big wave, throwing its occupants into the water. After they struggled to shore a second attempt was made to reach the yacht. They were successful this time, but not before a wave half filled the small boat while it was being launched through the breakers. The thoroughly wet and cold Miss Jones was taken aboard *Rosina*.

LUCY W. SNOW—1901

The schooner *Lucy W. Snow* was en route from Nassau, Bahamas to Providence, Rhode Island, on September 11, 1901, when she ran aground near the Moriches Life-Saving Station (west of Westhampton). The lifesavers rescued her captain and six-man crew. The schooner, her home port was Portland, Maine, was high and dry and attracted a large crowd of sightseers.

BELLE OF OREGON and ANTELOPE—1902

Belle of Oregon was once a famous American bark 185 feet long and 38 feet wide. She was built at Bath, Maine and launched in 1876. By February 2, 1902, when she was lost off Westhampton, she had been converted into a lowly barge. The barge *Antelope* was lost with *Belle of Oregon*. On May 3, 1905, the residents of Westhampton erected a monument in the northeast corner of the Westhampton cemetery in memory of A.W. Daly and two unknown men of the two barges. *Belle of Oregon*'s beautiful figurehead is on display at the Mariners' Museum at Newport News, Virginia.

ALICE REED—1902

The bark *Alice Reed*'s home port was New York City, but on December 3, 1902, she was en route from Turks Island, West Indies to Boston when she grounded at Napeague Beach. Lifesavers rescued ten men by breeches buoy. The bark and her cargo of salt were a total loss. A section of the starboard bow bulwark that was found on the beach in Montauk by Michael Hidalgo of Elmhurst, New York is on display at the East Hampton Town Marine Museum at Amagansett. Reed Hill was named after the bark.

JOHN C. FITZPATRICK—1903

The 1,277-ton, 242-foot long, wooden-hulled schooner *John C. Fitzpatrick* was launched in 1892, in West Bay City, Michigan. She carried freight between Great Lake ports for six years. In 1898, the relatively new four-master suffered the ultimate indignity of conversion from proud sailing ship to coal barge. After conversion, she was towed from the Great Lakes to the Atlantic Ocean, where she served in her menial role for the next five years.

On April 3, 1903, *Fitzpatrick* was en route from Philadelphia to New Bedford, Massachusetts, loaded with 2,400 tons of coal. She was owned by the Boutelle Transportation Company of Cleveland, Ohio, and was under tow by the tug *Sweepstakes*. The schooner-barge still retained her steam-powered equipment for hoisting anchor, transferring cargo, and operating bilge pumps. Captain George Davis commanded a crew of four men.

Off the village of East Hampton a tremendous explosion blew a massive hole in the barge's wooden hull. Burdened with her coal cargo, the barge plummeted to the bottom, carrying Captain Davis and his four-man crew with her. The disaster happened so quickly that the tugboat crew barely managed to cut the towline with an axe to avoid being drawn under by the sinking barge. In their opinion, the schooner-barge was maintaining too much pressure for her steam boiler, and it exploded. It may be that the owners stretched economy of operation too far in lack of maintenance of the only steam equipment the old schooer retained after her conversion.

Ron Barnes, a member of the Aquarians Dive Club identified the wreck in 1988 with his recovery of a bronze capstan cover engraved "John C. Fitzpatrick, American Ship Windlass Co., Providence RI, 1892. F.W. Wheeler & Co. Shipbuilder, West Bay City, Michigan." The scattered wooden wreckage lies in about 135 feet of water, about seven-and-one-half miles south of East Hampton. The wreck is referred to as the "Jug" because fishing trawlers recovered ceramic jugs in their nets after the wreck was discovered. All that remains of the century-old schooner, turned barge, is her wooden hull, collapsed and broken up, with scattered ribs and timbers extending only a few feet off the bottom.

SEACONNET—1905

The 188-ton fishing steamer *Seaconnet* out of Greenport ran aground between the Shinnecock and Tiana lifesaving stations on May 29, 1905. The 24-man crew used the steamer's lifeboats to reach shore. The survivors were given shelter at the lifesaving stations. The large fishing vessel was a total loss.

GOLDEN RAY 1905 and EDITH E. DENNIS 1911

Samuel Wyllys bought Plum Island, originally called Isle of Patmos, from the Montauk tribe in 1659, for "a coat, a barrell of biskitt, 100 muxes [iron drills used to make wampum beads from shells] and fish hooks."

During the Spanish-American War, the Army built Fort Terry as a coastal artillery base to protect the entrance to Long Island Sound. Some of the fort's brick buildings, locked and unoccupied, are still standing and are visible from the southern shore. Small batteries, where 3-inch and 5-inch guns were in place at one time, are still visible from the north, east, and south beaches. Large batteries of 14-inch guns were dug into the hills in the middle of the island's east end.

Plum Island is little more than a mile from Orient Point, the tip of Long Island's north fork. The strong currents of Plum Gut, the passage between Orient Point and Plum Island, are a hazard to navigation. In November 1905, the schooner *Golden Ray*, with a cargo of coal, sank in the middle of the dangerous channel. The two men on board, Captain Dick Bushnell and Jesse Howard, managed to take to a small boat before the schooner sank. Their boat capsized in the rough seas and they swam ashore on Plum Island.

The schooner was owned by J. Madison Wells of Greenport, Long Island. Wells replaced *Golden Ray* with the two-masted schooner *Edith E. Dennis* that sank in almost the same spot.

Edith E. Dennis was en route from New York to Shelter Island Heights with a load of coal on November 12, 1911, when she sprung a leak near Horton's Point Lighthouse. Captain Augustus Cook attempted to pass through Plum Gut to Gardiner's Bay where he intended to anchor and make repairs.

Heavy seas and gale force winds from the southwest had turned Plum Gut into a mass of boiling foam, and the schooner began to sink in 70 feet of water. Soldiers from Plum Island's Fort Terry saw the vessel in distress and turned on a 60-inch searchlight. In the light's glare, Captain Cook put his wife and child in the dory (a flat-bottomed boat with flaring sides) with the schooner's mate. That was the only boat, so Captain Cook and three crew members stayed on board the sinking schooner. When the small boat was within a 100 feet of shore it was capsized by a huge wave.

Captain Cook lashed himself to a piece of wreckage and after the schooner sank he washed ashore at Fort Terry. The soldiers untied the unconscious captain. When he regained consciousness and learned that his wife and child had not made it to shore, the half-crazed man walked the beach in a desperate search for his family and crew. Captain Cook was the sole survivor.

BUENA VENTURA—1906

On April 22, 1898, the U.S. Navy gunboat *Nashville* captured the Spanish steamer *Buena Ventura* (Good Venture.) The first prize ship captured by U.S. Navy warships in the Spanish-American War. U.S.S. *Nashville* captured three other Spanish vessels during the war.

The steamer's engine and boilers were removed and she was converted into a coal barge. During a storm in December 1906, *Buena Ventura* sank a mile-and-a-half east of Montauk Point Lighthouse. Her masts were above water after she foundered. Captain Olle Owarsond and seaman Charles Martin were rescued by a crew member of the tugboat, *Walter A. Luckenbach*, that had been towing the barge. Mitchell Bruso volunteered to row a small boat from the tug to the masts where he found the captain frozen to the topmast. Fighting his way through towering seas he went back to the sunken barge and found Martin frozen to a floating hatch. Three of the barge's crew drowned.

KEEWAYDIN—1906

The three-masted, British schooner *Keewaydin* was en route from New York City to Wolfville, Nova Scotia with 200 tons of coal. Captain Salter decided to anchor for the night in Long Island Sound, about two miles east of Southold, Long Island.

The seas were calm and the weather fair when Salter and his crew retired early on the evening of October 6, 1906. During the night gale force winds developed and by morning the rough seas broke the anchor loose and the schooner drifted ashore. The captain and crew made an effort to launch a boat, but could not, due to the booming breakers washing over her deck. The crew fired distress signals to summon help.

A surfman on patrol from the nearby Rocky Point Life-Saving Station spotted the ship on the rocky shore. After lighting his Coston signal flare to let the stranded sailors know their distress signals had been seen, he hurried to alert the station crew.

The lifesavers reached the site with rescue gear and a line was fired over the ship's rigging with the Lyle gun. Four men were brought ashore in the breeches buoy, but the fifth man was injured and was unable to climb into the buoy. He was rescued in the schooner's yawl which was hauled ashore by a line. The schooner's mascot dog was left aboard and perished. The crew, all Nova Scotians, saved nothing but the clothing they wore. The schooner was a total loss, but nine-tenths of her cargo was salvaged.

GEORGE P. HUDSON—1908

The 266-foot long, five-masted schooner *George P. Hudson* ran aground off Shinnecock Hills, Southampton on April 9, 1908. Heavy seas prevented the lifesavers from launching their surfboat, so the Lyle gun was used to fire a line to the ship. The ship was not in danger of breaking up, so the crew refused to be taken off by breeches buoy. However, Captain G.C. Gardner came ashore and made arrangements for a salvage company to refloat his ship. Although the stranded schooner was so high on the beach that sightseers could walk out to her, she was pulled off by salvage tugs ten days later. She was saved only to be lost later off Massachusetts when she ran into a submerged wreck and sank.

GEORGE CURTIS—1912

In a heavy fog on June 8, 1912, the 121-foot long, 194-ton fishing steamer *George Curtis* went on the rocks about five miles west of Montauk, near the Ditch Plain Life-Saving Station. The steamer began to fill with water as soon as she struck, and the vessel's crew quickly stripped her of everything that could easily be removed. Captain Charles Baldwin, of Shelter Island, Pilot

Lewis A. King ran aground near Montauk Light in 1887 because the schooner's captain mistook Montauk Light for Watch Hill Light on Rhode Island. Her cargo of dates was salvaged by locals who enjoyed date pudding as dessert for many months.

Above: Gale force winds drove the British schooner *Keewaydin* ashore in 1906, about two miles east of the village of Southold. Note the man being rescued by breeches buoy. *Courtesy of the Southold Historical Society.* Bottom: In 1908, the five-masted schooner *George P. Hudson* ran aground off Shinnecock Hills, Southampton. *Courtesy of the Long Island Maritime Museum.*

The passenger steamer *Kershaw* aground in 1918 off the village of East Hampton. *Courtesy of East Hampton Town Marine Museum.*

Above: In 1921, the freighter *Malden* grounded in 40 feet of water about one-mile north of Montauk Point Light. The ship was a total loss. *Photo by Bob Beattie.* Bottom: The worst Montauk Point maritime disaster occurred in 1951 when the fishing charter-boat *Pelican* capsized and 25 people drowned. The photo shows the overloaded boat leaving the dock on her last charter. *Courtesy of Albert R. Holden.*

George Ross, of Greenport, and the crew were taken off and brought to Promised Land, then transported to Greenport by the steamer *Amagansett*, where they were paid off and discharged.

BESSIE C. BEACH—1912

Amagansett's village flagpole was formerly the 45-foot topmast of the three-masted schooner *Bessie C. Beach* until it was replaced by a steel pole in 1950. The ship, en route from St. John's, New Brunswick to Philadelphia on December 6, 1912, ran aground at the Highlands (now Devon), Amagansett. Captain Mackay and his five-man crew were rescued, but his 32-year-old schooner quickly broke up in the surf. The schooner's cargo of spruce lath (narrow, thin strips of wood) was scattered for miles along the shore.

LOUISE BLISS—around World War I

In 1891, Noyack Bay, near Sag Harbor, was selected for submarine torpedo tests. The E.W. Bliss Company felt the shallow water, lack of tidal current, and land-locked environment made the small bay perfect for testing torpedoes that were manufactured at their Brooklyn factory. The torpedoes were shipped to Sag Harbor in four sections, where they were assembled. Robert A. Hanna, U.S. Army, retired, was in charge of the test program and lived on Sag Harbor's Main Street.

The 140-foot long, 40-foot wide, steel-hulled barge *E.W. Bliss* was used as a platform for firing the torpedoes, with dummy warheads, at the target at a speed of 45 miles per hour. After a test, the torpedoes would float to the surface and be retrieved by smaller vessels.

On May 1, 1909, the Sag Harbor *Corrector* reported that the steam collier *John B. Dallas* was hit by an erratic moving torpedo that punctured her hull below the water line. The collier, that had been discharging coal alongside *Bliss* when the mishap occurred, had to be beached to keep from sinking.

In September 1914, a torpedo retrieval vessel was struck by a torpedo and badly damaged. After World War I torpedo testing in Noyack Bay gradually diminished, but during the 30 years that the Bliss Company was in Sag Harbor, 15 vessels were used for the program. One caught fire and sank about 150 feet from shore in Noyack Bay. The small amount of wreckage remaining is in about 15 feet of water.

The authors were told the name of the wreck is *Louise Bliss*, a vessel used to retrieve the torpedoes for reuse. Some torpedoes missed the net and their dummy warheads still lie on the bottom of the bay. One was recovered by scuba divers in the 1980s.

KERSHAW—1918

The stranding of the Merchants and Miners passenger liner *Kershaw* is unusual because many residents of East Hampton aided in the rescue of her crew.

On March 12, 1918, the 1,767-ton steamer was en route from Newport News and Baltimore to Providence and Boston. She was carrying a cargo of Old Taylor Rum, tobacco, flour, and peanuts when she encountered gale-force winds and ran aground on a sandbar 175 yards off the beach, just opposite the end of Ocean Avenue, in the village of East Hampton.

Violent waves prevented surfboat rescue by the Coast Guard (three years earlier the Life-Saving Service became part of the new Coast Guard). They tried twice, but the first boat capsized and the men almost drowned returning to shore. The second managed to remove seven or eight passengers and crew, but as it reached shore the boat capsized. William Collins, a member of the Coast Guard, suffered two broken ribs.

Using a Lyle gun, the Coast Guard fired a line over the ship. Because of the large waves a hawser was run from the ship's masthead over the top of a building and fastened to the ground. The breeches buoy line was attached to the bumpers of automobiles belonging to East Hampton residents. The volunteers drove their cars up and down Ocean Avenue, hauling the men to shore and sending the empty breeches buoy back again in record time.

Working with the Coast Guard crews from the Georgica, Amagansett, and Napeague stations, the volunteers worked all day rescuing the passengers and crew members. Various accounts of the disaster state there were from 71 to 164 passengers and crew on board. When they reached shore and were released from the breeches buoy the Red Cross provided hot coffee to the grateful survivors. They were taken to local hotels and given dry clothes and accommodations. Captain James McDorman came ashore the next day, leaving only the ship's engineer on board.

Kershaw provided excitement for the locals for three weeks. Then, the ship was pulled off by Merritt-Chapman salvage tugs after two-thirds of her cargo was thrown overboard to lighten her. So many peanuts were recovered by local children that the stores were unable to sell any for months. While the children gathered peanuts, their fathers collected barrels and bottles of rum. Hundred-pound sacks of flour floated in, and only the outside quarter-inch of the flour was wet.

LAKE DEVAL—1920

The United States Shipping Board freighter *Lake Deval* ran aground two miles west of the village of Southampton in a heavy fog on March 12, 1920. She was en route from Texas City to Boston with a cargo of sulfur. When first sighted by a member of the Meadow House Club she was listing badly from the beating she was taking from the pounding seas. A few hours later the fog thickened so much that the freighter could not be seen from shore. The ship's crew communicated with men on shore by sending Morse code with the freighter's fog horn. A shift in the wind helped to right the ship. Her captain and 33-man crew were rescued.

U.S.S. OLYMPIA—1921

Each summer, early in the 20th century, the Navy held maneuvers in Gardiner's Bay and Fort Pond Bay. In 1921, a formation of eight warships was steaming through 42-foot-deep water when the cruiser *Olympia* struck a rock near Shagwong Reef off Montauk Point Lighthouse. The rock extended up from the bottom to within 18 feet of the surface.

Emerson Taber of Three Mile Harbor, East Hampton, who was checking his lobster pots and witnessed the incident, later said: "They tried to take me to Newport as a witness. The captain swung her around and ran on Cerberus Shoal in 11 feet of sand.

Her upper deck was just awash. They got 25 or 30 Navy boats and divers to get [her] off, and managed to do that 30 days later. I took my lobster pots out."

The shoal the cruiser's captain ran onto was named after the British frigate *Cerberus* that grounded there in the 18th century. In 1778, during the American Revolution, the British warship was destroyed by her crew in Narragansett Bay to keep her from being captured by French warships. A pile of ballast stones marks her grave on the bottom of the Bay.

MALDEN—1921

The 5,054-ton freighter *Malden* ran aground off Fire Island in February 1920, but was refloated. Near midnight on September 17 of the following year, her captain John Gertsen was giving Montauk Point a wide berth in dense fog after his previous experience with Fire Island. The small collier *Jonancy* was heading south when she collided with the north-bound *Malden*. There was no loss of life, but the collier's bow tore a massive opening in the freighter's port side. The collier had a crumpled bow but was in no danger of sinking; the freighter's condition was questionable.

At 12:28 a.m., *Malden* sent out an "SOS" that was received by a Navy radio station where it was relayed it to the Coast Guard cutters *Acushnet* (at Woods Hole, Massachusetts) and *Gresham* (at New York). *Gresham* quickly got underway, but *Acushnet's* radio operator was not on duty and the cutter's crew was alerted by telephone, but not until 6:30 a.m. Later the Navy would demand an explanation for the delay and the Coast Guard responded that regulations required a continuous radio watch be maintained only when a cutter was at sea. At dock, emergency messages were to be delivered by telephone. The Navy had been informed of the procedure two years earlier.

With the delay in receiving the emergency message, *Acushnet*, the closest cutter to the disaster, did not arrive at the scene until 2:30 p.m. that afternoon. By then, *Malden* was under tow by the Scott Wrecking Company's tug *Guardsman*. The cutter placed a hawser aboard the tug and assisted in the tow. At 7:25 p.m. the freighter grounded on a sand shoal and the hawser from the tug parted. The following morning the freighter was refloated but grounded for the last time approximately one-mile north of Montauk Point Lighthouse in about 40 feet of water.

A radio message gave *Malden*'s condition: "grounded forward and afloat aft. Ship listed to port 17 degrees and port bulwarks and port side of main deck under water for full length. Holds number one, two, three full, four partly full, five dry, engine and boiler rooms dry. Steam on one boiler. Last high water, vessel shifted position and *Acushnet* and *Guardsman* tried tow her ashore, but failed. Now holding her in favorable position and we are filling all double bottom tanks. Collision damage does not, as far as seen, appear serious for temporary repairs. Ship lies in exposed position and it is necessary to discharge port cargo and close all openings. Will advise later our decision after low water this afternoon, crew still on board."

The salvage tug picked up divers and small barges and returned to the freighter to remove cargo and patch the hull. However, a two-day storm further damaged the hull and the insurance underwriters abandoned the plan to refloat the ship. Salvors were ordered to strip what they could.

Captain Gertsen of *Malden* and *Jonancy*'s third mate, Clarence W. Colbeth, who was on the bridge and in command of the collier at the time of the collision, were tried for violation of Article 16 of the International Rules of the Road.

Article 16 reads: "Every vessel shall, in a fog, mist, falling snow, or heavy rainstorms, go at a moderate speed, having careful regard to the existing circumstances and conditions. A steam vessel hearing, apparently forward of her beam, the fog signal of a vessel the position of which is ascertained shall, so far as the circumstances of the case admit, stop her engines, and then navigate with caution until danger of collision is over."

Captain Elisha T. Rogers of *Jonancy*, who was not on the bridge at the time of the collision was charged with negligence and inattention to duty. The verdict was guilty for the charges of violation of Article 16 against Gertsen and Colbeth, and inattention to duty against Rogers. The charge of negligence against Rogers was dismissed. The licenses of the three men were suspended for a period of 30 days.

NORTHCLIFF—1923

In May 1923, the three-masted schooner *Northcliff* was en route from Turks Island, West Indies to Buckport, Maine when she encountered dense fog and a southwest gale off the south shore of Long Island. The schooner ran aground on a sandbar two or three miles west of the Georgica Coast Guard Station. Captain William McCloud and his six-man crew rowed ashore in a 13-foot dinghy.

The five-year-old *Northcliff* was 150 feet long, with a 35-foot beam, and about 300 tons. The schooner's three masts were snapped off near the deck by the gale-force winds. *Northcliff*, owned by Stanley Soley of Parrsboro, Nova Scotia, and her cargo of 400 tons of salt was a total loss. The hull, spars, rigging, and sails were sold for $100 to two East Hampton men.

In 1939 part of the hull was still visible not far from where she went ashore, about one-half-mile west of Georgica Pond Inlet.

COOT—1928

In March 1928, in a dense fog, the 125-foot long, 34-foot wide *Coot* struck a rock, breaking her rudder and damaging her screw-propeller. The captain grounded the vessel one mile east of Old House.

The vessel lay on the beach for 45 days. Her cargo of codfish was removed and when a nor'easter struck the crew managed to pull her off the beach without paying salvage tugs to do the job. That recovery without cost provided her owners, Chesebro Brothers of New York, with some solace.

WILLIAM N. PAGE—1931

During a storm and dense fog, the collier *William N. Page* ran aground at Westhampton Beach on January 4, 1931. The following day, even though the storm winds continued, a surfboat from the Tiana Life-Saving Station managed to reach the stranded ship after a hard pull and offered to take the 40 members of her crew ashore. Although they had all been working the pumps all night, the crew rejected the offer and elected to stay with Captain A.D. Parcell and the stranded ship.

Constant wave action tore away the ship's rudder and a slight leak developed in the hull. The water did not rise high enough to put out the fires in the boilers, so they continued to supply steam to the collier's pumps.

The first attempt to refloat the ship at high tide on January 7 failed and the crew and two tugs, *Relief* and *Willett*, from the Merritt-Chapman salvage company prepared for a long, hard battle. Salvage was hampered by gale-force winds, fog, and heavy seas, but after 3,000 tons of coal were removed to lighten the vessel, she was pulled off the sandbar on January 16.

RARITAN SUN—1935

An oil spill washing ashore and fouling a pristine sand beach is the dread of every seaside community. With modern electronic navigation aides a tanker running aground is less likely to happen. The 189-foot long tanker *Raritan Sun* did not have radar, loran, or GPS to show her position in relation to shore in dense fog on July 14, 1935, and ran aground between Montauk Point and Ditch Plains. Oil began to seep out of her rock-punctured steel hull.

At the next high tide, two Coast Guard cutters tried to pull the tanker off but the hawsers snapped and the locals feared the ship would break up. Eventually, the tanker was refloated and the threat to the environment did not materialize.

The damage that can result from an oil spill was not fully appreciated until 1967, when the supertanker *Torry Canyon* ran aground and broke in two off Land's End, the southwestern point of England. Thousands of tons of crude oil blackened the beaches of Cornwall and killed thousands of marine organisms.

PELICAN—1951

The worst maritime disaster for Montauk Point occurred in 1951. Within sight of Montauk Point Lighthouse the fishing charter-boat *Pelican* capsized on September 1. The boat's owner and captain, Edward Carroll, of Staten Island, was lost along with 44 passengers; only 19 survived. A Coast Guard investigation determined that the 42-foot long boat was overloaded. The boat should have only had 20 people aboard, not 63.

Due to rough seas, Carroll had decided to return to port, but ten miles from Montauk Point one of the two engines failed. When the overcrowded, underpowered boat met the riptide off the Point she had difficulty making way. When she was struck on the starboard side by three big waves, passengers panicked, rushed to the port side, and the boat capsized. Only one of the passengers wore a life jacket, because Carroll never told them to put them on. Some passengers were thrown into the water and others were trapped below in the cabin.

Three close by fishing boats managed to rescue the few survivors. *Pelican* did not sink; later, when the half-submerged boat was towed back to the dock at Montauk, ten bodies were recovered from her cabin. For several days others were recovered in the waters around Montauk Point, but some were never found.

Today, Coast Guard regulations strictly limit the number of passengers for charter boats depending on the size of the vessel.

U.S.S. *CHENANGO*—1960

The largest vessel to run aground on Eastern Long Island was a veteran of Guadalcanal, Tarawa, and other Pacific World War II action. The 533-foot-long aircraft carrier U.S.S. *Chenango*, was under tow in Long Island Sound by the tug *Port Jefferson* on February 18, 1960. The tug fought mountainous waves and 60 mph winds until the towline parted, driving the warship ashore near Horton's Point Lighthouse in Southold, Long Island.

The decommissioned aircraft carrier, earlier sold for scrap for $351,000, was being towed from the mothball fleet at Boston to Brooklyn.

While a Coast Guard cutter stood by, two salvage tugs pulled the 11,000-ton warship off the sandbar six hours after the mishap. Only four men were aboard the carrier and none were injured.

Hundreds of North Fork residents watched the salvage operation, including a busload of school children who were happy to be let out of class for the excitement of a close-up view of an aircraft carrier.

AGAPI—1964

The 10,000-ton, 500-foot long, Lebanese registered freighter *Agapi* ran aground on November 7, 1964 on a sandbar in Plum Gut, just east of the Orient Point Lighthouse. The vessel loaded with scrap steel was en route from New Haven, Connecticut to Japan. Drawing about 26 feet, the large ship grounded in 16 feet of water. Men from the Merritt, Chapman & Scott salvage company unloaded her cargo of steel, and the 210-foot long salvage tug *Curb* pulled her off on November 26. The Merritt-Chapman salvage company of New York had merged with the Scott salvage company of New London, Connecticut. The freighter was towed to City Island, New York for a hull inspection.

DEBRA ANN—1989

The trawler *Debra Ann* went down in Shinnecock Inlet on January 24, 1989 after a 10-foot wave broke over the boat's stern. The Coast Guard rescued two crewmen but a third, Theodore Kip of Flanders, was lost.

ELI—1989

Even with today's sophisticated electronics, disasters at sea occur. At 12:58 a.m. on March 21, 1989, the 73-foot long commercial fishing vessel *Eli* ran aground about three quarters of a mile west of Shinnecock Inlet at Hampton Bays. The vessel was returning to her dock at Hampton Bays with 25,000 pounds of fish, after a one-day offshore fishing trip.

According to the Coast Guard, *Eli* ran aground while on auto pilot when the crew member in the wheel house fell asleep while the vessel was in a heavy rain heading for the inlet.

The three-man crew struggled to get the wooden-hulled vessel off the beach and back into deep water, but they were unsuccessful. They abandoned the boat at 3:00 a.m. and walked ashore. Captain Mel Moss, of East Quogue, said "... I walked off, I didn't get wet."

A Coast Guard 44-footer arrived at the scene and prepared to pull *Eli* off the beach. However, the Coast Guardsmen determined there was not enough water for them to pull her off without jeopardizing their boat and crew. *Eli* was destroyed by the fury of the waves.

A few months earlier, Toby Miller, of South Jamesport, a crewman on *Eli*, was a crewman aboard the fishing vessel *Evening*

Prayer when she ran aground on the outer shoal of Shinnecock Inlet. Miller and two other men clung to the *Evening Prayer*'s pilot house for nearly two hours, pounded by eight-foot seas, before they were rescued by a Coast Guard helicopter.

SHINNECOCK ONE—1991

"Catch of the Day Dooms Boat" was a headline in the March 15, 1991, Long Island *Newsday*. Two days before, the fishing trawler *Shinnecock One* had hauled aboard a World War II vintage torpedo. Vinnie Farrell, a mate on the vessel, said the torpedo came to rest leaning on a piece of equipment with its warhead against the deck. He admitted, "We had been joking that we had a bomb aboard, but we didn't take it that seriously."

The 3,500-pound torpedo was equipped with a 1,200-pound warhead, so a state of emergency was declared. The Hampton Bays Fire Department evacuated the Dune Road area from Shinnecock Inlet to Tiana Beach.

The torpedo was identified as an American type, probably fired in a training zone near Block Island. Rough seas with up to 14-foot waves made it impossible to remove the torpedo. The trawler was declared a hazard and a team of Navy, Coast Guard, and Air National Guard personnel sank the vessel with C-4 explosive charges in 60 feet of water about two miles west of the Shinnecock Inlet buoy.

On March 18, Navy divers set a timed explosive charge and detonated the torpedo. Coast Guard officials said "the torpedo could have damaged 500 Hampton Bays homes if it had gone off on the surface."

ALASKA, VOLUNTEER STATE, AND HOOSIER STATE—1993

In 1993, the 300-foot dredge *Alaska* was at the end of a five-month job of pumping some 1.4 million cubic yards of sand onto the Westhampton barrier beach to fill a 2,600-foot wide breach and bolster the eroded beach, about two miles east of Moriches Inlet. *Alaska* was about one-mile offshore with two tugboats, *Volunteer State* and *Hoosier State*.

Despite threatening weather forecasts, the dredge's owner, Chicago-based Great Lakes Dredge and Dock Company, chose not to tow the dredge back to port to ride out the storm. Ironically, the dredge's project was completed several hours before the storm hit.

On November 28, at about 10:00 a.m. the crew of the dredge notified the Coast Guard that three of her five anchor lines had parted overnight in 8- to 12-foot seas and winds gusting up to 50 miles per hour.

The larger of the two tugs, *Volunteer State*, tried to secure the dredge, but fouled her propeller in two lines. The smaller tug rescued the crew of *Volunteer State* and tied the unmanned tug to the dredge. About an hour later the dredge's crew radioed that the last two anchors had broken loose and the dredge, with *Volunteer State* still tied to her, was drifting ashore. The smaller *Hoosier State* alone was not powerful enough to prevent the dredge and the other tug from grounding.

Hoosier State, while trying to save the dredge, had difficulty maneuvering in the huge breakers. The Coast Guard asked the two men aboard the tug if they wanted to be lifted off by helicopter, but they said no. But when the engine room of *Hoosier State* flooded, the tug lost power and ended up broadside to the waves and capsized.

The tug's captain, James Dennis Hatcher of Florida, was not found by the Coast Guard helicopters, but seaman William Moore of New Jersey remained afloat and was plucked to safety by a Coast Guard helicopter.

The capsized tug sank and settled upright on the bottom. When the dredge grounded, *Volunteer State* came free and was towed up on the beach by a line attached to a bulldozer that had been moving sand on shore. The dredge's 18-man crew were uninjured and remained aboard the stranded vessel. They were joined by a Coast Guard officer and a crew member from a salvage company that was trying to refloat the dredge. Both were dropped aboard the dredge by helicopter.

The following morning a shroud of mist and fog lifted from the beach, exposing the dredge with its two cranes and pump houses towering over the beach cottages. While attempting to put new lines aboard the dredge, another tugboat stranded on the same sandbar. Two other tugs arrived on the scene late the same day to refloat the stranded vessels, but salvage efforts were hampered by continued high seas and shallow water.

Great Lakes Vice President Steve O'Hara said he thought the dredge would be able to ride out the storm, but the storm was far more intense than predicted.

The dredge was loaded with 100,000 gallons of fuel oil and there was concern that the oil would be spread upon Westhampton beaches and flow through the inlet into Moriches Bay, fouling the water and coating migratory birds. However, the Coast Guard removed most of the fuel and the dredge and stranded tugs were refloated.

Alexander La Valle ran aground near the village of Southampton in 1874. The ship was a total loss. *Courtesy of the Suffolk County Historical Society.*

The schooner *Lucy W. Snow* ran aground near the Moriches Life-Saving Station in 1901. *Courtesy of Harry Huson.*

Below: A large piece of unidentified wreckage washed ashore at Westhampton Beach, after a severe storm. *Photo by H. Keatts.*

Top: Horton Point Lighthouse without a porch. The automated light tower, added in 1933, is on the right. *Courtesy of the Southold Historical Society.*

Middle: The phoenix gargoyles on the Horton Point Light function as downspouts to carry rainwater from the light tower's roof. The name gargoyle is derived from "gargouiller," old French for "a gargling sound." The mold used to produce the new phoenix gargoyles is on display inside the lighthouse museum. *Photo by H. Keatts.*

Bottom: the lighthouse in 1997. *Photo by H. Keatts.*

EASTERN LONG ISLAND LIGHTHOUSES

HORTON POINT LIGHTHOUSE

When Built: 1857
Location: Horton Point, Southold
Still on site: yes
Accessible to public: yes

The distance from Plum Gut at the mouth of Long Island Sound and Mount Sinai is 42 nautical miles, a stretch known to mariners for its rocky shoals and exposed underwater boulders. The shoals are particularly dangerous because they extend as far as a mile and a half into the Sound, and rise abruptly from safe depths of more than 25 feet. Close to shore, boulders are exposed at low tide.

BEACON

The need for a warning beacon along the perilous stretch of waterfront was recognized as early as 1756, according to a popular belief in Southold Town. It is said that was the year a 24-year-old former surveyor named George Washington recommended that a navigational light be erected at Horton Point. His choice was the "Cliff Lot" of Barnabas Horton's original 1640 land grant, on a cliff 65 feet above high water, the site of the present lighthouse. There is some basis for the legend. Augustus Griffin, in his compendium of local history and old-time gossip, *Griffin's Journal*, 1857, referred to a visit by Washington. However, by then Washington was no longer a young surveyor. He was Colonel of the Virginia Militia, en route to Boston via ferry from Greenport to New London.

While waiting for the ferry at Greenport, Washington spent

several hours at the Booth Inn. A small, bronze plaque marking the event is mounted on the face of a six-foot boulder at the northeast corner of Main and Sterling streets:

This tablet commemorates
The presence here of
Col. George Washington
Who in 1757, stopped at the
Inn of Constant Booth
Which then stood
Near this spot

The actual location of Booth's Inn was somewhat removed from the boulder. The *Atlas of Long Island,*(1873) shows it at the intersection of Sterling Street and Sterling Avenue, facing Sterling Harbor. There is no historic plaque there. Constant Booth's Inn was removed to Orient where it is part of the Oyster Ponds Historical Society.

Griffin makes no mention of Washington stopping in Southhold Village, but Warren Hall, in *Pagans, Puritans, Patriots of Yesterday's Southold* (1975) cites his claim that the visit was actually a year earlier, as confirmed by Virginia records, and Washington did stop at Southold. His purpose was to deliver correspondence to Ezra L'Hommedieu from a cousin William Chevalier de Peyron, Washington's friend in Virginia. Once stopped, he might have taken time for a view of the Sound from Horton Point before proceeding to Greenport for the ferry. It is more certain that he did commission construction of the beacon 33 years later, while president, but funding was not available to build the beacon until 1855.

LIGHTHOUSE CONSTRUCTION

On July 24, 1855, Charles H. Paine sold 8.2 acres of farmland called Cliff Lot on Horton Point to the United States for $550 while Franklin Pierce was president. In 1826, Joshua Horton had lost the land for nonpayment of taxes. The current lighthouse was constructed during Pierce's administration, but it was October 15, 1857, when it went into operation. That was 100 years after Washington may have identified the need, and by then the president was James Buchanan.

After a granite foundation was laid, brick was used to construct a rectangular two-story keeper's residence attached by a cut-stone arched windway to a square, slightly tapering three-story tower. In the 1880s, the windway was closed-in, and a second story was added between the structures, creating space for an assistant keeper's dormitory. About that time, the gracious north porch was added across the original keeper's residence. The tower was whitewashed until both the dwelling and tower were covered with white stucco. The 57-foot-high tower was capped by a circular iron railing and black iron octagonal lantern with a copper dome. It was necessary to climb 29 steps, then two seven-step ladders to reach the lantern room. A simple watch room with a stove and door to the iron balcony was beneath the lantern room. Although the square tower construction was not uncommon, it provided additional visual identification that distinguished it from lighthouses with rounded or octagonal towers designed to withstand high winds. About 40,000 bricks went into the structure that cost $12,212 to build. The cornerstone was laid June 9, 1857.

Horton Point Lighthouse.
Illustration by Vincent Quatroche, The Greenport Art Studio.

Illumination was provided by an Argand whale oil lamp with two wicks designed by a young lieutenant in the United States Army named George Meade. The prisms of a bee-hive-like, 3rd order, fixed Fresnel lens around the lamp magnified and condensed the light into a narrow beam. The lens was perfected by French physicist Augustine Fresnel in 1822. The Army officer who designed the oil lamp later found his way into the history books as General George C. Meade, commander of the Federal forces at Gettysburg.

LIGHTKEEPERS
Records show that there were eight keepers of the light in the 76 years of its manned operation:

William Sinclair	6/04/1857 - 4/13/1861
A. J. Tillinghast	4/13/1861 - 10/19/1866
Barnabas Pike	10/19/1866 - 4/15/1869
Theron Squire	4/15/1869 - 6/01/1871
Daniel Goldsmith	6/01/1871 - 2/24/1877
George S. Prince	2/24/1877 - 9/10/1896
Robert E. Ebitts	9/10/1896 - 5/01/1919
George Ehrhardt	5/01/1919 - 6/30/1938

The list of eight ignores Keeper Stella Prince, daughter of the sixth keeper George S. Prince, a Civil War veteran and recipient of the Medal of Honor. She was born and raised at the lighthouse. When her father died, she was appointed assistant keeper under his replacement, Robert Ebbitts (also a Civil War veteran). He served from September 10, 1896, to May 1, 1919, but in 1903, he was injured in a 30-foot fall when his ladder collapsed while he was painting the tower's walls. During Ebbitt's lengthy convalescence, President Theodore Roosevelt appointed Stella as his interim replacement. She served until her resignation in 1904 to marry another Long Islander, George Herbert Terry of Orient, the cook on *Black Eagle* out of Orient.

The last keeper, George Ehrhardt, had served as assistant keeper of Orient Point Lighthouse, keeper of Plum Island Lighthouse, and keeper of Long Beach "Bug" Lighthouse. Prior to his lighthouse service he was a member of the famed U.S.

Seventh Cavalry. His first assignment was to care for Custer's horse Comanche, the sole survivor of the Battle of the Little Bighorn in 1876. Ehrhardt fought at Wounded Knee in South Dakota in 1890, the last major battle of the Indian Wars. He was also present for the storming of Moro Castle in Cuba during the Spanish-American War.

AUTOMATION

In 1863, because whaling was decreasing and because of the demands of war, whale oil became so expensive that the lanterns were converted to lard oil fuel which caused much work for the keepers, removing soot from the lamp and lenses. In March 1883, kerosene replaced lard oil, and on January 28, 1907, kerosene oil vapor became the standard fuel, but the Fresnel lens was unchanged. That served until June 30, 1933, when the lighthouse was decommissioned as an economy move and the lamp and Fresnel lens were removed and stored in a Coast Guard warehouse in Maryland, where the lens was misplaced and never seen again despite persistent efforts to retrieve it, but the need for a beacon was not ignored. An automated 100,000-candlepower revolving electric lamp with a green beam that could be seen at a range of 14 miles was installed on an iron and steel skeleton tower 50 feet in front of the lighthouse. That ended what Elizabeth Horton Goldsmith, daughter of an assistant light keeper, termed "the romantic and hectic family life at Horton Point Lighthouse."

Keeper George Ehrhardt stayed in residence and watched over two automated lights (Horton Point and Shinnecock Lighthouses) until the 1938 hurricane blew a large portion of the roof off the keeper's residence and he retired. The federal government disposed of the furniture and fixtures, but Ehrhardt's wife and daughter Marguerite managed to save brassware and other items now on display at the lighthouse museum.

The automatic light was replaced in about 1960 with a Crouse Hinds Type DCB-10 Rotating Beacon that was designed as an aircraft beacon. Two revolving beams of light were produced by a 500-watt lamp and two semaphore lenses set 180 degrees apart. The 94-pound unit revolved at six RPM, producing a flash at ten-second intervals.

Community interest in the beloved lighthouse never wavered in the years following its 1933 closing. In January 1934 it was conveyed to the Southold Park District for one dollar by the U.S. Department of Commerce. However, the federal government retained the right to repossess the property to have access to the light. During World War II, the tower was used as a Coast Guard lookout for enemy aircraft and submarines, and military personnel were housed in the lightkeepers' quarters. After the war, vandals took delight in stripping the old structure of anything that could be torn loose and decorating the walls with graffiti. Doors were welded closed, but they were pried open and the destruction resumed until the Korean War brought the lighthouse into service again. It was manned by civilian volunteers for the Ground Observer Corps of the Air Force.

RESTORATION

In January 1976, a $40,000 restoration was begun by the Southold Historical Society as part of the Southold Park District's bicentennial project. It included the installation of plumbing, electric wiring, and heating. Early in July 1977 the keeper's residence, converted to a museum, was opened to the public. George Wagoner, director of the Society, served as resident curator of the museum. It features the original yellow pine flooring and one of the six original fireplaces. Central heating was installed and five other fireplaces were bricked up. A permanent display of exhibits dating as far back as colonial days include harpoons, scrimshaw, powder horn, a whale tooth, and a saw made from the bill òf a sawfish. Charles Payne, who sold the eight acres of the lighthouse to the U.S. government in 1855 is memorialized by the display of his scrimshaw walking stick. Marine paintings on loan to the museum and lighthouse logs written by the keepers dating back to 1857 are also displayed.

An anonymous diver donated 22 Spanish silver coins from the 18th century that were recovered from Long Island Sound off Horton Point. Another donor, a Cutchogue resident, contributed a bar of silver bullion she recovered in 1986 at the edge of Peconic Bay in Jamesport, using a metal detector. The mint mark "Cerro de

Pasco" stamped in the ingot identified its source as a mining town in the Andes above Lima, Peru that had operated since 1639.

In the spring of 1978, the Coast Guard replaced the automatic light that was installed when the lighthouse was closed in 1933 with an FA-251 electronic light controlled by an electric eye. Also, a radio direction-finding transmitter and tower were installed behind the lighthouse. The range of the new light was 20 miles, a 40 percent improvement over the old one. Gradual restoration of the old structure continued, but its lantern remained dark. In May 1990, the FA-251 light was placed in the restored lantern room and the lighthouse was recommissioned. After being dark for 57 years, the lighthouse again displayed its beam on June 9. The light gives a slow flashing green-tinged glow every ten seconds, with a range of about 14 nautical miles. The steel tower was displaced by a flagpole, set on its old foundation.

A postmark and stamp, both featuring a Horton Point Lighthouse etching by local artist Joy Bear, were issued on June 9, 1990. They commemorated Southold Town's 350th anniversary and the 200th anniversary of President George Washington's 1790 commissioning of the lighthouse.

In 1991, the radio-direction finding transmitter and tower were dismantled and buried behind the lighthouse.

In 1993, the north porch was reconstructed from original plans, and the iron stairs connecting the balcony, which encircles the lantern, with the watch room below was restored.

GARGOYLES

One of the features of the original lighthouse was ten gargoyles covering the downspouts on the dome of the lantern room. They were missing in 1995, but Bob Kaelin, a volunteer of the Southold Historical Society recalled them from his childhood. He was under the impression that they were in the form of a lion's head, but the ensuing search proved them to be the heads of the legendary phoenix, the bird that lived for 500 years, then rose from its own ashes to live again. A story about the Southold Historical Society's search for the gargoyles, was printed in *The Suffolk Times* July 6, 1995 issue. Wayne Wheeler, president of the U.S. Lighthouse

Society, based in San Francisco, read the story and called Cliff Benfield, the present volunteer curator of the lighthouse museum. Wheeler told Benfield that he remembered seeing a gargoyle in Shore Village Lighthouse Museum in Rockland, Maine. Benfield contacted the museum's curator, Ken Black, and was told the gargoyle was one that the U.S. Lighthouse Board had cast in bronze to cover rainspouts for all lighthouses.

A Hauppauge Long Island company contacted a Brooklyn caster who made a mold of the phoenix gargoyle and using a lost wax process cast ten new ones for the Horton Point Lighthouse. As with all restoration, the Southold Park District shared the cost with the Southold Historical Society. The copies of the original phoenix gargoyles that graced the dome of the once-doomed lighthouse were in place by Memorial Day, 1996, and symbolized the lighthouse's resurrection from obscurity to a place on the National Register of Historic Places. Today, the exterior of the lighthouse is identical to the earliest photographs of it taken in 1871.

The treasured landmark is back on the job of warning Long Island Sound navigators away from treacherous shoals and boulders. The Horton Point green beacon flashes its warning every ten seconds. The Coast Guard maintains the operating lantern, while the grounds, museum, and the apartment above the museum are maintained by the Southold Town Park District and the Southold Historical Society. The nautical museum provides education and entertainment for throngs of schoolchildren, residents, and tourists.

The Southold Park District and the Southold Historical Society have accomplished their mission for the aged lighthouse with its long history. It is a remarkable history that, so far, ranges from the early days of our country's history to the present, a legend of life and death before rising from the ashes to live again.

OPEN TO THE PUBLIC

The lighthouse now houses the Southold Historical Society Nautical Museum and is open to the public on Saturday and Sunday from 11:30 a.m. to 4:00 p.m. from Memorial Day to Columbus Day. Cliff Benfield said, "About 5,000 people visit each year."

LONG BEACH BAR LIGHTHOUSE (BUG LIGHT)

When built: 1871; rebuilt 1990
Location: Long Beach Bar at entry to Orient Harbor
Still on site: yes
Accessible to public: no

*E*ighteen years before there was an Orient Point Lighthouse at the eastern tip of Long Island's North Fork, a new lighthouse went into operation only a few miles southwest, at the entry to Orient Harbor. It marked the deep water between Long Beach and Shelter Island for boats sailing between Orient Point and Orient Harbor, Greenport Harbor, or the Peconic Bays. After passing the lighthouse, boats followed channel markers between Shelter Island's Hay Beach Point and Cleve's Point in East Marion on the North Fork. They were guided by an unmanned light into Greenport Harbor, a deep water harbor that served as a shipbuilding center in World War II. Although Long Beach Bar Lighthouse marked the shoals at the end of the sandy Long Beach peninsula, the stubby structure set on stilts became better known as Bug Light because it looked so much like a spindly-legged insect walking on the water.

CONSTRUCTION

The wave-swept lighthouse, built in 1871, was a 26- by 26-foot, three-story Victorian-style lightkeeper's house built on a rock foundation. The light tower protruded above the roof, with a railed watch tower around the peaked-roof lantern room. Three bedrooms and a kitchen were provided for the lightkeeper and his family, and a basement furnace protected them against cold winters. Re-provisioning by going ashore every three or four days was no problem—except when the bay was frozen or filled with drifting ice. Then, the diet was from cans for a week or more, even as long as a month, as in 1936.

The winter of 1917-1918 was one of the coldest on record for Eastern Long Island. From late December to mid-March the bays were frozen solid enough for mail delivery twice a day across Great Peconic Bay from Good Ground (Hampton Bays) to New Suffolk, a distance of eight miles. During the 46 day record freeze, a newspaper described the plight of one pedestrian, Bug Light's keeper: "Keeper Erhardt, of the Long Beach Lighthouse, had a close call Wednesday. In an attempt to walk ashore on the ice, he soon found himself on an ice floe. His danger was seen by Captain Charles Fournier who telephoned to Chief of Police Theodore Howard in Greenport. Adolph Johnsen got the big oyster boat *Magician* out and went to the rescue, but the man was able to step out on hard ice just before the rescuers reached him."

Long Beach Bar Lighthouse.
Illustration by Vincent Quatroche, the Greenport Art Studio.

RENOVATION

In 1924 the Coast Guard concluded that the spindly legs supporting the lighthouse were inadequate. A concrete foundation under the keeper's quarters reinforced it, but that eliminated the open space under the structure. It no longer resembled an insect walking on water, but its name never changed. Even after the Coast Guard decommissioned it in 1948, the darkened structure was fondly referred to as Bug Light.

A group of 13 Orient residents had hopes of one day restoring the lighthouse. In the early 1950s they purchased it in the name of their organization, jokingly referred to as the Orient Marine Hysterical Society. Although there was no restoration, children did go out in small boats to paint the walls and wash windows. The society never accomplished its objective, but its members did enjoy the privileges of ownership, shared with the locals who found it a great place for fishing.

ARSON

On the night of July 4, 1963, a local boater, Jay Helm, was headed for Deering Harbor after watching a fireworks display. As he approached Orient Harbor, the sky lit up with a glow that seemed to be a ship on fire, until he realized that it was Bug Light ablaze. He knew that the old wooden structure was doomed, and his reaction echoed all who knew the venerable old relic, "It was terrible when we realized it was the Bug Light." But that was mild compared to the grief of retired Lightkeeper William Follett, who served there for the ten years before it closed, "Oh, gosh, I was sick, just so sick when I heard she was gone. I loved that place."

All that was left after the fire were the foundation and evidence that a flammable liquid had been poured throughout the structure. The perpetrator remains unknown, and it is not known whether the act stemmed from malicious intent or mindless revelry intended to contribute to the night's fireworks. Regardless of which it might be, the culprit would have been dealt swift, severe justice on the North Fork.

The Suffolk Times published in its July 3, 1997, edition the report of Frank Andreiuolo, 78, that he was visiting friends, Carl and

Dorothy Schaub at their home just inside the entrance to Gull Pond in Greenport when Bug Light was destroyed. He stated that he and his host were cleaning up after a barbecue on Schaub's front lawn when they saw a huge flash at about 10:00 p.m. They thought a boat had blown up and went out to help aboard Schaub's 27-foot Owens, with Schaub's son Gary aboard. They got as close as they could to the flames and realized it was a building, not a boat. "They were right there," Andreiuolo said of two young men he saw on the rock foundation of the lighthouse. "They were screaming and hollering and cheering; they were having a great time."

Andreiuolo stated that after five minutes, the two youths realized they were being watched. Then they jumped off the rocks into a 14-foot speedboat that out-distanced Schaub's powerful Owens. "Carl wanted to catch them," Andreiuolo said. "He was really upset they had burned it."

It is hard to understand why, if the story is true, neither Andreiuolo nor Schaub, or even Schaub's son Gary saw fit to reveal it 34 years ago, particularly when concerned Orient residents offered a $200 reward for information leading to the apprehension of those responsible for destroying the lighthouse.

> West beyond the tip of Long Beach Point
> Once stood old "Bug Light";
> And for exactly a hundred years;
> the government kep her shining bright.
> ...
> It was known far and wide
> As a landmark at the entrance to Peconic Bay;
> Yachtsmen and seafarers alike;
> Would pass her night and day.
> ...
> It happened one night around ten o'clock
> In fact, on July 4, 1963;
> When persons with no community pride;
> Turned a day of celebratin into a tragedy.

> *They soaked her down with gasoline*
> *These people who aren't known by name;*
> *And set it afire to go up in smoke;*
> *And leave their souls to live in shame.*
> —George H. Morton, *Old Bug Light*

RESTORATION

For the next 26 years, only its concrete foundation graced the rocky site of the fire-gutted Bug Light. The lighthouse was only a memory, but the urge to restore it lived on. In November 1989, a dedicated group of North Fork and Shelter Island residents formed the East End Seaport Museum and Marine Foundation. Its aim was to restore Bug Light in appearance and function to its former glory. The objective was to start construction on July 4, 1990, the 27th anniversary of its destruction by fire.

The volunteers raised $140,000 in less than a year and the "almost-replica" Bug Light was built in three sections at the Greenport Yacht and Shipbuilding Company by volunteer workers; Stephen Clarke, the company's owner, donated his facility. Sixty tons of rip-rap was placed around the base of the lighthouse and in early August a Shelter Island ferry carried a cement truck and pumping equipment to the old lighthouse foundation where ten yards of cement was added as reinforcement. On Wednesday, September 5, 1990, sail and power boats gathered to watch the first floor of the little wooden house as it slid down the yard's rails like a ship, while a U.S. Navy band played. They followed as it floated by barge to the lighthouse site. A heavy duty marine crane first lifted it from the barge, then gently deposited it on the concrete and steel foundation that had been prepared to receive it. The second story followed and was lowered with precision till it set on top of the first floor. Then, the 258-mm, solar-powered light was lowered on top, 63 feet above the water, to complete the restoration.

That evening, the re-lighting of Bug Light was celebrated with a formal ceremony, a 21-gun salute, music by a Navy band, and a fireworks display. The entire process from start of construction to re-lighting took only 60 days, after 42 years of darkness. The East

End Seaport Museum and Marine Foundation maintains the building and the Coast Guard maintains the light. Boats entering Orient Harbor are now greeted every six seconds by its white light flashing the greeting that local mariners interpret as, "Welcome to Orient Harbor—courtesy of East End Seaport Museum and Marine Foundation."

The high spirits that were stimulated by re-opening the lighthouse were dampened in 1997 by evidence of severe damage to the structure by the combined forces of wind, wave, ice, storm, hurricane, and the salt-laden environment. After only seven years, inspectors were greeted by damaged roof shingles, split caulking, the access ramp broken, and the steel basement door driven in by wave-driven tree limbs. The alarm system had already been replaced twice because its sensitive wiring needed protection against the harsh elements of the site.

The East End Seaport Museum and Marine Foundation quickly responded with a call for $38,000 in donations and a major volunteer effort to correct the deficiencies. With the benefit of experience, technological advances, the generous contributions of donors, and experienced volunteer help, the resulting project should far outlast the 1990 effort.

Other lighthouses have been rebuilt by the Coast Guard, but Bug Light will enjoy the distinction of being the only one funded and constructed by volunteers.

Top: Long Beach Lighthouse became known as "Bug Light" because the stilts that supported the stubby structure made it look like a bug. *Courtesy of Antonia Booth, Southold Town Historian.*
Bottom: Later, the lighthouse's stilts were boxed in. *Photo taken by George Morton in 1953.*

Orient Point Lighthouse under
construction in 1899. Top: June 6.
Above: August 2. Right: August 20.
Courtesy of the National Archives.

Left: Orient Point Light - house under construction in September 1899. *Courtesy of the National Archives.*

Bottom: Orient Point Lighthouse photographed in 1996 by H. Keatts.

Plum Island Lighthouse in 1884 *(top, courtesy of the National Archives)* and in 1996 *(bottom, photo by H. Keatts).*

ORIENT POINT LIGHTHOUSE

When built: 1899
Location: Oyster Pond Reef/Plum Gut/Long Island
Still on site: yes
Accessible to public: no

Orient Point marks the eastern end of Long Island's North Fork, about 15 miles short of neighboring Montauk Point on the South Fork. Like Montauk Point, it consists of terminal moraine, the deposit left by the receding glacier as the Ice age came to a close. Unlike Montauk Point, Orient Point does not front on the Atlantic. Instead, it faces little Plum Island, separated only by Plum Gut. The Gut connects Long Island Sound with Gardiners Bay to the south, or Montauk and the open Atlantic to the southeast. Unlike Montauk, its lighthouse is not a slender needle perched high on a bluff. It is a stubby, wave-swept structure at sea level, affectionately known as the "Coffee Pot."

Orient Point Lighthouse.
*Illustration by Paul M. Bradley Jr.,
Lighthouse Graphics.*

Currents of five to six knots converging from both directions produce wild waters in the Gut, particularly when the tidal current is counter to the wind. The depth of its channel is more than 100 feet, but outside the channel the dangerous, rocky bottom is less than 10 feet deep. The offshore Orient Point Lighthouse is built at the end of a stretch of rocks, only ten feet deep, known as Oyster Pond Reef. That underwater hazard, marked by the lighthouse, stretches almost one third of the way across the Gut.

The need for a lighthouse was recognized three years before its construction, when the beacon off Orient Point on the west side of Plum Gut was carried away by ice. The Commissioner of Lighthouses proposed that it be replaced by a lighted beacon and fog 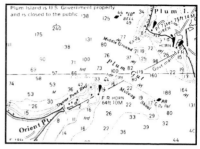 signal at $5,000 estimated cost. That was either grossly underestimated or major changes were included because on June 4, 1897, Congress approved $30,000 for the construction.

CONSTRUCTION

Instead of excavating a foundation, the uneven contour of the rocks of the reef was leveled to provide a stable base for the structure. Cast-iron sections of curved plates with flanges on the concave (interior) surface were cast in New York City and shipped to the Orient Point Wharf Company, the current site of the Cross Sound Ferry terminal. The plates were floated to the reef, where they were assembled and laid in place, one course at a time, to form a 32-foot-long caisson, 25 feet in diameter with bolts through the interior flanges. It was filled almost completely with concrete, with the top left unfilled to provide space for equipment and supplies. Then the tower was set on top of the caisson. On October 26, 1898, a gale swept away a second course of plates that had been sunk in position to reinforce the caisson. It also damaged 19 of the first course of plates and broke 20 beyond repair. That convinced the Commissioner of Lighthouses to install about 600 tons of riprap stone to reinforce the base of the structure.

The black tower, with a white band midway, is 45 feet tall with a diameter of 21 feet at the base and 18 feet at the top. Its shape has aptly been described as a "conical spark plug," with a circular watch deck on top that supports the circular lantern. The same cast iron plates with flanges construction was used on the walls of the tower as on assembly of the caisson. The tower is lined with brick, three feet thick at the bottom, tapering to a smaller thickness at the top. Access to the wave-washed tower is by ladder to the first floor, which is encircled by a covered gallery. Window and door openings were provided for living quarters on the first two of three stories, but now, with no need for keepers, those openings are covered with steel plates to discourage vandalism. Four round ports light the third floor. The watch deck and lantern levels are also encircled by walkways protected by railings, but without cover. The broad white band above the walkway provides daytime identification of the light.

Circular cast iron stairs, built into the tower walls and separated from the living quarters by a sheet metal wall, provide access from each floor to the lantern level. The slanted, lantern roof is covered with sheet metal with a ball ventilator at the peak.

When the light went into operation on October 20, 1899, Norwegian-born N.A. Anderson was appointed its first keeper at $600 annual salary. In December, he was joined by Daniel McDermott of Ireland, whose salary as his assistant was $450 a year. Anderson remained at his post until 1919.

PRESERVATION

In 1939, the Coast Guard took over responsibility for the lighthouse and automated it in 1966. Only four years later, the Coast Guard announced plans for its demolition because it was rusting away and listing. That made it a hazard for personnel servicing the light, and repair was not economically feasible. By the end of the 1970 season the old "Coffee Pot" was to be demolished by a U.S. Navy disposal team, and replaced with a simple, stem beacon.

Widespread protests by mariners who treasured the beacon and members of the community who dreaded the loss of their historical landmark influenced the Coast Guard. Initially, it offered to postpone demolition until a private group could take over the lighthouse. Then, after a survey by engineers from New London, the lighthouse was permitted to operate for three more years, until October, 1973. Observers were pleasantly surprised then, when workers began repairs instead of demolition. The surface of the lighthouse was sandblasted, then covered with a 10-year preservative coating and epoxy base finish coat. Holes in the cast-iron caisson base were filled with concrete and the rest of the lighthouse was restored.

On June 1, 1978, the 108-year-old Plum Island Lighthouse was closed. The history of that old granite lighthouse, built in 1869-70, actually went back to its predecessor, a 40-foot rough stone tower, built on land purchased for that purpose by the Federal government in 1826. To compensate for the loss of its 350,000-candlepower beacon and 14-mile visibility, an automated beacon was installed at Plum Gut. At the same time, the Orient Point Lighthouse was automated to operate by remote control from New London. It is now illuminated by a 190-mm lantern, 26 ⅞ inches high and 19½ inches diameter, rotated by a motor-driven turntable.

PLUM ISLAND LIGHTHOUSE

When built: 1826; rebuilt 1869-70
Location: western end of Plum Island, on Plum Gut
Still on site: yes
Accessible to public: no

*P*lum Island lies 110 miles east of New York City, about 1.5 nautical miles from Orient Point, Long Island, and approximately 10 miles from Connecticut. It is 2.9 miles long and 1.7 miles wide at the western (widest) end. The Dutch named the island after the beach plum that grows along the shore. The early occupants, the Circhug Indians, owed allegiance to Wyandanch, Sachem of the Montauketts. He conveyed ownership of the island to Samuel Wyllys in the following deed (original spelling retained): "Know all men by these presents that I, Wyandanck, the Montauk Sachem, for me and my heirs forever, for and in consideration of a coat, a barrel of biskitt, 100 muxes (iron drills used to make wampum beads from shells) and fish hooks, at these subscribing by mee, received of Samuel Wylls and his heirs forever; I, the said Sachem, hereby declare myself to bee the rightful owner of the sayd Island and I covenant with the said Samuel Wyllys, his heirs and assigns, that I will never molest him or his assigns in the possession of same and will prohibit my men from doing so, by killing any of his cattle that shall bee put upon it. And for the true performance hereof, I have set my hand at Gadiner's Island, April 27, 1659."

(Signed) Wyandanck
His X mark

For two centuries, Plum Island was devoted to farming and raising cattle and sheep, under private ownership. By 1826, it was the property of Richard Jerome and his wife. On August 29, 1826, the United States Government bought three acres on the western end of the island for $90 to erect a 40-foot high, rough stone lighthouse tower.

LONESOME

In the early 1840s, teenager Sarah Bowditch shared the lonely existence of Plum Island with her grandfather Henry Conklin, keeper of the lighthouse. Her mother died at her birth and she was raised by her grandparents. The sensitive young girl never adjusted to the lonely existence of lighthouse life. A collection of poems written in her late teens disclose the extent of her suffering from confinement on Plum Island. As a 17-year-old in 1841, she eloquently expressed her plea for escape:

> *Lend me your wings, my gentle dove,*
> *O lend them for a while.*
> *Fain would I spread them wide and fly*
> *Far from this dreary isle.*
> *My soul is sick of solitude.*
> *I long afar to flee*
> *From the ceaseless roaring of the waves*
> *And the pounding of the sea.*
> *No friends, no pleasures have we here*
> *The long hours to beguile.*
> *Lend me your wings, my gentle dove,*
> *O, lend them for a while.*

Sarah did escape. In 1845 she married Benjamin K. Mulford.

By 1868, the tower and keeper's dwelling were in such bad condition that the inspector of lighthouses recommended in his *Annual Reports* that the 42-year-old lighthouse be rebuilt: "Both the tower and keeper's dwelling are in bad condition and should be rebuilt. The tower, built in 1827, leaks badly; the masonry is soft and crumbling; the lantern is of the old pattern ... with small lights ... It is thought the old buildings are not worth the money which would be required to put them in good order, and it is therefore proposed to rebuild them...."

REBUILT

The rebuilding was completed in 1870 with a whitewashed,

octagonal tower housing a Fourth Order Fresnel lens atop the peak of a granite block keeper's dwelling. The year 1869, when reconstruction started, appears at the base of the tower. The 350,000-candlepower light had a range of 14 miles.

Plum Island Lighthouse.
Illustration by Vincent Quatroche, The Greenport Art Studio.

Only eight years later, the slate roof of the dwelling house leaked so badly that the slate roof was replaced by a shingle roof, eliminating the problem. At the same time, the height of the fog bell was raised about ten feet to improve its audibility in fogs and storms.

The United States Government purchased the entire island in the 1890s and constructed Fort Terry as a coast artillery post. It was considered important to the defense of Long Island during the Spanish-American War and served in both world wars as a training camp. The Army went so far as to build the now defunct Plum Island Rail Road on the island to move submarine mines to and from ships.

OFF LIMITS

After the war, the Army Chemical Corps assumed charge of the island, but on July 1, 1954, Plum Island was transferred to the United States Department of Agriculture. A high-containment laboratory was opened in 1956 to study hoof-and-mouth disease and other domestic animal diseases of economic significance. There are about 350 employees, mostly commuting from Orient Point, but visitors are not allowed on the island.

The Plum Island Lighthouse was closed in June 1978 as an economy measure. In its place, a small unmanned beacon, Plum Gut Light (LLN 937.50), was installed. To compensate for the loss of Plum Island's powerful beam, Orient Point Light (LLN 940), operated from New London was upgraded. The Fresnel lens and clockwork mechanism were removed from the lighthouse and are featured in an impressive display at the East End Seaport and Marine Museum in Greenport.

EROSION

Erosion is attacking the historic lighthouse. Its old generator building overhangs the cliff, which is eroding at the rate of one foot per year. Although the two-story lighthouse is still solid and weathertight, paint is peeling, the flooring has caved in, and rooms are covered with crumbling asbestos. Minimum maintenance only is being provided.

Efforts to obtain government assistance in restoring the old structure have been to no avail. Laboratory management's response to such requests is, "the agency is not in the business of restoring lighthouses." *Newsday's* June 8, 1997, issue reported that a group of lab employees, interested in restoring the lighthouse, were warned that it would raise problems of liability. They were advised to incorporate as volunteers, but not until Department of Agriculture attorneys determined if the agency could legally work with restoration volunteers. That discouraged the employees from further pursuit of the project out of concern for their jobs.

There is still hope for the old granite lighthouse that marked the treacherous waters off the western point of Plum Island for 108 years, but it does not run high.

LITTLE GULL ISLAND LIGHTHOUSE

When built: 1806, rebuilt 1868
Location: between Plum Island and Fishers Island
Still on site: yes
Accessible to public: no

*L*ittle Gull Island is only two acres in size, but for more than 190 years it has protected maritime traffic in the hazardous passage between Long Island Sound and Block Island Sound. That channel, called The Race, is notorious for the turbulence caused by conflicting currents of the two sounds. The average flood velocity is 2.9 knots and it ebbs at 3.5 knots, but either can reach 5 knots. Other than for about one-half-hour at slack tide, there are always rips and swirls. They are particularly heavy during foul weather, especially when a strong wind opposes the current or the current bucks a heavy sea.

ORIGINAL

The treacherous channel claimed so many ships by the early 1800s that the Lighthouse Board ordered construction of a lighthouse on the tiny island to mark the southern edge of The Race. The Little Gull Island 50-foot-high lighthouse called the "Key to Long Island Sound" was lighted in 1806 with a fixed, white beacon that had a range of only eight or nine miles. The lighthouse was one of the earliest projects completed after the Federal Government assumed responsibility for aids to navigation.

The solid masonry tower was topped by a dome-shaped, 10 feet high by 10 feet in diameter, glass-enclosed lantern room. A wood-burning stove protected the panes against frosting on cold winter nights. A large house was attached to the tower and there was a separate building for oil storage. There were also hog pens and a small barn for animals.

Illumination was provided by 14 whale oil lamps, seven larger than the others, backed by parabolic nine-inch, silver-plated copper reflectors. A metal tube enclosed in an outer wick-tube extended through the bottom of each lantern to provide air for a tubular wick mounted around the air-tube. The wick was raised or lowered by a pointed rod through a small slot in the wick-tube.

Until a lighthouse was erected on Race Rock, off New London, Connecticut in 1878, Little Gull Island Lighthouse alone protected navigation through The Race.

On September 23, 1815, a hurricane inflicted severe damage to the lighthouse. According to Willard E. Rackett, who heard the story from his great-grandfather Noah Rackett II, the tide was so high that a pig, swept from its pen, was rescued through a window of the keeper's house. Damage to the lighthouse was so severe that $30,000 was spent to build a wall of loose rock about its shoreline to protect against the fury of another hurricane.

Benjamin Thomas Dering, Superintendent of Construction during the building of the wall, wrote in his journal (now in the Jermain Memorial Library, Sag Harbor): "These islands were purchased of William Jarome by the U.S. in 1805 for $800 for the purpose of erecting a lighthouse. It was thought more practical to place it on the small island which then contained not more than three quarters of an acre.... The islands take their names from the great number of gulls that frequent them in Summer ... The lighthouse was erected in 1804 at the expense of $15,000. In 1807 a wall was erected on the NW part of the island to protect it from the encroachment of the sea. [During] The hurricane of September 1815 more than one-half of the upland of the island was swept away. The sea approached within four feet of the foundation of the lighthouse and leaving a perpendicular bank of 15 feet from the level of the shore. It also undermined the dwelling house, half of which hung over the bank. During the awful storm ... only one woman with her four children witnessed the scene. [Her husband, the keeper, was on the mainland.] After the storm, three commissioners surveyed the island and decided that a circular wall was needed to protect against erosion. The wall was erected in 1817 and was 300 feet in circumference and 100 feet in diameter. The wall was seven feet thick at the bottom and three and one-half feet at the top. The height of the wall was 22 feet and a four-foot high railing on the top. The cost of building the wall was $24,500. The workmen 28 in number appear cheerful and happy and work very hard. But here as in every part of the country rum is a great article little could be done without it. Soon shall we be a drunken nation. Yes now half of the country staggers."

Work on the wall started May 19, 1817; and was completed August 15, 1817.

On Friday, June 28, 1817, President James Monroe left New London in a sloop-of-war, in company with four cutters, intending to sail into Gardiners Bay, but the wind failed and he transferred to a cutter and stopped at Little Gull Island during construction of the wall. Dering wrote of the unprecedented event, "I quickly blackened my shoes ... buttoned my coat and met him on the shore ..." The president went to top of the lighthouse.

In 1856, a 2,000-pound fog bell was installed, but even with the light and fog signal, ships still stranded in the shallows around Little Gull Island.

REPLACED

After 62 years of service, the 1806 lighthouse was replaced by a taller, block granite tower and a powerful Second Order Fresnel lens was installed to increase the range of its beacon. Cast iron was used for the central column, stairs, and watch deck flooring. It was one of the last masonry structure lighthouses built on the East Coast. The use of cast iron, the distinctive granite block door lintel carved with the date 1868, and the Italian influence were a departure from traditional lighthouse design, a bridge between the old and the new.

The circular granite base of the lighthouse is about 19 feet in diameter. The inside of the tower is lined with brick. The thickness of the walls, including granite and brick, is 5 1/2 feet at the base and

2 feet at the top. A cast iron column through the center of the tower supports the cast iron circular stairway and the top of the column supports the cast iron floor of the watch deck. At the top of the 91-foot tower, the diameter is 12 feet. The door to the tower, facing north, is reminiscent of Italian design, with protruding granite blocks on either side. Four windows at four different levels, facing four different directions, spiral up the 91-foot-high tower to illuminate the 96-step circular stairway during the day. The 12-sided lantern room is covered by a sheet metal, ogee-(reverse curve or "S") shape roof topped with a ventilator ball. Lard oil was burned in the lamps until 1883, when they were replaced by mineral oil lamps. In 1907, the oil lamps were replaced with an incandescent oil vapor lamp, similar to a Coleman lantern. The keeper pumped up pressure in the lamp before lighting the mantle.

Little Gull Island Lighthouse.
Illustration by Paul M. Bradley Jr., Lighthouse Graphics.

A three-story dwelling housed the head keeper on the first floor, the assistant on the second, and the second assistant on the third floor, with a spiral staircase connecting the three floors. Each floor had two bedrooms, a kitchen, and a sitting room; the only sources of heat were the kitchen stoves.

On a freezing morning in February 1918, a cry for help alerted Keeper Eugene Merry to a man in the distance, adrift on an ice floe. Merry and his two assistants launched the station's row boat and made the rescue after two hours of winding through the ice-choked waters.

The 1938 hurricane damaged or carried away the oil tanks, fog signal building, the out house, and the boat house. Keeper Edgar Whitford stated that during the height of the storm he watched waves breaking at eye level from the building's second floor. The outbuildings were rebuilt following automation of the station.

During World War II the Army installed a 16-inch gun emplacement at Fort Michie on nearby Great Gull Island. The Army artillerymen alerted the head keeper at Little Gull Island whenever they were going to fire practice rounds. He protected the lantern glass from concussion by climbing outside and covering it with blankets.

On April 20, 1944, fire destroyed the living quarters. The blaze started in the paint locker and spread quickly, with the light tower acting as a chimney, drawing heat and smoke out the top. Intense heat shattered the glass in the lantern and damaged the Fresnel lens. The living quarters were replaced with a one-story structure.

In May 1978 the 110-year-old lighthouse was automated. It looks the same, but there is no keeper to tend its 17,000-candlepower Second Order Classical, 1,000-watt lamp and DCB-24 lens. Still, it projects a fixed, white beam 18 miles, a 306 kHz radio beacon 20 miles, and a piercing horn that bites through dense fog.

The old Fresnel lens was stored in 31 crates until 1997. Then, thanks to the efforts of Gail Fuller, curator of the U.S. Coast Guard, that valuable relic was transferred to the nearby Greenport East End Seaport Maritime Museum on permanent loan. It was assembled by volunteers and mounted on an eight-foot-high pedestal for display. The visual impact of the massive lens is awe-inspiring. It almost reaches the ceiling of the two-story room, dwarfing the three- to four-foot-high Fourth Order lens that served in the Little Gull Lighthouse from 1868 to 1925.

Keeper Edgar Whitford's son Ed spent his summers and school vacations at the light station. He fished, caught crabs, and watched ships and fishing boats as they sailed past. Occasionally they visited neighboring islands. When Ed returned to the island in 1992, his first visit in nearly 50 years, he reminisced: "There wasn't a day that went by that something didn't happen which was different and exciting. I guess we never felt deprived being out there. We always thought we were special, being the lighthouse keeper's kids. We grew up not caring about crowds, and to this day, I feel uncomfortable in a crowd. I feel very comfortable and at peace out here."

The original keeper's dwelling is gone, replaced by a separate building to house generating equipment and two small fiberglass storage sheds. The lighthouse is essentially sound, although the tower lining and some of its interior metal structure is cracked. But, with the help of modern technology, it still protects navigation between Long Island Sound and Block Island Sound.

Little Gull Island Lighthouse in 1928 with the three-story living quarters that was destroyed by fire in 1944 (top and center, courtesy of the National Archives) and in 1996 with the one-story structure that replaced the old one *(bottom, photo by H. Keatts).*

Race Rock Lighthouse
under construction
in October 1875
*(courtesy of the National
Archives)* and in 1996
(bottom, photo by H. Keatts).

RACE ROCK LIGHTHOUSE

When built: 1878
Location: .6 miles southwest of Race Point, Fishers Island
Still on site: yes
Accessible to public: no

ace Rock is a mostly underwater ledge of rocks, one 12 feet by 4 feet, others smaller, located .6 miles southwest of Fishers Island. It lies on the turbulent stretch of water called The Race (originally Horse Race) that connects Long Island Sound and Block Island Sound, southeast of New London, Connecticut. The mean velocity of tidal currents through The Race is 3.3 knots, and at times much greater, with prevailing strong rips and swirls. When currents confront strong wind or heavy seas, the rips are particularly severe. Race Rock lies three to thirteen feet deep in that maelstrom.

It was chosen as the site of a lighthouse because it was a navigational hazard that claimed an average of one shipwreck a year for eight years between 1829 and 1837. Captain Andrew Mather of the United States revenue cutter *Wolcott* assisted the vessels ashore on Fishers Island. He knew of "several more to go entirely to pieces, and in some instances with loss of life, and a great deal of property." In his opinion, the danger of passing through The Race stemmed from vessels misjudging the strength and direction of the tides. The *New York Journal of Commerce* carried his observations that are as valid today as the day they were written: "Vessels bound eastward in the night generally run down near Plum Island and the Gull Islands; and when abreast of the latter, they steer the sound course, which is E. by N.; and too many of them are not aware of the strength and course of the flood tide. The first half-flood sets NW, the last half about W.NW; consequently, when steering E. or E. by N., they have a strong tide on the starboard bow, which cuts them over to the northward; and, instead of making, as they supposed, an E. or E. by N. course, they are making a NE. by E. or NE. course, which often carries them on Race Point from which runs far out a reef of rocks under water."

It would have been preferred to build the lighthouse on land, at the tip of Race Point, but the decision was properly influenced by the 1838 report of Lieutenant George M. Bache in his study of the area: "... much benefit might be derived from a light upon Race point, if the navigation in its neighborhood were free from obstructions; but in addition to the reef which extends for some distance off from Fisher's [sic] Island, the dangerous rock, called Race Rock, lies at a distance of nearly three-fourths of a mile from it. It is difficult, in hazy weather particularly, to form an accurate estimation of the distance of a light; and vessels judging from the bearings of one on Race point, that they had given it a sufficient berth to clear all dangers, might be decoyed upon the rocks; its erection therefore is not recommended."

In response to the high frequency of disasters, and influenced by Lieutenant Bache's assessment, Congress appropriated $3,000 in 1838 for construction of a lighthouse at Race Rock. However, those funds were never expended.

DISASTER

While the fate of a lighthouse at Race Rock was being weighed in Washington, the steamer *Atlantic* neared Fishers Island from New York Harbor shortly after midnight on November 26, 1846. Captain Isaac K. Dustan kept the ship's whistle blowing through a cold, November storm. Nine miles off Fishers Island, a steam pipe burst, disabling the steamer. She anchored at once, but the heavy seas left her passengers concerned for their safety. One, who would have been a passenger was Daniel Webster of Marshfield, Massachusetts. He was one of many who had canceled passage because of the stormy night. Including the crew, there were 59 aboard when the ship began to drag her anchor toward the dangerous shore of Fishers Island.

Atlantic was forced into the breakers at about 2 a.m., and at 4:30 a.m. she hit a ledge with an impact that broke both her anchor cables. The ship broached and began to break up almost instantly. Terrified passengers clutched whatever they could to keep them afloat, but of the 39 passengers and 20 crew, only 14 made it to shore alive.

In a strange aftermath of the sinking, Fisher Island residents visiting the scene heard the weird tones of a bell tolling in the surf. It was the ship's bell lodged between the rocks, tolling a requiem for the 45 victims whenever the waves broke over it. Six years later, the clipper ship *John Milton* was lost on the south shore of Long Island, west of Montauk Point. Her ship's bell, like *Atlantic*'s, mourned victims of the disaster until it was removed for installation in the East Hampton Presbyterian Church.

Atlantic's loss added to the reputation of Race Rock as a killer that needed containment by a strategically located lighthouse. In 1852, the Lighthouse Board reported: "Various efforts have been made, and numerous appropriations expended, in endeavoring to place an efficient and permanent mark on this point. Buoys cannot be kept on it, and spindles have hitherto only remained until the breaking up of the ice in the spring."

That report was followed by a $7,000 appropriation in 1853 for a beacon on Race Rock, that culminated only in a day beacon completed in 1856.

Congress appropriated $8,000 in 1854 for construction of a lighthouse, but only $1,600 was expended, and that was mostly in surveys. In a solid statement of support, Congress appropriated $90,000 "for a lighthouse at or near Race Point."

After preliminary surveys that cost $6,528.57, an additional $10,000 was appropriated in 1870. By then, the Board had determined that $200,000 would be required to build the lighthouse and an additional $150,000 more was approved in 1871. That was the year construction finally started.

Awesome problems confronted engineer Francis Hopkinson Smith and his construction foreman, Captain Thomas Albertson Scott. Smith also built the government seawall at Governor's Island and the foundation for the Statue of Liberty in New York

Harbor. Captain Scott was the head of the Scott Wrecking Company, and a master diver. He did the submarine work on many of Smith's lighthouses. Others claimed Race Rock was impossible, but Smith and Scott proved it could be done by doing it, although it took seven years to complete.

Twenty eight years later, an open water lighthouse was constructed at nearby Orient Point in only two years using caisson pre-fabrication technology. While construction of Race Rock Lighthouse was underway, the Lighthouse Board developed the cast-iron caisson foundation for use at such sites. A caisson, made of pre-fabricated iron plates bolted together on site, formed a shell that was filled with concrete, to provide a rigid, heavy footing.

CONSTRUCTION

With the help of divers, the ledge was made approximately level with broken stone and riprap. Then a wall of 10,000 tons of riprap was built in an oval around the rock. The irregular stones averaged four tons each. A circular space, 60 feet in diameter, was cleared in the middle of the oval and a wood and iron framework was lowered into it. In the resulting cofferdam, a 9-foot-deep base of concrete was laid in four concentric layers, stepped like a wedding cake. The three-foot-high bottom layer measures 60 feet in diameter. Three feet wide cylindrical bands of half-inch iron were used to accomplish the stepping. The upper surface of the concrete is only eight inches above mean low water. That phase of construction was completed in November 1871.

The foundation supports a 57-foot-diameter, 30-foot-high conical pier. It is made of heavy masonry backed with concrete, and houses cisterns and cellars for the lighthouse above. The pier is crowned by a projecting coping 55 feet in diameter. A granite building for living quarters, one-and-a-half stories high, rises above the pier, with a light tower ascending from the center of the front of the house. The tower is square at the base and octagonal at the tower walk level. It carried a Fourth Order Fresnel lens, alternating white and red flash electric light of 90,000-candlepower. Its height of 67 feet above sea level and 45 feet above land provided 14 mile visibility. A heavy, masonry landing pier, 53 feet long and 25 feet wide, offers access to the lighthouse by boat on the north side of the lighthouse.

By April 1871, more than $95,000 was spent. Construction bids were so high that contracts could be let only for the landing, encroachment of the foundation, and only two courses of the pier. The encroachment alone used 8,000 tons of stone weighing eight to ten tons each. It was estimated that $75,000 more would be needed to complete the pier and dwelling. The additional funds were appropriated and the lighthouse construction continued.

COMPLETION

Bad weather, lack of materials when they were needed, and contract disputes impeded progress. Two workmen lost their lives during the project and living quarters for the workmen were twice damaged by storms, but the lighthouse was completed in 1878 at a total cost of $278,716. Its completion marked the end of masonry lighthouses on wave swept sites. It was also one of the last 19th century lighthouses to follow the Gothic Revival architectural style.

Race Rock Lighthouse.
Illustration by Paul M. Bradley Jr., Lighthouse Graphics.

Thomas A Carroll of Noank, Connecticut was appointed keeper of the light in 1880. Whenever he left the lighthouse, he rowed home across the sound and returned in the same manner. He was marooned ashore for several days by a severe storm in 1788. He believed it was his duty to row out to the lighthouse even though the waves were high and dangerous. The following spring his body washed ashore at Groton Long Point, Connecticut.

In 1895, a second-class siren and auxiliary bell were installed in response to the need for a fog signal. Both were unsatisfactory and the siren was discontinued on June 8, 1897. The bell continued in use until the following February, when a first-class siren was installed. It gave a group of two powerful blasts twice a minute, but mariners found it at times inaudible when approaching from eastward, south of Fishers Island.

The lighthouse operated until 1979, when it was automated and the Fresnel lens was replaced by a rotating 24-inch beacon (DCB-224) that flashes red every ten seconds, with a range of 19 miles. The structure, itself, is remarkably sound, with foundation, walls, and rock much the same as they were in 1879. Only the sash and door are new and the roof has been replaced.

Race Rock Lighthouse is a credit to the men who designed and constructed it. Their skill and determination provided a vital aid to navigation where others claimed it was impossible. Technology has passed them by in the completion of such a project, but Francis Hopkinson Smith and Captain Thomas Albertson Scott are the two who made Race Rock Lighthouse happen.

GARDINERS ISLAND LIGHTHOUSE

When built: 1854
Location: Gardiners Island
Still on site: no
Accessible to public: no

Not far away we saw the port,
The strange, old-fashioned, silent town,
The lighthouse, the dismantled fort,
The wooden houses, quaint and brown.
—Longfellow, *The Fire of Driftwood*

Gardiners Island enjoys a rare distinction along the busy Atlantic seaboard. It has survived since 1639, not only as a privately owned island, but also the property of the same family. The Island is the first English settlement in what is now New York State. It lies at the eastern end of Gardiners Bay, between the two fluke-like peninsulas of eastern Long Island.

Lion Gardiner, the original English settler, acquired the island from the resident Indians in much the same way that the Dutch purchased Manhattan Island. He received 3,000 acres for one large black dog, some powder and shot, and a few Dutch blankets. Later, a land grant from King Charles I of England provided proof of ownership under British law. The Indians called the island Manchonacke (Island of Death), but today it is not known why. When Gardiner paddled around the island it reminded him of the Isle of Wight in England, so he christened his island Isle of Wight, but it has always been known as Gardiners Island. The 3,000-acre island is claimed to be the only real estate still intact as part of an original Royal Land Grant from the King of England.

After the "Pequot War," between the Pequot Indians of Connecticut and the English and their Indian allies, Lion Gardiner developed a close friendship with Wyandanch, an Algonquin Indian living near Montauk Point (see the Introduction to Eastern Long Island). Wyandanch's group of Indians were called Montauketts by the English. Wyandanch's brother was sachem (chief) and with Wyandanch's help Gardiner purchased the island from Yovawan, the sachem of Pomanocc.

The plantation-type operation set up on the island by Lion Gardiner raised herds of cattle and sheep and produced crops such as corn, wheat, fruit, and tobacco.

AMERICAN REVOLUTION

During the American Revolution, the island provided safe harbor for the ships of Admiral Marriot Arbuthnot, Great Britain's Commander-in-Chief of North America. Gardiners Bay was a perfect haven—with a diameter of six miles and a depth of three and one-half to seven fathoms. It was more than adequate to maneuver the largest warships in the fleet. Plum Gut, between Plum Island and Gardiners Island, provided harbor entry from Long Island Sound.

The British used the island to provision their ships during the War of 1812, in preparation for their attack on Washington, and burning the United States Capital. Playing host to the enemy cost the Gardiner family dearly in popularity with their American neighbors but they retained ownership of their island, passing it from generation to generation for over 350 years.

CONSTRUCTION

Its strategic location at the opening to Little Peconic and Great Peconic Bays made Gardiners Island an ideal location to build a lighthouse for navigation through Plum Gut. In August 1851, the Federal Government paid the Gardiner family $400 for a site on the sand spit at the north end of the island.

Gardiners Island Lighthouse was constructed in 1854, with a Sixth Order (lowest power) Fresnel lens installed. The fixed, white light was only 33 feet above sea level, all that was needed in the confined bay area. At that height, the beam was visible to an observer at sea level more than six miles away.

The 1876 Atlantic Coast Pilot stated, "The light-house ... is a circular brick tower, 26 feet high, painted brown, and attached to the keeper's dwelling, which is of the same color."

EROSION
During the great blizzard of March 12, 1888, Block Island Sound breached the sand spit, and tides and current commenced to slowly erode the unstable land at the base of the lighthouse.

On June 22, 1893, Jonathan A. Miller of East Hampton was appointed keeper of Gardiners Island Light to replace Josiah P. Miller, at an annual salary of $560. Erosion by then had progressed so much that in March 1894 Miller received the following instructions: "You are hereby directed to extinguish your light until further orders from this office, pending contemplated repairs to site. Captain Latham has been instructed to remove all your stores and supplies to New London. You can live on shore, but you will frequently visit your station, and make written report to me of the

Map courtesy of the
Town of East Hampton.

condition in which you find it. Keep your sail boat for this purpose."

While the U.S. Lighthouse Service deliberated whether to move the structure elsewhere, it was destroyed by a storm. The last remnants of the 40-year-old Gardiners Island Lighthouse washed away in December 1894. The construction of a fort was begun on the sight during the Spanish American War, but the war ended before the fort was finished. The fort, although never completed, was given the name "Fort Tyler Military Reservation." No guns were emplaced and no troops were ever billeted at the fort.

The old fort was given to the New York State park system in 1924, but the state returned it to the War department 12 years later.

During World War II and after, the fort was used by aircraft for gunnery and bombing practice, leaving it in ruins. Today, Fort Tyler is known as "The Ruins." As a result of erosion, the site is now an island, separated from Gardiner's Island by about one and a quarter miles of water.

> *There she sat without a buyer*
> *This structure known as old Fort Tyler;*
> *Sitting in waters, peaceful and calm;*
> *In the 40's she felt the wrath of bombs.*
>
> *Now almost after a hundred years*
> *There is no one to shed any tears;*
> *No State or government will go in hock;*
> *To save this old piece of rock.*
>
> *There she sits as if with no name*
> *As for me, I think it's a shame.*
> —George H. Morton

WARNING

In the 1980s, sport divers recovered practice bombs that missed the fort and landed in surrounding waters. Some are iron or lead and once contained a shotgun shell that fired white powder into the air when striking the ground. Others pose a serious threat because they contain powerful explosives. Military explosives become unstable and extremely dangerous when submerged in water. That prompted the Suffolk County police emergency services section to issue a warning: "Collecting unexploded bombs from a military target range off Gardiners Island is dangerous and illegal."

Other navigational aids have replaced the Gardiners Island Lighthouse. Nothing is left to see, but it earned its place in American lighthouse history with 40 years of reassurance to navigators in need of guidance through Long Island's dangerous Plum Gut.

CEDAR ISLAND LIGHTHOUSE

When built: 1839; rebuilt 1868
Location: Cedar Point, East Hampton Town
Still on site: yes, damaged by fire
Accessible to public: no

There is no Cedar Island in the waters off Eastern Long Island. There was one as far back as Colonial times, and it lay 200 yards off the tip of Cedar Beach, on the South Fork of Long Island. It contained three acres and a grove of 40 or 50 of the cedars that gave the island its name. Over the years, storms and tides washed away two-thirds of the island, and denuded it of trees. Then nature reversed the erosion with the fierce hurricane that struck the Northeast on September 21, 1938. The 200-yard strait between the island and Cedar Beach disappeared, connecting the two with a sand spit peninsula that remains. Cedar Island became Cedar Point, but the lighthouse retained its name.

Rip tides, fierce storms, fog, and shifting sandbars make the narrow passage past the tip of Cedar Island (or Point) extremely hazardous. An early example of the dangers of navigating in the tight confines and wild action of Eastern Long Island waters was the sinking of the Swedish brig *Fahlum* on October 28, 1809, when she struck a rock off Plum Island and went down off Cedar Island.

STAKE LIGHTS

As least as far back as the War of 1812, "stake (or pole) lights" were maintained by agents and owners of whale ships and brigs that headed into or from the then great whaling port of Sag Harbor. Those early signals were whale oil lamps mounted on oak piles hammered into the sides of the channel leading to Gardiners Bay. A local resident tended the lamps with refueling, trimming wicks, lighting them at dusk, and turning them off at dawn. That navigational aid was continued through the Revolutionary War.

During the war, heavy British sea traffic prompted a group of patriots to remove or re-set the channel lights to confuse the enemy and create disaster. That kept the British busy replacing the signals, but the colonists followed with another, more deadly strategy. They refloated an old schooner and created the impression of a ship loaded with cargo. A British warship discovered it, without sails and drifting with the tide. The find was moored in the midst of three other British vessels in preparation for exploring her hold. The booby-trapped decoy exploded when a hatch cover was lifted, killing the entire boarding crew and setting another ship afire.

With the increase of marine traffic after the war, a more permanent light was needed to replace the series of channel lights between Gardiners Bay and Sag Harbor Bay. On August 13, 1838, the United States Government bought the three-acre island, populated by a grove of about 45 red cedar trees, from East Hampton Town for $200. At the East Hampton Town meeting of April 2, 1839, it was voted: "... that the money in the hands of the Supervisors, arising from the sale of Cedar Island, be appropriated, as much as deemed necessary, to the contingent expenses of the town."

The first Federal lighthouse on the island was a wooden building and tower built in 1839. Its lantern, equipped with highly polished mirrors, emitted a steady white beam.

PRESENT LIGHT

In 1868, the present lighthouse replaced the 29-year-old structure with granite instead of wood. The 2 ½ story L-shaped main house is about 33 feet square with a four-story tower about eight feet square at the end of the "L". A square railing protected the lookout walk around an octagonal beacon capped with a conical roof.

The architecture is a Victorian example of Boston granite-style construction. The contractor, W. & J. Beattie Company, Fall River, Massachusetts, owned a quarry that probably provided the granite that was used. The walls are two-foot-thick granite blocks, and the 1868 construction date adorns the area above the main doorway in granite relief. Another doorway, about seven feet wide, probably provided means for storing a small rowboat inside. Downspouts at the corners of the house carried rain water to a cistern in the cellar. Some of the downspouts still remain. A five-foot-wide granite walkway encircles the lighthouse.

Cedar Point Lighthouse.
Illustration by Paul M. Bradley Jr., Lighthouse Graphics.

A Sixth Order Fresnel lens provided a fixed white beam with an 11-mile range, but not even the most intense light signal could penetrate the dense fog of Eastern Long Island bays. Ship captains asked for, and got, an audible fog signal added to the rebuilt lighthouse. It was a bell operated by clockwork that served for 60 years before an automatic fog signal replaced it.

By the start of the 20th century, heavy storms and strong tidal action had eroded the original three-acre island to less than a third that size. The lightkeeper, Charles J. Mulford of East Hampton, appealed to the Lighthouse Service Board for reinforcement of the disappearing shoreline. In 1904, 4,000 tons of riprap (boulders closely interlaced) were deposited on the northern exposure. Two years later, 2,000 additional tons were added. Keeper Mulford was a Civil War veteran with a wooden leg and he kept extra legs stored in the large attic of the lighthouse. Several of Mulford's spare legs were destroyed in the fire that swept through the old lighthouse 70 years later.

The blizzard of January 24, 1908, covered the island with a high tide that swept much of the riprap away, but left the sturdy lighthouse intact. That led to the construction of a breakwater that may have stemmed the rate of erosion, but by 1937 only 0.947 of the island's original three acres remained, and all the beautiful cedar trees were gone.

CLOSING

The lighthouse was decommissioned in 1934 and was turned over to the Treasury Department for disposition as "surplus property." It was replaced by an automatic light over a 57-foot skeleton tower on an adjacent breakwater. Its green light, flashing every four seconds, is visible five nautical miles away. The last keeper of the light, William S. Follett, also later served as the last keeper of Bug Light. Both of Follett's lighthouse commands were victims of arson, one within nine years of the other.

On January 12, 1937, the lighthouse was auctioned for $2,002 to Phelan Beale, of Bouvier & Beale, New York City attorneys. For his money, Beale obtained 0.947 acres of island, without trees but with a nine-room lighthouse, a boat house, an oil house, and a small generating plant, probably installed at the turn of the century. Although the lighthouse was structurally strong, it lacked modern conveniences such as running water and a heating system. Beale planned to install them, then make it available to his 20 employees for fishing and swimming during summer vacations.

On September 21, 1938, a fierce hurricane filled in the 200-yard strait separating the island from the mainland with a sand spit that converted the island from Cedar Island to Cedar Point.

Five years later, Beale sold the lighthouse to Mrs. Isobel Bradley, an interior designer from Connecticut. She added guest houses, a wharf, and a new generator building for her residence (the lighthouse) and the guest cottages. Her investment was amply protected by a kennel of dogs under a Japanese kennel master. In 1957, after Mr. Bradley died of a stroke, Mrs. Bradley sold the lighthouse to Suffolk County for incorporation into Cedar Island County Park.

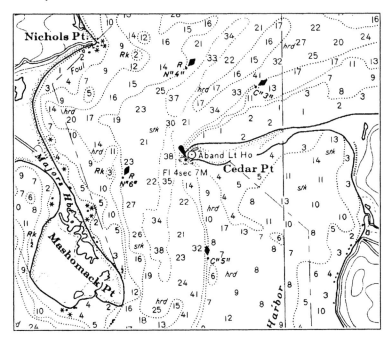

Like other decommissioned lighthouses, the lighthouse was frequently vandalized, and on June 6, 1974, it was set afire by arsonists. The estimated damage of $50,000-$100,000 included destruction of the roof and the oaken interior. Even heavy granite walls cracked from the heat of the blaze. The old lighthouse was still structurally sound, and Park Commissioner Charles Dominy had the burned-out roof replaced, and windows and doors sealed shut.

FOILED RESTORATION

In 1989, Suffolk County leased the 131-year-old structure to the Sag Harbor Whaling and Historical Museum, on a renewable, five-year, no-fee arrangement. The museum launched a drive for funds to restore the interior of the lighthouse, reopen it to the public, and have the Coast Guard maintain the beacon. Three years later, a November 1992 issue of *Newsday* revealed that the fund raising project had been abandoned, in part because of disappointing results. Of greater significance, however, was the failure of the museum and county to agree on a means of access to the lighthouse. George Finckenor Sr., curator of the museum and Sag Harbor historian, said, "They wouldn't put a road in there for us," adding that the road would have cut through the nesting grounds of endangered sea birds. The birds that killed the project, according to a member of the Sag Harbor Whaling Museum, were piping plovers, a triumph of conservation over history.

The automated flashing green beacon that replaced Cedar Island Lighthouse serves the needs of those sailing the narrow channel to Sag Harbor. But the darkened tower of the deactivated lighthouse still stands as a symbol of the days when trimming a wick meant the difference between safe passage and disaster.

Above: Cedar Island Lighthouse 1996 *(photo by H. Keatts)*.
Below: Montauk Lighthouse, at Montauk Point, the easternmost point of Long Island, is the island's most photographed landmark. The white, rectangular observation tower was used during World War II to sight for gun emplacements and watch for German submarines. A concrete gun emplacement (on the right) fell to the beach as the cliff eroded away. *Photo by H. Keatts.*

Shinnecock Lighthouse in an undated photo, *courtesy of Tim Griffing.* Bottom: In 1948, the deactivated lighthouse which had stood for nearly a century was demolished. The tower begins to fall (left; courtesy of Pat Shuttleworth) and (right) breaks in two before hitting the ground (*photo by Edwin Kurant; courtesy of Tim Griffing).*

MONTAUK LIGHTHOUSE

When built: 1796
Location: Turtle Hill, Montauk Point
Still on site: yes
Accessible to public: yes

> The eastern end of Long Island, the Peconic Bay region, I knew quite well too—sail'd more than once around Shelter Island, and down to Montauk—spent many an hour on Turtle Hill by the old lighthouse, on the extreme point, looking out over the ceaseless roar of the Atlantic.
>
> —Walt Whitman, *Specimen Days*

*L*ong before there was any thought of a lighthouse, Montaukett Indians recognized the value of the hill at the end of Montauk Point as a signal point to call council meetings. Their name for it was Womponamon, an Algonquin word meaning "to the east." The settlers who followed named it Turtle Hill because the high bluffs resemble the carapace of a huge turtle. During the seven-year British occupation of Long Island during the American Revolution, the Royal Navy maintained a huge fire on the hill as a signal for their ships that were blockading Long Island Sound.

After the war, the new nation recognized that commerce based on safe coastal navigation was essential to the future of the country. That meant that dangerous waters along the seaboard had to be equipped with warning beacons for safe navigation, particularly during storms or hours of darkness.

George Washington left his mark on the far-eastern tip of Long Island on April 12, 1792, with his approval of the act to erect a "Light House on Montok [sic] Point." The act was passed by the

Second U.S. Congress in 1791, and was signed by Secretary of State Thomas Jefferson. When President Washington approved construction of Long Island's first lighthouse, he predicted that it would last for 200 years. Congress appropriated $255.12 to buy land on Montauk Point's Turtle Hill, 65 feet above the Atlantic, for a warning beacon to alert passing ships away from its rocky shore. The site, between Block Island Sound to the north and the open Atlantic to the south and east was ideal according to historic preservationist Robert J. Hefner in a *Long Island Historical Journal* article: "Perhaps its foremost appeal was as a landfall for ships bound to New York from Europe. These vessels could take bearings from Montauk Point and use its light to conduct themselves from the Atlantic to safe anchorage northeast of Gardiners Island, or in Gardiners Bay. The light would guide ships on their way in or out of Long Island Sound, and those bound eastward in the Atlantic for Newport, New Bedford, and the Vineyard Sound. Also, Montauk Point was high enough to allow a tower to serve as a landmark within the Sound, especially to guide ships through the Race to New London and other mainland ports."

CONSTRUCTION

The site was selected and the original structure was designed by Washingon's friend Ezra L'Hommedieu. Of four companies that submitted bids to build the lighthouse, New York bricklayer John McComb, Jr.'s $22,300 was the lowest. Further to his credit, he had already built a lighthouse at Cape Henry, Virginia, and another at Eaton's Neck, New York. McComb started almost immediately, hauling heavy blocks of "brown Chatam stone" from Connecticut to Montauk and digging a 13-foot foundation to support the 96-foot-high light tower.

On June 7, 1796, the first stone of the foundation was laid. By November 5, 1796, the tower and a small house for the keeper and his family were completed. Nine cedar cisterns were also constructed to hold the whale oil used to fuel the lantern. However, the ship carrying the whale oil went aground at Napeague Beach 14 miles down the coast and the lamps of the new lighthouse were not lighted until the spring of 1797. It was the fifth built by the United States.

A sketch titled "A View of The Light House at Montauk Point" by Jeane McComb bears a description of the original structure by John McComb, Jr.: "The lighthouse stands 130 yards above high water mark. The hill is 65 feet above the water and the light is elevated above the level of the sea 155 feet. The oil vault is 30 feet from the Light House. The dwelling house is 32 feet above the water & 150' from the Light House."

The lighthouse was an 80-foot-high octagonal tower, tapering from 28 feet diameter at the base to 16 feet at the top. The walls were nine feet thick at the base and three feet at the top. A 10-foot-high, octagonal lantern room glazed with storm panes topped the tower. Smoke from 13 whale oil lamps on two tiers in the middle of the room vented through a large copper exhaust that protruded above the roof. In 1838, a new system of 18 lamps was installed, each backed by a 14-inch polished metal reflector, increasing the range to 20 miles. A brick addition was also added to the 16- by 34-foot keeper's dwelling. In 1849, a 15-lamp chandelier with 21-inch reflectors replaced the 18 lamps, with their smaller reflectors.

The President of Yale University visited the lighthouse in 1804 and wrote: "Perhaps no building of this useful kind was ever erected on this side of the Atlantic in a spot where it was more necessary for the preservation of man."

In 1857, a First Order lens designed by the French physicist Augustin Fresnel was received, requiring a 14-foot addition to the tower with a service room beneath for the revolving apparatus. The Fresnel lens, 12 feet high by six feet in diameter, increased intensity of the light by refraction through a series of concentric glass rings. The complex lens resembled a huge beehive encircling one 4-wick lamp that replaced the 15 lamps that were installed in 1849. The resulting beam was visible 35 miles at sea. In order to distinguish the light from a new light at Shinnecock, farther west on the south shore, the normally fixed light was changed to a beam that was interrupted every two minutes by a brilliant flash followed by darkness.

One of Long Island's worst maritime disasters followed almost immediately after the Montauk Point light change. Ephriam Harding, captain of the full-rigged sailing ship *John Milton*, was unaware of the change because he was returning to New Bedford, Massachusetts from a two-year voyage. Nor was he aware of the opening of the new Shinnecock Lighthouse, farther west on the island, with a fixed beam. After sailing eastward along the Long Island south shore through strong gales and a thick snowstorm, he saw the steady Shinnecock light. Mistaking it for the familiar Montauk beacon, he continued east, then turned to port and headed north into what he expected would be Block Island Sound. Instead, early Saturday morning, February 20, 1858, his ship drove into the rocky Long Island south shore, about five miles west of Montauk Point. All 26 men aboard died. The next morning showed wreckage piled on the rocks and along the beach in a frozen mass of masts, spars, sails, officers, and crew.

An iron balcony and iron stairway were also added in 1860 renovations, increasing Montauk's tower height to its current 110 feet. Other improvements included constructing a double dwelling for keepers and an oil house adjacent to the tower, with an enclosed hallway connecting both to the tower.

In 1873, a foghorn was permanently installed to cut through the dense fog that frequently blanketed Montauk Point for days. When visibility drops below five miles, the horn bellows its message for two seconds every five seconds. Its earsplitting signal, sounding steadily for a week or more was reported to leave listeners pleading for relief and homes with pictures hanging crooked on the walls.

To facilitate visual identification during daylight hours, the sparkling white tower of the lighthouse was coated in 1900 with a broad band of brown paint that covered the middle third of its surface. It is renewed with metallic paint and the rest of the tower is whitewashed each year.

Repairs were required in 1903 on the clockwork mechanism of the light's flash panel. They were so extensive that the Lighthouse Board decided to replace the Fresnel lens with a revolving 3.5 order bivalve Fresnel lens. It was only 54 inches in diameter, and produced three times the candlepower of the original lens.

Kerosene replaced whale oil as the lamp fuel in the late 19th century. In 1939, the Lighthouse Service was combined with the

United States Coast Guard that then took over operation of the light. During World War II the Coast Guard Artillery Firetower was added to the site as part of the East Coast Defense Shield. The lamps were converted to electricity in the 1940s, but not until the 1960s was it used to revolve the lens. That was a task that until then had been performed by the keeper cranking up the weights of the old 80-pound clockwork mechanism every three hours.

Since 1987, a converted DCB-224 1,000-watt airport beacon has produced a 300,000-candlepower beam that rotates once every ten seconds in a pool of mercury (to reduce friction). Two flashes occur in every rotation because the lamp is double sided. That increases the flash frequency from the octagonal tower room to once every five seconds. The light turns on ½-hour before sunset and off ½-hour after sunrise. However, when visibility is under five miles, it is used with the fog horn. There is no need to tend the automated beacon, but the 54 panes of glass in the octagonal light room must be kept clear by manual labor. To ensure that the light will be seen 19 nautical miles (about 22 statute miles) at sea on a clear night, the housekeeper of the lighthouse must climb the 130 steps up the circular stairway that leads to the viewing platform.

> *The lanterns shine*
> *From Montauk's lighthouse o'er the brine;*
> *High-looming like a sheeted ghost*
> *That lonely column lights the coast.*
> *On sedgy marsh, on weedy rock*
> *On the wild sea-bird's passing flock,*
> *On sand-beach desolate and low,*
> *Enshrouded by the pallid snow,*
> *It cast a radiance serene,*
> *Illuminating the rugged scene.*
> —Issac McLellan, *The Lost Ship,* 1858

GOURMET DINING

For many years the lighthouse was desolate and often inaccessible. The only land access was a 20-mile-long rock road that connected it with the nearest village, East Hampton. The keepers and their families were virtually isolated from society, except for a few visitors who, during the summer months, were attracted by the excellent fishing off the point. There was a period, after Patrick T. Gould was named keeper in 1832, when the tedium of life was relieved by paying guests who found Gould's epicurean meals the most lavish between Boston and New York. Two customers, Theodore N. Porter and John King, both of New York, noted in 1838 that Gould had treated them to "… a most admirable supper, rendered thrice as welcome by the dreary region through which we had wended our way hither." The gourmet meal included wild goose, broiled chicken, and fried and raw oysters, according to an October 17, 1854, entry in the guest register kept by the keepers.

Sometime in the 1840s, Walt Whitman turned up by sloop from Greenport with a party of young people. He described his visit in a Brooklyn newspaper: "We rambled up the hills to the top of the highest, we ran races down, we scampered along the shore, jumping from rock to rock. We threw our hats in the air, aimed stones at the shrieking gulls, mocked the wind and imitated cries of various animals!"

Following their unwitting acceleration of bluff erosion, Whitman and his friends sought one of Patrick Gould's fabled meals. Unfortunately, earlier guests had emptied the larder, and the group had to settle for a chicken that they roasted on the way back to Greenport.

In 1852, the Lighthouse Board took over the nation's lighthouses, and imposed regulations that no longer permitted operation of dining establishments by the keepers.

In 1860, the lighthouse's wooden floors and windows were torn out and replaced by iron, and new iron decks and doors were installed.

EROSION

The lonely existence of lightkeepers persisted until the early 1900s, when droves of tourists in motor cars descended on the area, creating a new problem, the rapid erosion of the bluff between the lighthouse and the sea. By clambering up and down the slope, they destroyed retaining vegetation and disturbed unstable soil that became gullies under the onslaught of winds and rain—gullies that disappeared only when their walls cascaded down into the ocean.

The problem of erosion was recognized before construction of the lighthouse began. Turtle Hill, including its fragile bluff that fronts on the Atlantic, consists of a mixture of sand, silt, clay, and gravel referred to by geologists as glacial till. It provides little resistance to attack by the heavy winds and storms that drive in from the open sea. That is why it was set back 297 feet from the eastern edge of the bluff that overlooks the Atlantic. But only four months after construction started, the local Superintendent of Lighthouses, Henry P. Dering, reported to Washington that the soil being washed away in gullies near the foundation of the lighthouse was a menace to the future of the tower. As a result, stone dams were built across four gullies on Turtle Hill and the dams were filled with loose stones to control the erosion. However, by 1868, the original set-back of 297 feet was reduced to 200 feet. It was down to 105 feet by 1944, and only 55 feet by 1989, despite a 100-yard section of erosion control installed during the 1960s.

In 1944, a heavy storm washed away a 12-foot section of the bluff, prompting the Army Corps of Engineers to pile large stones at the base of the bluff as a breakwater. But the ocean was not the problem, so much as wind, rain, and the heedless traffic of tourists over the loose soil. The most promising solution came, not from a government agency but from a concerned woman named Giorgina Reid, from Jackson Heights, Queens. As a summer resident of Rocky Point on the north shore of Long Island, she knew the devastating erosion of its high cliffs by the furious storms of Long Island Sound. Her solution was a system to grow vegetation on the face of an eroding bluff, with a slope of no more than 45 degrees, but only after the base of the bluff was reinforced against storm waves. The system was patented (#3,412,561) on November 26, 1968. Mrs. Reid's sense of humor is reflected in her book on erosion control, *How to Hold Up a Bank*.

In the fall of 1969, the Coast Guard gave Mrs. Reid permission to try her method, reed-trench terracing, at Montauk Point. By

1985, she and her husband Donald had firmly terraced the entire eastern and north-eastern faces of the bluff with what looks like a series of steps with wooden risers. Behind and below each riser is a deep trench filled with withered reeds, not to grow, but to absorb and retain rainwater that might otherwise form gullies to carry off the soil during heavy precipitation. The result is a moist environment that favors the growth of beach grass, shrubs, crownvetch, and any vegetation that can take root and feed on the decaying reeds and lumber.

During World War II, the Army Corps of Engineers installed massive boulders interlaced as closely as possible at the base of the bluff, a type of protection called riprap revetment. To supplement that, the Coast Guard lined the area between the boulders and the slope terracing with gabions (wire cages filled with stone), a new development. They let water flow through them without disturbing the soil behind them, instead of resisting the sea and giving way to its superiority as riprap revetment does.

Coast Guard Petty Officer W. Gene Hughes, formerly in charge of the light, claimed that Mrs. Reid's method halted erosion at the light permanently. That claim seems justified by the fact that no damage occurred in the treated areas of the bluff after a December 1992 storm, described as the worst in 30 years. However, the battle is far from over. The untreated south bluff of Turtle Hill is in an area that was ceded to New York State in 1957. It is now under the jurisdiction of the state's Parks, Recreation, and Historic Preservation Commission. Competing projects and funding limitations have denied funding for erosion control of those bluffs. They will continue to threaten the lighthouse with destruction until New York State, some other governmental agency, or private funding can support their reed-trench treatment.

During World War II, the lighthouse became part of the Eastern Defense Shield guarding New York from possible Axis invasion. That shield included adjacent Camp Hero's Gun Battery 112, with its two 16-inch guns. The guns are gone, but their concrete structures can still be seen only a short walk down the beach.

TRANSFER

Friday, September 12, 1986, marked the end of an era and the beginning of another for the ancient lighthouse. Two hundred observers, including Montauk schoolchildren, gathered on the lighthouse lawn at one o'clock that afternoon while the Coast Guard lighthouse staff stood at attention and the Coast Guard band played under sunny skies. Boatswains Mate First Class W. Gene Hughes, keeper of the lighthouse, opened the ceremony with its transfer to the Montauk Historical Society. He ordered the Coast Guard flag lowered and the Historical Society flag, designed by Montauk artist Frank Borth, raised. In a symbolic gesture, he presented the society's president, Peggy Joyce, with a commemorative plaque. Representing the society, Dick White presented a painting of the lighthouse to Hughes' wife.

The emotional ceremony ended 189 years of government operation of the lighthouse. Hughes, the last of its 34 consecutive keepers, acknowledged that there was a structure to be transferred only because of Giorgina Reid's dedicated erosion control system described earlier. In recognition of her perserverance and the success of her efforts, County Legislator Gregg Blass presented her with a framed letter from President Ronald Reagan. It described her outstanding achievement and praised her for helping to save the great monument.

The property is leased from the Federal Government for 30 years, free of charge, with the society assuming responsibility for all maintenance.

AUTOMATION

Three months later, maintenance was reduced by automating the light with lasers, photo cells, and remote control switches that kept a 1,000-watt bulb glowing 24 hours a day. The lighthouse museum (Montauk Marine Display) includes the Fresnel lens that was replaced, early lamps and lenses, ship models, charts, photographs and early drawings, including a 1797 sketch of the lighthouse that was sent to George Washington when it was completed.

Washington's prophesy has been more than fulfilled, and the Montauk Point Lighthouse is still in service after 200 years. How much longer it will continue to dominate the eastern end of Long Island depends on the success of the Montauk Historical Society in enlisting continuing public and private financing to support erosion control and maintenance.

Montuak Lighthouse.
Illustration by Vincent Quatroche, The Greenport Art Studio.

OPEN TO THE PUBLIC

The lighthouse is open for viewing from 10:30 a.m. to 4:50 p.m. on weekdays and 10:30 a.m. to 5:00 p.m. on weekends. Tower tours are available.

Walt Whitman's affection for one of the most historic landmarks on Long Island is imbedded in six lines of his immortal 1888 poem *Leaves of Grass*, subtitled "From Montauk Point":

> I stand as on some mighty eagle's beak,
> Eastward the sea absorbing, viewing
>   (nothing but sea and sky),
> The tossing waves, the foam, the ships in the distance,
> The wild unrest, the snowy, curling caps-that inbound
>   urge and urge of waves,
> Seeking the shores forever....

SHINNECOCK (PONQUOGUE) LIGHTHOUSE

When built: 1858
Location: Ponquogue Point, Hampton Bays
Still on site: no
Accessible to public: no

*N*o record of Eastern Long Island lighthouses would be complete without the Shinnecock Lighthouse, situated on Ponquogue Point, Hampton Bays. Nothing but memories remain of the 170-foot-high, red-brick structure that warned navigators away from catastrophe on Long Island's southern seacoast for 74 years. It holds a special place in the hearts of those who lived in the shadow of the majestic tower and basked in the international recognition it focused on their community.

It will never be known how many ships were spared by the warning beacon, but history has recorded the tragic circumstances that almost certainly drove a fine clipper ship to her destruction under full sail a few miles east of the lighthouse.

CONSTRUCTION

Until January 1858, the south shore of Long Island was unprotected by a lighthouse from Montauk Point to Fire Island. Early in 1857 the United States Government purchased 10 ¼ acres of Ponquogue Point, near what was then the village of Good Ground (now Hampton Bays), from Edward H. Foster. Construction followed quickly on a spread crib structure of treated 12" x 12" yellow pine timber laid below high water level to support a cut stone foundation, approximately 18 feet deep. All building materials were transported from New England by boat through Peconic Bay to Canoe Place, then to Ponquogue by wagon. At that time, there was no Shinnecock Canal.

Shinnecock Lighthouse.
*Illustration by Vincent Quatroche,
the Greenport Art Studio.*

The tower was 170 feet high to the top, 160 feet to the light. It was constructed of red brick, tapering from 7 feet 10 inches thick at the base to 17 ½ inches at the top. The extreme outside dimension of the base was 26 feet 2 inches, with a three-tiered stone base that added 2 feet 5 inches to the diameter. At the top the extreme diameter was 13 feet 5 inches. Interior diameter was a uniform 10 feet 6 inches. Fifteen rooms in a three-story structure at the base of the lighthouse provided living quarters for the keeper and two assistants.

The 260,000-candlepower, glass-enclosed, fixed Fresnel lens was imported from France. It burned whale oil shipped in hogsheads, that was later replaced by lard oil, then a kerosene wick lamp. It was visible 20 miles at sea when the lighthouse went into operation at sundown, January 1, 1858. It was not only visible to ships at sea but also proved to be a deadly attraction for migrating birds who dashed themselves to death against the lighthouse and the windows of the lantern room. A wire mesh provided protection for the light, but not for the birds. Thousands of migrating geese, ducks, and other species perished in that fashion during the 74 years the lighthouse was in operation. A kerosene vapor lamp, with a 27-mile range, was installed in 1912.

DISASTER

The sleek clipper ship *John Milton* was an object of beauty as she glided out of New York Harbor, headed for San Francisco on December 6, 1856. Although the voyage around Cape Horn would be long and hazardous, Captain Ephraim Harding had no concern. He was experienced, his 1,445-ton ship was sound, and he had a good crew. He knew the Atlantic coast, but what he didn't know was that change would begin to occur early the next year with construction of the Shinnecock Lighthouse.

Five months later, *John Milton* cast anchor just inside the Golden Gate Bridge. After a short stop at Callao, Peru, the return voyage was interrupted to load cargo at the Chincha Islands, off the southeastern coast of Peru. By February 14, 1858, the ship anchored in Hampton Roads, Virginia, waiting for orders from her owners. Although the Shinnecock Lighthouse was already six weeks old, receipt of that news was never recorded in the ship's log as being received.

Captain Harding was cheered by the success of his voyage as he headed along the south shore of Long Island for New Bedford, Massachusetts. He and his 25-man crew would be spending the weekend ashore after 14 and a half months at sea.

On Thursday, February 18, 1858, the ship's log book for the day recorded "strong gales and thick snowstorm." The rest is conjecture, but is the only logical explanation of what followed. Seven weeks earlier, while *John Milton* was beating her way northward through the Atlantic, the new Shinnecock Lighthouse went into operation. To the best of Captain Harding's knowledge, the only lighthouse east of Fire Island was at lands end, Montauk. Its steady beam signaled the beginning of open water through which he would head north to Block Island Sound, then to his New Bedford home port. To compound his problem, Shinnecock's light was steady and Montauk's fixed beam was converted to a flashing light the year before.

Early Saturday morning, February 20, mistaking Shinnecock for the Montauk light he knew and trusted, Captain Harding gave it a wide berth. Past the light he headed north into what he thought was open water and drove his ship, with all sails set, into rocks about five miles west of Montauk Lighthouse. Several hours after the wreck, Life-Saving Station Keeper Thomas J. Mulford rode his horse along the beach from his own station to one further east. His vision was impaired by the storm that was still blowing, but he sighted the fragments of the wreck including two of its small boats and other wreckage including a seaman's chest that contained the ship's log.

John Milton ashore. *Harper's Weekly*, courtesy of Albert R. Holden.

There were no survivors. The bodies of Captain Harding and four others were never recovered, but ice-caked corpses, were mingled with rigging and cargo along the shore. The bodies of three mates, and 18 sailors washed ashore and were buried in a common grave in the old South End Burying Ground, East Hampton. Mrs. Mary Esther Mulford Miller wrote in her booklet *An East Hampton Childhood* (1938) that Reverend Stephen L. Mershon preached a moving funeral sermon from the Book of Job: "Terror take hold of him as waters; a tempest stealeth him away in the night. These are cast on the shore of a stranger, but a shore where there are those who feel all men are kindred."

The community reflected that sentiment in the numbers in which they turned out to mourn the lost sailors. The bell of the clipper ship was presented to the East Hampton Presbyterian chapel known as Session House, where it rings to this day in the service of that church.

A white marble monument was erected over the common grave. The inscription reads: "This stone was erected by individual subscriptions...to mark the spot... of the crew of the ship John Milton... Thy way, O God, is in the Sea."

.

The *Suffolk Weekly Times* published a report of the disaster in February 1858, including a description of the wreck site by Miss Cornelia Huntington of East Hampton: "... In the general crash which must have succeeded in grounding of the vessel, the ship's bell was dislodged from its setting and became poised on two beams projecting from the bow, which when morning came, was all that was left of the vessel, and there, swaying with every swell, it tolled out the requiem of the departed. This relic of that awful scene was fortunately secured e'er it slid from its resting place into the surging deep, and finally came into the hands of the church

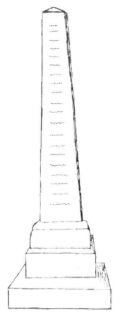

John Milton monument in the old South End Burying Ground, East Hampton.

authorities of East Hampton, who caused it to be suspended in the belfry of the new session room. Last Sunday, December 5th, its voice echoed for the first time o'er the resting place of those who in life were so familiar with its tones."

The following excerpt is from Miss Huntington's poetic tribute to the tolling of the ship's bell in memory of those who lost their lives in the disaster:

> *Ring out, ring out thy pealing notes;*
> *Thou strange mysterious bell;*
> *Whose voice in mournful music floats*
> *O'er sea, and plain and dell;*
> *They will not wake who erst did spring*
> *From slumber, at thy summoning.*

> *They will not hear, whose gladsome tones*
> *in gleeful gushing answered thine;*
> *Nor heed the wintry wind that moans*
> *Above the spot where they recline;*
> *The laughing lips are mute and still*
> *The light heart's pulseless on the hill.*

About the time *John Milton* was lost, another ship, the whaler *Washington* of Sag Harbor approached Shinnecock Lighthouse, returning from a long voyage to the Pacific. Captain Henry Babcock had taken the sun at noon the day before, and knew exactly where his ship was when the light was sighted. He was convinced that although the light appeared to be Montauk's, it was sighted too soon. Overriding the protestations of his crew, who were anxious to get home, he ordered, "Tack ship and stand offshore." The next morning proved the wisdom of his decision.

William H. Elliston memorialized Captain Babcock's wisdom in the poem *Captain Henry's Christmas Gift*. The following are selected stanzas:

> *Two years before when they set sail*
> *The Montauk Light beamed bright*
> *The Ponquogue had been built since then*
> *They knew not of this light.*
>
> *The* John Milton *with forty men,*
> *Some weeks before in frost,*
> *Thought Ponquogue Light was Montauk Light*
> *Struck shore and all were lost.*
>   ...
> *The captain was a jolly man;*
> *Loved people, he loved fun.*
> *He was in charge of a whaling ship,*
> *The good ship* Washington.
>   ...
> *Two years in South Pacific,*
> *Their task became a bore.*
> *With loaded ship they headed home,*
> *Home to Sag Harbor's shore.*

Because that night was Christmas Eve,
With spirits they were gay.
Each one wished to hurry home,
To be there Christmas Day.

A furious storm was raging,
A tumultuous typhoon.
As the wind did blow, the ship did rock,
Mad waves smashed on the dunes.

...

The man on watch came rushing in
Half frozen from the night!
"It's good news men, we're almost home,
Just saw the Montauk Light!"

The captain rushed out on deck.
"My friend, this could not be."
But he too saw the steady light.
"I don't believe," said he.

...

The captain knew he'd checked the sun
At noon the day before.
This could not be the Montauk Light,
They must go some miles more.

He talked then with his officers,
He then talked to the crew.
They all agreed t'was Montauk Light,
"Come on and push her through."

"My calculations are correct!"
He loudly then did shout.
"We'll tack the ship and stand off shore,
We'll have to ride it out."

...

Alone the captain walked the ship;
His eyes were straight ahead.
He then went to his officer,
And this is what he said:

"You will be home for Christmas
With your children and your wife.
I've wrapped each one a secret gift.
The precious gift of life!"
. . .
At break of dawn, all stood on deck.
They shook down to their socks.
Five hundred yards ahead of ship
Was a solid mass of rocks!

DESTRUCTION

For the next 74 years the Shinnecock Lighthouse served as a mariner's beacon. Only technology and economics took her out of service on August 1, 1931. Captain George Thomas was the last lightkeeper. By then, the main shipping channels were well-marked by non-tended lights and a structural steel tower was erected 1 ¾ miles east of the old tower. It emitted an automatic, red flashing light. Seven years later the steel structure was demolished by the hurricane of September 21, 1938, but the original lighthouse, then 84 years old, still stood. Fifteen months later the destroyed steel tower was replaced by another, about ¾ mile southwest of the original.

Local residents and those from nearby communities joined forces to save the historic lighthouse. On August 23, 1941, Rear Admiral L.C. Covell, assistant commandant of the U.S. Coast Guard laid a cornerstone dedicating the Shinnecock Station at Ponquogue Point, Hampton Bays. It also included the 2 ½-story combination administration and dwelling building and the equipment and boathouse structure.

Despite the best efforts of its staunch supporters, the old lighthouse was ordered destroyed. At 10:30 a.m. Thursday, December 23, 1948, man accomplished what nature had been unable to do for 90 years. The tower finally tumbled after her brick wall base was replaced with support timbers, then the gasoline-soaked supporting timbers were set afire and burned through. It was a sad moment for those who had fought for its survival to witness almost a century of history disappear into a field of smoking red bricks.

Nine-year-old Tim Griffing witnessed the demolition. Forty-nine years later, he told one of the authors that the project engineer drove a stake in the ground and said "the top of the tower will hit somewhere near this spot." Griffing said the prophesy was proven correct when the top of the fallen tower struck the stake, driving it out of sight.

The Bell Tolls

APPENDIX A
SIGNIFICANT LIGHTHOUSE SOCIETIES

Great Lakes Lighthouse Keepers Assoc.
c/o Henry Ford Estate
4901 Evergreen Road
Dearborn, MI 48128-1491

The Association, a nonprofit organization, was incorporated in 1983. Its purpose is to facilitate the accumulation and exchange of information about the histories of lighthouses and their keepers so that life at Great Lakes stations may be accurately interpreted, their history preserved, and a new generation of preservationists developed.

Each Great Lakes area is headed by a coordinator who serves to accumulate information and to keep the membership informed of the history and changes in each area. The coordinators organize conferences to share information about the lighthouses and their keepers, to discuss and illustrate restoration projects and to seek ways to address issues of common concern in their area. Cruises are periodically arranged to offshore lighthouses for viewing, photographing, and fellowship.

The *Beacon*, their quarterly publication, contains articles, photographs and drawings of Great Lake lighthouses. The publication also includes member news, coverage of their conferences and cruises, and other items of interest.

The Association has received a 30-year license from the Coast Guard to restore and use the light station on St. Helena Island in the western Straits of Mackinac. The light station, built in 1873, serves as a center for educational seminars and work parties.

Outer Banks Lighthouse Society
301 Driftwood St.
Nags Head, NC 27959
(919) 441-4232

U.S. Lighthouse Society
244 Kearny St., 5th Floor
San Francisco, CA 94108
(415) 362-7255

The United States Lighthouse Society is an 11,000-member non-profit historical and educational organization incorporated to educate, inform, and entertain those who are interested in America's lighthouses, past and present.

Although the almost 300-year-old era of manned light stations in this country has come to a close, those remaining symbols of our maritime heritage should be preserved for the enjoyment of future generations. With this in mind, the U.S. Lighthouse Society was founded to assist in the restoration and preservation of America's lighthouses.

The Society publishes a 48-page glossy quarterly magazine, *The Keeper's Log*, that is "the thread that binds the Society." The first section is historical in nature, featuring a famous American lighthouse cover story, a human interest article, and usually a foreign lighthouse story. Other subjects explored in this section are history of lightships, fog signals, and excerpts from old Keeper's logs. The second section is contemporary, covering events in the various Districts (New England, Great Lakes, Gulf Coast, etc.), listing groups looking for caretakers of their lighthouses, and even an occasional lighthouse for sale.

With the *The Keeper's Log*, members also receive an eight-page Society Bulletin detailing the Society's projects, regional and international lighthouse tours, and products for sale. The Society organizes frequent tours, including an annual Maine pilgrimage, and maintains a comprehansive research library and archives.

APPENDIX B
THE U.S. LIFE-SAVING
SERVICE HERITAGE ASSOCIATION

The Association was a result of the first Lifesaving Station Symposium held in September, 1995 at the Cape Cod National Seashore in Massachusetts. The National Park Service's Maritime Initiative and the Hull Lifesaving Museum organized the two-day symposium. The meeting provided an opportunity for private and public owners and managers of these unique properties to meet, communicate, and exchange ideas. The attendees created the Association to promote, preserve, and interpret the history of the U.S. Life-Saving Service (USLSS) and related organizations.

Association membership benefits include:
- receive a quarterly magazine, *Wreck & Rescue*, on the Life-Saving Service and Coast Guard
- help save the remaining lifesaving stations, boats, and equipment
- learn about the latest in historic preservation activities, new books, and special opportunities to visit lifesaving stations
- periodic newsletters with updates of activities
- an annual members' meeting with station tours
- learn about great shipwrecks, rescues, and maritime history

Join the U.S. Life-Saving
Service Heritage Association!

Membership is open to all. There are four membership categories with dues ranging from $25 to $500.

U.S. Life-Saving Service Heritage Association
P.O. Box 75
Caledonia, MI 49316-0075

BIBLIOGRAPHY

ACKERMAN, Kenneth D. "Deep-Sea Diving A Century Ago." *Invention & Technology*, Spring 1994.

ADAMS, James Truslow. *Memorials of Old Bridgehampton*. 1916. *History of the Town Of Southampton*. 1918.

ANNUAL REPORT *of the Operations of the United States Life-Saving Service*. Government Printing Office, 1894.

ARMSTRONG, Warren. *White For Danger*. The John Day Company.

BAILEY, Paul. *Treading Clams*. Long Island Forum, 1965.

BARNETT, J. Paul. "The Lifesaving Guns of David Lyle." *Wreck & Rescue*, No. 5, Summer 1997.

BAYLES, Donald M. *Horton's Point Lighthouse*. Unpublished manuscript, 1997.

BEAR, Joy. "The Lighthouse Keeper's Grandaughter: Plum Island, 1840-1844." *Long Island Forum*, August 1984.

BEAVER, Patrick. *A History of Lighthouses*. The Citadel Press, 1971.

BEERS, Burton F. *World History*. Prentice Hall, 1991.

BEHRENS, David. "Keepers Of The Light." *Newsday*, August 6, 1990.

BELL, Mary Conklin. "Wreck of the John Milton." *Long Island Forum*, April 1944.

BENSON, Frederick J. Research, *Reflection and Recollections of Block Island*. The Utter Company, 1977. "Wreck of the schooner Nahum Chapin." Unpublished.

BESTON, Henry. *The Outermost House.* Rhinehart, 1928.

BLEYER, Bill. "Montauk Point Lighthouse: A Beacon to Tourists, Too." *Newsday*, May 22, 1987. "Show Time: A Long Island Lighthouse Group Is Becoming A Beacon For Tourists." *Newsday*, June 17, 1996.

BOTTING, Douglas. *The Seafarers: The Pirates.* Time-Life Books, 1978.

BRADY, Edward M. *Marine Salvage Operations.* Cornell Maritime Press, 1960.

CHARTUK, Bob. "Lighthouse stands test of time." *Suffolk Life*, November 30, 1983.

CLIFFORD, Candance. *Inventory of Historic Light Stations.* National Park Service, History Division (418), 1994.

COLEMAN, Tim and Soares, Charley. *Fishable Wrecks & Rockpiles.* MT Publications, 1989.

COMES, Clarence Russell. "Peconic's Old Gristmill." *Long Island Forum*, June 1954.

CURLEY, Bob. "Nature, History and Legend Define Block Island." *Coastlines*, September/October 1997.

DELATINER, Barbara. "Restoring Lighthouse In Montauk." *Newsday*, November 19, 1995.

DEWAN, George. "By George, It's Still Here." *Newsday*, June 2, 1996.

DUGAN, James. *The Great Iron Ship.* Harper & Brothers, 1953.

DUNBAUGH, Edwin L. "The Loss of Metis." *Steamboat Bill*, No. 169, Spring 1984.

ELDREDGE, Kay. *East Hampton: A History and Guide.* Random House, 1985.

FIELD, Van R. *Wrecks and Rescues on Long Island.* 1997.

FINCKENOR, Sr., George A. "Cedar Island, Is it or Isn't It?" *Long Island Forum*, May 1989.

FISH, John Perry. *Unfinished Voyages: A Chronology of Shipwrecks.* Lower Cape Publishing, 1989.

FREEDMAN, Mitchell. "Lighthouse Lovers Kindle Old Flame." *Newsday*, September 5, 1996. "Special Day for Montauk Lighthouse." *Newsday*, May 30, 1997.

GARDINER, Sarah Diodati. *Memories of Gardiner's Island.* 1947.

GARDNER, J. Howland. *The Development of Steam Navigation on Long Island Sound.* The Steamship Historical Society of America, Inc., 1994.

GENTILE, Gary. *Shipwrecks of New York.* Gary Gentile Productions, 1996.

GONZALEZ, Ellice B. *Storms, Ships & Surfmen.* Eastern Acorn Research Series, 1982.

GRIFFIN, Augustus. *Griffin's Journal: First Settlers of Southold.* Augustus Griffin, 1857. *Grolier Electronic Publishing*, Inc., 1993

HABERSTROH, Joe. "The Light at the End." *Newsday*, June 2, 1996. "Saving a Light That's Going Out." *Newsday*, June 8, 1997.

HALL, Warren. *Pagans, Puritans, Patriots of Yesterday's Southold.* Cutchogue-New Suffolk Historical Council, 1975.

HALSEY, William. *Sketches from Local History*, 1935.

HAMILTON, Harlan. *Lights & Legends.* Wescott Cove Publishing Company, 1987.

HEDGES, H.P. *History of East Hampton*, 1897.

HENDRICKSON, Richard G. *Wind in the Fish's Tail.* Amereon House, 1996.

HOCKING, C. *Dictionary of Disasters at Sea.* Lloyd's Register.

HOLDEN, Albert R. *A Pictorial History of Montauk.* Holden's Publications, 1983.

HORTON, H.P. & Squires, Harry B. "Ships That Struck in the Night." *Long Island Forum*, May 1948.

HUGNENIN, Dr. Charles A. "Wreck of the Circassian in 1876." *Long Island Forum*, August 1956.

HUNTER, Lois Marie. *The Shinnecock Indians*. Buys Brothers, 1950.

JENNY, James. *Shipwrecks of New England: Their Lure and Lore*. Rowe Publications, 1981. *In Search of Shipwrecks*. A.S. Barnes & Co., 1980.

KEATTS, Henry C. *New England's Legacy of Shipwrecks*. American Merchant Marine Museum Press, 1988. *Guide to Shipwreck Diving: New York & New Jersey*. Pisces Books, 1992. *Beachcomber's Guide (from Cape Cod to Cape Hatteras)*. Gulf Publishing Co., 1995.

—and FARR, George C. *Dive into History, Volume 1: Warships*. Pisces Books, 1990.

—and SKERRY, Brian. *Complete Wreck Diving*. Watersport Books, 1995.

KENDALL, Connie Jo. "Let There Be Light: The History of Lighthouse Illuminants." *Clockworks*, Spring 1997.

KERN, Florence and Voulgaris, PA1 Barbara. *Traditions, 200 years of history*. Bicentennial publication by the Coast Guard Historian's office, July 1990.

KIMBALL, Carol W. "Demise of the Larchmont." *Sea Classics Special*, 1976.

KOBBE, Gustav. "Heroes of the Life-Saving Service." *Century Magazine*, Vol. LV, 1898.

LACEY, Robert. *Ford, The Men and the Machine*. Little, Brown and Co., 1986. "Lighthouse Demolished at Shinnecock Last Thursday." *The County Review*, December 30, 1948.

LIVERMORE. *History of Block Island*. Originally printed in 1877, The Block Island Committee of Republication, 1961.

LUTHER, Captain Brad W. *Ten Years at Ten Fathoms*.

MCADAM, Roger Williams. *Salts of the Sound*. Steven Daye Press, 1939.

MCDONALD, John. "Catch of the Day Dooms Boat." *Newsday*, March 15, 1991.

MAGILL, Frank N., Editor. *The Nobel Prize Winners, Vol. 1.* Salem Press, 1989.

MAIZIE. *Block Island Scrapbook.* Pageant Press, 1957.

MILLER, Mary Esther Mulford. *An East Hampton Childhood.* 1938.

MINTZ, Phil. "Stormy Search: Dredge ripped from anchors; tugboat crewman missing." *Newsday,* November 29, 1993.

MITCHELL, Joseph. "Dragger Captain, a Profile." *The New Yorker,* January 11, 1947.

MORRIS, Paul C. & QUINN, William P. *Shipwrecks in New York Waters.* Parnassus Imprints, 1989.

NOBLE, Dennis L. "Warfare Against the Sea." *Nautical Collector,* Winter 1995.

O'CALLAGHAN, E.B. *Journal of the voyage of the sloop Mary.* J. Munsell, 1866.

OVERTON, Jacqueline. *Long Island's Story.* Doubleday, Doran & Co., 1929.

PENNY, Anne P. "Venerable Shinnecock Lighthouse." *Long Island Forum,* October 1947.

PILAT, P.R. "Wreck of the Circassian Is Recalled in 1934 Story." *The News,* December 25, 1959.

POST, Richard H. *Notes On Quogue: 1659-1959.* The East Hampton Star, 1959.

QUINN, William P. *Shipwrecks Around New England.* The Lower Cape Publishing Co., 1979.

PRIME, Nathaniel S. *History of Long Island.* Robert Carter, 1845.

RATTRAY, Jeannette Edwards. *Ship Ashore.* Yankee Peddler Book Company, 1955. Records of the Town of East Hampton, Volume VI.

ROSS, Holland F. *Great American Lighthouses.* The Preservation Press, National Trust for Historic Preservation.

SCHEINA, Dr. Robert. *Coast Guard History.* Commandant's Bulletin 16-85.

SCHMITT, Frederick P., and Schmid, Donald E. *H.M.S. Culloden.* The Marine Historical Association, Inc., 1961.

SHEARD, Bradley. *Beyond Sportdiving.* Menasha Ridge Press, 1991.

SHEPARD, Brise. *Lore of the Wreckers.* Beacon Press, 1961.

SHEPARD, Edith H. "The Cruel Winter." *Long Island Forum,* March 1983.

SKERRY, Brian.
"R.I. Ship: A Study In Irony & Bad Luck." *Underwater USA,* September 1994.

SMITH, Arthur. *Lighthouses.* Houghton Mifflin Co., 1971.

SMITHERMAN, Laura. "A Foghorn Salute To Lighthouse." *Newsday,* August 4, 1996.

SNOW, Edward Rowe. *Amazing Sea Stories Never Told Before.* Dodd, Mead and Co., 1954.

SPARGO, Margaret. "The Larchmont Disaster." *Tidings,* July 1991..

SQUIRES, Harry B. "Wreck of the 'Money Ship,' 1816." *Long Island Forum,* May 1947. Notes in the archives of the Suffolk County Historical Society.

STEELE, Joel Dorman and Esther Baker. *A Brief History of the United States.* American Book Co., 1885.

STICK, David. *Graveyard of the Atlantic.* University of North Carolina Press, 1952.

THOMAS, Lowell. *Raiders of the Deep.* Doubleday, Doran & Co, Inc., 1928.

THOMPSON, Benjamin F. *History of Long Island.* E. French, 1839.

THOREAU, Henry. *Cape Cod.* Norton, 1951.

TOOKER, James E.
"Wreck of the Circassian." *Long Island Forum,* January 1939.

TORREY, F.P. *Journal of the Cruise of the United States Ship Ohio.* Samuel N. Dickinson, 1841.

VANDERWOUDE, Carol Ann. "Fresnel—Genius of Illumination." *Sea Frontiers*, Vol. 27, No. 6, November/December 1981.

WACKER, Tim. "Bug Light Whodunit Smolders On." *The Suffolk Times*, July 3, 1997. "Battening Bug Light's Hatches." *The Suffolk Times*, August 28, 1997.

WALTER, Helen Penny. *"Pon Quogue Lighthouse: 1858 - 1948."* A typed manuscript is in the Suffolk County Historical Society. "Song of a Civil War Veteran." *Long Island Forum*, March 1982.

WEAVER, K.D. "Daytripping First Family Charms New Shoreham." *The Block Island Times*, Vol. XXVII, No. 34, August 23, 1997.

WHEELER, Wayne C. "The History of Fog Signals, Part 2." *The Keeper's Log*, Vol. VII No. 1, Fall 1990.

WICK, Steve. "Bug Light To Shine Again." *Newsday*, April 22, 1990. "Lighthouse vs. Erosion." *Newsday*, February 21, 1989. "Stranded In A Strange Land." *Newsday*, October 28, 1997. "The Colonial Collision." *Newsday*, November 2, 1997. "A Man Named Lion." *Newsday*, November 9, 1997. "The Settler and the Sachem." *Newsday*, November 10, 1997. "Wyandanch, Ever an Enigma." *Newsday*, November 11, 1997. "Gardiners Island: What Next?" *Newsday*, November 12, 1997. "Sag Harbor's Heyday." *Newsday*, February 9, 1998.

WILBUR, C. Keith. *Pirates & Patriots of the Revolution*. The Globe Pequot Press, 1984.

WILMERDING, Gus. "Trawler Runs Aground as Helmsman Sleeps." *Hampton Chronicle*, March 23 1989.

WOOD, Clarence Ashton. "Gull Light's Keeper in 1833." *Long Island Forum*, March 1944. "Torpedo Boat at Southold, 1814." *Long Island Forum*, June 1944.
"Stella Prince, Lighthouse Keeper." *Long Island Forum*, July 1948.

YEAGER, Edna Howell. *Around The Forks*. It Publishing Corp.

ZAYKOWSKI, Dorothy Ingersoll. *Sag Harbor: The Story of an American Beauty*. Amereon, Ltd., 1991.

The Bell Tolls

INDEX

Commodore, 59-64
"Coffee Pot", 277, 279.
    See also Orient Point
Lighthouse.
Coimbra, 55, 165, 167, 168
Conkling, Capt. Jeremiah, 126
Cook, Capt. Baldwin, 141
Cook, Surfman Samuel A., 221
Cooper, Capt. Huntting, 83
Cooper, Robert, 53
Coot, 254
Corey, Robert N., 79
Crasper, Surfman Levi, 181, 182
Culloden, H.M.S., 85-98
Daboll, Caladon, 41
Dalen, Niles Gustav, 36, 37
Daniel Webster, 222, 223
Davidson, Carlton, 93, 95-97
Daylight, 230
Debra Ann, 257
Dickens, Charles, 32, 44
Eagle 17, U.S.S., 129, 131
Edith E. Dennis, 246, 247
Edward Quesnel, 220
Edwards, Capt. Samuel S., 235
Eli, 257
Ellen, 240, 241
Elliston, William H., 81, 322
Elmiranda, 236, 237
Elsie Fay, 115, 234
Escort, 238, 239
Europa, 231
E.W. Stetson, 239
Experiment, 228
Fahlum, 301
Fair Helen, 84
Fallon, Mary, 96

Fanny J. Bartlett, 235
Farrell, Vinnie, 258
Field, Van, 234
Finckenor Sr., George, 305
Flying Cloud, 223
Fresnel, Augustin, 38
Fulton, Robert, 65-68, 70
Gardiner, Abraham, 88
Gardiner, Lion, 51, 52, 297
Gardiner, Lyon, 218
Gardiner, Robert David Lion, 53
Gardiner, Sarah Diodati, 218
Gardiners Island Lighthouse, 297-300
Gate City, 193-198, 240
Gem, 237
George Appold, 6, 233, 234
    See also "Shoe Wreck."
George Curtis, 248, 249
George P. Hudson, 248
Golden Ray, 246, 247
Gould, Keeper Patrick T., 223
Gordon, Capt. Charles T., 190
Great Eastern, 99-109
Green, Capt. Barney R., 83
Green, Henry, 160-162
Gregory, M.H., 227
Griffin, Augustus, 263, 264
Griffin, Surfman Henry, 242
Griffing, Tim, 325
Hall, Warren, 264
Hallock, Selden H., 179
Harding, Keeper Silas H., 24
Halsey, Surfman, William, 183-185
Hand, Capt. David, 83
Haynes, Halsey, 59

Hedges, Capt. Carl, 119-121
Hegeman, Don, 92
Helen, 219
Henry, 221, 222
Hesperus, 10
Hill Baxter, 228
Holden, Albert R., 320
Hoosier State, 258, 259
Horton Point Lighthouse, 61, 162, 225, 238, 246, 256, 263-270
Howell, Surfman Samuel H., 141
Huntington, Cornelia, 321
Independent, 240
Jacob C. Thompson, 228
Jacobs, Andy, 237
Jagger, Franklin, 160-162
James A. Potter, 229
James, Joshua, 23, 24
James T. Abbott, 231
Jane N. Ayers, 240
Jeffers, Capt. Samuel, 91, 95
Jessup, Capt. Franklin C., 176
Jessup, Winfield, 184, 192
John & Lucy, 215
John C. Fitzpatrick, 244, 245
John D. Buckalew, 230
John Milton, 6, 176, 293, 308, 317-321
Joseph F. Loubat, 235, 236
Joyce, Peggy, 315
Kaelin, Bob, 269
Keene, Robert, 81
Keewaydin, 247, 248
Kershaw, 250, 253
Kiah, Keeper Jerome G., 25, 26
Knight, Paul, 95, 97
Koppleman, Peter, 237

Kuss, Betty, 96
Lake Deval, 251
Larchmont, 8
Lawrence, John, 223
Lawson, Keeper Lawrence O., 25
Lewis A. King, 232, 233
Lewis, Ida, 48, 49
Little Gull Island Lighthouse, 285-300
Live Oak, 218
Long Beach Bar Lighthouse, 266, 271-275.
  See also "Bug Light."
Longfellow, Henry Wadsworth, 10, 12, 99
Lord Byron, 84
Louis Philippe, 221
Louise Bliss, 249
Lucy W. Snow, 244
Ludlow, Gordon, 145
Lykens Valley, 169-174
Lyle, Captain David A., 19, 20
Lynch, Patrick, 127
McCauley, 238, 239
Madonna V, 123, 124
Majestic, 221
Malden, 252, 253
Maria Louisa, 217, 218
Markham, Richard, 158
Mars, 133-135
Mary, 216, 217
Mary Milness, 224
Massachusetts, 224, 225
Massachusetts Humane Society, 19, 22, 23
Merritt, Israel J., 9
Metis, 8